THE EUROPEAN UNION S

General Editors: Neill Nugent, William E. Pater

The European Union series is designed to provi
on the European Union, ranging from general introductory texts to
definitive assessments of key institutions and actors, policies and policy
processes, and the role of member states.

Books in the series are written by leading scholars in their fields and reflect
the most up-to-date research and debate. Particular attention is paid to
accessibility and clear presentation for a wide audience of students, practitioners
and interested general readers.

The series consists of four major strands:

- General textbooks
- The major institutions and actors
- The main areas of policy
- The member states and the Union

The series editors are **Neill Nugent**, Professor of Politics and Jean Monnet
Professor of European Integration, Manchester Metropolitan University, and
William E. Paterson, Director of the Institute of German Studies, University of
Birmingham.

Their co-editor until his death in July 1999, **Vincent Wright**, was a Fellow of
Nuffield College, Oxford University. He played an immensely valuable role in
the founding and development of *The European Union Series* and is greatly
missed.

Feedback on the series and book proposals are always welcome and should be
sent to Steven Kennedy, Macmillan Press, Houndmills, Basingstoke, Hampshire
RG21 6XS, UK or by e-mail to *s.kennedy@macmillan.co.uk*

(continued overleaf)

The Political Economy of Monetary Union

Malcolm Levitt and
Christopher Lord

First published 2000 by
MACMILLAN PRESS LTD
Houndmills, Basingstoke, Hampshire RG21 2XS
and London
Companies and representatives
throughout the world

ISBN 0–333–71710–4 hardcover
ISBN 0–333–71711–2 paperback

A catalogue record for this book is available from the British Library.

Copy-edited and typeset by Povey–Edmondson
Tavistock and Rochdale, England

10	9	8	7	6	5	4	3	2	1
09	08	07	06	05	04	03	02	01	00

Printed in Hong Kong

 Published in the United States of America by
ST. MARTIN'S PRESS, INC.,
Scholarly and Reference Division
175 Fifth Avenue, New York, N.Y. 10010

ISBN 0–312–23189–X

European Union Series
Series Standing Order
ISBN 0–333–71695–7 hardcover
ISBN 0–333–69352–3 paperback
(*outside North America only*)

You can receive future titles in this series as they are published by placing a standing order. Please contact your bookseller or, in the case of difficulty, write to us at the address below with your name and address, the title of the series and one or both of the ISBNs quoted above.

Customer Services Department, Macmillan Distribution Ltd, Houndmills, Basingstoke, Hampshire RG21 6XS, England

---

Contents

List of Tables, Figures and Boxes

Tables

Figures

Boxes

Chapter 1

Introduction

During the first weekend of May 1998 the heads of government of the European Union met in Brussels to appoint the first president and executive of the Central Bank, and to confirm that stage three of monetary union would have a founding membership of Austria, Belgium, Finland, France, Germany, Ireland, Italy, Luxembourg, the Netherlands, Portugal and Spain. On 31 December, the last financial trading day of 1998, the EU's finance ministers met to fix the exact rates by which national moneys of the eleven would be converted into euro. Although it is a common perception that there will be no single currency until the euro is issued as notes and coins, the legal position is that the national currencies of the eleven are now irrevocably fixed together and will only continue to exist until 2002 as subdivisions of the euro.

Yet popular perception is not without wisdom: the formation of the euro remains an unfinished story. Not only will its physical introduction as notes and coin be a considerable undertaking and one that may substantially alter the self-understanding of the European peoples, there is also the all-important question of whether the euro will ever become a truly single currency in the sense of being the only legal tender in all member states of the EU.

In addition, the full institutional implications may only be worked out through the practice of monetary union itself. While arrangements for the making of monetary policy are fairly tightly specified in advance, those for fiscal coordination could develop in various ways: at one extreme they could involve little more than a few rules of good neighbourliness between states; at the other they could yet result in the construction of an ambitious system of economic government around the Council of Ministers. It is to this unknown that politicians usually refer when they argue, sometimes bitterly, over the question of whether monetary union must inevitably lead to political union.

One point on which supporters and opponents of a single currency would probably agree is that it is a dramatic development in the process of European integration. Both groups would

1

acknowledge its potential to change market structures and political institutions at both the national and European levels. They clearly part company, though, in their predictions of what those effects are likely to be, and in their assessments of their desirability. Without coming down on either side, this book seeks to clarify the debate. Its aims are as follows:

- To provide a dispassionate view of the possible economic costs and benefits of monetary union.
- To show how and why monetary union came about.
- To set out the treaty provisions that establish monetary union, and explain their significance.
- To analyse the institutional mechanisms by which monetary union is managed, and explore their implications for the wider political system of the European Union.
- To explore the place of monetary union in European integration.

The most important aspects of monetary union are to be found in the Treaty of European Union (TEU), negotiated by the heads of government at the Maastricht European Council in December 1991. It is this document which sets out the statute of the European Central Bank, the qualifying criteria for countries to join the single currency, the principal obligations on member states, the roles to be played by other EU institutions, and rules for linking the euro to other currencies. However the TEU was only the last stage in a long history of attempts to commit the European Communities to monetary union, and only the first in the often difficult birth of the euro. A summary of the full chronological development of monetary union is set out in Tables 1.1 and 1.2.

What is different about monetary union?

One way of beginning to understand what is different about monetary union is to compare it with the political economy of the other major initiative in European economic integration in the last fifteen years of the twentieth century: the single market programme. The single market programme commanded a relatively easy intergovernmental consensus; its ratification encountered little opposition from domestic publics and parliaments (with the exception of Denmark); and it rapidly caught the public imagination

Table 1.1 *Chronology of monetary union negotiations, 1988–91*

1988	
January–February	French and Italian governments propose collaborative approach to monetary management in EU
February	German foreign minister suggests that a monetary union should take form of European Central Bank and single currency
June	Hanover European Council remits question of monetary union to the Delors Committee of National Central Banks
1989	
April	Publication of Delors Report
June	Madrid European Council. Agreement to hold intergovernmental conference on monetary union; and that stage one of EMU should start on 1 July 1990
November	Fall of the Berlin Wall. First British counter-proposal: a system of competing currencies
December	Strasbourg European Council: firm agreement reached to open IGC on Monetary Union before end of 1990
1990	
April	Kohl and Mitterrand propose an IGC on political union
June	Second British counterproposal: hard ECU plan
October	Rome European Council 1: agreement that stage two of EMU would start on 1 January 1994
December	Rome European Council 2: opening of IGCs on monetary union and political union
1991	
December	Maastricht European Council. The IGCs on monetary and political union conclude and a text is agreed that becomes the basis of the new Treaty of European Union

Table 1.2   *Chronology of monetary union since Maastricht*

1992	
June	First Danish referendum
September	First ERM crisis, French referendum
1993	
June	Second Danish referendum
July	Second ERM crisis
August	ERM bands widened to plus or minus 15 per cent
1994	
January	Start of stage two and establishment of European Monetary Institute
1995	
December	Madrid European Council agrees Commission's green paper on transition to single currency
1996	
November	Italy returns to ERM
December	Dublin European Council agrees main outlines of Stability and Growth Pact
1997	
June	Amsterdam European Council adopts Stability and Growth Pact
1998	
May	Brussels European Council confirms initial membership of stage three and appoints the first executive board of ECB
1999	
January	Stage three starts
2002	
January	Notes and coins for single currency to be introduced
March	Deadline for withdrawal of national currencies

as a means of reviving the dynamic potential of European integration. In contrast the proposal for a single currency split the member states; it contributed to a 'ratification crisis' that called public acceptance of an 'ever closer union' into question; and over the subsequent five years it struggled into existence through a mixture of sometimes messy political compromises and fiscal austerity measures which tested the public's preparedness to make sacrifices for the construction of a new European policy.

Closer inspection of the historical record suggests that monetary unification has long been the *enfant terrible* of the integration process, in contrast to its apparently well-behaved sibling, the single market. The EC tried and failed to create a monetary union once before, in the 1970s. It then established a European Monetary System (EMS) with an Exchange Rate Mechanism (ERM) of semifixed currencies in 1979. No sooner, however, had this been assigned the role of providing a 'glide path' to full monetary union than it broke up in a prolonged crisis during 1992–93.

Yet the governments of several member states kept returning to the challenge of monetary integration, however forbidding the 'lessons of history'. Quite as striking as its many difficulties and upsets is the fact that the majority of EU governments have rarely felt comfortable outside some system of exchange rate stabilisation for very long: until the early 1970s this was provided from outside Europe by the US-led Bretton Woods system; it was then provided by the 'snake' in the early 1970s and the ERM from 1979. For many years, therefore, the relationship between European governments and monetary integration resembled the Greek legendary figure of Sisyphus, condemned in the underworld to roll a stone up a hill, only for it to roll back down before he could reach the top, and the effort had to start all over again, continuing for eternity.

A policy goal that is at once compulsive and full of constraints promises to be unusually rich in what it can tell us about the overall process of European integration: about motives for assigning policies to the European arena; and about the difficulties of doing so. A rich array of possible motives for monetary union will be encountered during this work: the pursuit of economic gain through further market integration; aversion from certain kinds of economic and political risk; the need to find some way of providing various international public goods; the pursuit of domestic policy objectives by other means; a belief that policies and commitments can be made more credible if developed in a supranational setting; a wish to respond to changing geopolitical realities by binding the governments of the EU even more firmly into a consensual pattern of interstate relations; and a belief that a single currency would be an important catalyst to political system building at the European level.

But what of the alternative suggestion that monetary union is an unusually rich case study in the difficulties of integration? At first sight the contrast between the ease of creating a single market and the difficulty of moving towards a single currency maps on to the distinction between negative and positive integration (Tinbergen, 1965). That is to say, the single market was relatively easy to achieve because it merely entailed the removal of restrictions to cross-border interactions between the economies and societies of the EU. The single currency, on the other hand, is a more difficult undertaking because it involves the construction of new institutions and policies. There may be some truth in this, but it should not be exaggerated. On the one hand many of the difficulties of monetary union have been associated with market relationships, particularly the need to sustain the credibility of markets over long periods of time; on the other hand, the course of its institutionalisation has sometimes run smoothly, perhaps the most striking example being the intensification of contact between European central bankers through the operation of the ERM, and the role this played in facilitating consensus on how a full monetary union should be constructed.

There is, however, a further difference that may explain why monetary union has proven a politically more difficult undertaking than the single market: the sequencing and salience of costs and benefits. In the case of the single market many of the benefits were 'up-front' (raised investment expectations), while many of the costs (economic restructuring) were either diffuse or rarely attributed to the programme. In contrast the important costs of monetary union have been been made explicit through the need for countries to make sacrifices to meet the qualifying tests, known as the 'convergence criteria'. Moreover they have had to be paid as 'down payments' before the single currency can even begin to produce benefits.

Another way of comparing the single market and the single currency as initiatives in the political economy of European integration is to consider their relative importance. This is often simply answered by suggesting that the single market is the more important because the single currency would not otherwise have happened.

However the direction of causation may not be quite as clear cut. An element of monetary integration had been in place since the end of the 1970s, and this may have facilitated the single market programme (see p. 33 below).

It is likewise possible that monetary union has been far more important than the single market in politicising the process of European integration. The controversies that have been so powerfully stirred by the proposed abolition of national currencies have, however, done far more than produce a simple polarisation for and against integration. They have had two more subtle effects: they have powerfully raised public consciousness of the presence and importance of the European arena; and they have brought in their wake a whole new vocabulary and means of thinking about European integration that often challenge the assumption that we are faced with a simple choice between rule by the nation state and rule by the EU. This book suggests that the following are amongst the flexible notions that have reached a wider public audience as a result of monetary union: the idea that the EU may function alongside nation states as a 'non-state political system'; that it may be constructed according to various speeds or geometrical patterns; and that countries can ease themselves into 'one size fits all' policies through convergence criteria.

A final way of enquiring into the significance of monetary union is to consider what it means for the conceptual toolbox available for the study of economic and political science. Those who invented the study of international political economy argued that it would be impossible to understand an economically interdependent world without combining the study of states and markets (Gilpin, 1987; Strange, 1988). Yet this suggestion, academically innovative in its time, must seem strangely quaint for those who have followed the unfolding story of monetary union. In contrast to the dichotomy between states and markets, it seems very difficult to explain monetary union except as the product of a triangle of forces: it was only proposed at all because it served the objectives of key member *states*; it only took the form that it did because it was mediated through *EU institutions*; and it only survived by maintaining *market credibility*. This might argue for a new field of study, perhaps known as European political economy, in which an attempt is made to theorise the distinctive character of interactions between states, markets and the institutions of the EU.

Debates about monetary union

Needless to say, the various actors who participated in the shaping of monetary union were affected by different combinations of motives. The result has been to open up two lively debates that the reader might like to keep in mind while reading this book: one debate centres on whether economic or political factors dominated during the creation of monetary union; the other on whether monetary union was primarily invented to serve 'state interests' or to promote the development of new supranational structures. Perhaps the most interesting possibility, though, is that both debates are based on 'false opposites'. Economic and political motives for monetary union dominated at different stages, and both made distinctive contributions to the initiative. Likewise the supranational entrepreneurship of the European Commission in promoting monetary union, and the new forms of institutional centralisation such as the European Central Bank, can be seen as serving particular kinds of state interest.

Structure of the book

Chapter 2 defines monetary union, shows how it differs from a mere fixing of currencies, and analyses its benefits, costs and risks. The rest of the book then follows an interdisciplinary format with chapters on the political history of monetary union (Chapters 3–5) and its institutional implications (Chapters 12–15) written by Christopher Lord, and those on the economics of monetary union (Chapters 6–11) written by Malcolm Levitt.

Chapter 3 shows how proposals for monetary union between 1987 and 1989 were influenced by a series of *evolutionary* changes that had long been maturing within the political economy of European integration, namely the interaction between market integration, political preferences for exchange rate stability and discontent with the ERM. Chapter 4 shows how the coalition in favour monetary union was then reinforced by *revolutionary* change in the international political system after November 1989. It also concludes that it did matter that the initiative was handled through the institutions of the European Community, with their distinctive arrangements for agenda-setting, bargaining of preferences and decision-taking. Chapter 5 examines the politics of implementation between 1992 and 1998, particularly the interaction between domestic strategies of adjustment and continued efforts at European level to shape the composition and institutions of monetary union.

Chapters 6–11 analyse the economics of monetary union. Chapter 6 considers and critiques the Maastricht Treaty as a model of monetary union. Chapter 7 discusses the economics of implementation, with special attention being paid to the qualifying criteria. Both chapters demonstrate that the Maastricht model was incompletely defined by the TEU and that significant detail needed to be filled in later. Chapter 8 analyses what will be involved in managing the euro area by means of a common central bank and a single monetary policy rule. It also considers early indications of the monetary strategy to be pursued by the ECB. Chapter 9 introduces the all-important issue of fiscal coordination, the degree to which it is required by a monetary union and the possible means of achieving it. Chapter 10 analyses the factors that might promote the use of the euro as an international currency and the effects of any such development. Chapter 11 considers the relationship between the euro and the integration of capital markets and financial services. Overall the economics chapters introduce the reader to several theoretical tools that are useful to the understanding of monetary unions: optimum currency areas, fiscal federalism and the importance of central bank credibility are just three examples. Yet throughout the emphasis is on policy applications and what monetary union will mean for business actors, notably those involved in the financial sector.

Chapters 12–14 are concerned with the interaction between monetary union and the institutional development of the EU. Chapter 12 examines the effects of inserting a new form of executive power into the EU's institutional order in the shape of a European Central Bank that is federal in structure and, arguably, more independent than any previous central bank. Chapter 13 looks at the effects of monetary union on the established executive institutions of the EU, the so-called Commission–Council tandem. Chapter 14 discusses issues of representation and accountability, and the likely role of the European Parliament under monetary union. Throughout the aim is to establish how these various bodies will fit together to provide a monetary union with its own institutional subsystem within the wider political order of the EU. Chapter 15 concludes with an overview of the role of monetary union in the process of European integration, picking up themes that have been foreshadowed in this introduction: the relative contribution of different forces and types of actor; the place of monetary union in the continuing construction of the EU's political system; the consequences for state–society relations in national arenas; implications for the EU as an international actor; and the issue of flexible integration.

Chapter 2

What is Monetary Union?

This chapter reviews the meaning and nature of monetary union, including the role of the single currency. It then considers the potential benefits: completion of the single market; increased economic integration, efficiency and growth; lower inflation; and the potential global role for the euro. Next it considers the principal risks and costs involved in the adoption of a single monetary policy by the various and varied European economies. Finally it considers the economic conditions, policies and institutions needed to sustain monetary union.

The meaning of monetary union

A monetary union between two or more states exists when:

- the value of a unit of the currency used in state A has a fixed relationship to the value of the currency unit used in state B;
- this fixed relationship is enshrined in law (for example a treaty between sovereign states);
- the states participating in the monetary union are subject to a single monetary policy, set and implemented by a single common central bank.

The first condition by itself describes a *fixed exchange rate regime*, as when two countries agree to maintain a stable exchange rate between their respective currencies. This may require massive intervention by the central bank of country A to support the currency of country B if it comes under attack in the foreign exchange markets. If the currency of country B is sold in large quantities against that of country A's currency, central bank A responds by buying up the currency of B to preserve its value. The characteristic of a fixed exchange rate regime is that separate national central banks (NCBs) remain in existence, each with their own gold and foreign exchange reserves, which they promise to use by intervening in the market to maintain their locked exchange rates. In the above example, if central bank A offers a large amount of its own currency to prop up currency B, it is expanding its own money supply. Meanwhile central bank B will attempt to maintain the locked parity by selling its gold and foreign exchange reserves to buy its own currency.

By contrast, in a *monetary union* the common central bank has a monopoly of monetary policy, it focuses on the aggregate money supply of the union as a whole, although the notes and coins circulating in each country might have different symbols on them (for example pictures of the respective heads of state). NCBs lose the right to determine domestic monetary policy and become operating agencies of the common central bank. Consequently, if holders of currency denominated in country B symbols exchange them for currency denominated in currency A symbols, the *aggregate* money supply of the monetary union as a whole is unchanged. NCB A will be indifferent to offering its currency in exchange for currency B in unlimited quantities at the fixed conversion rate: their joint money supply is merely redistributed and there is no change in their gold or foreign exchange reserves. This distinction between a fixed exchange rate regime and a monetary union is important and often misunderstood: in the period 1 January 1999 to 1 January 2002 a *monetary union* will exist but not a fixed exchange rate regime, even though distinct national notes and coins will continue to exist until 2002. There will be a single monetary policy regime, operated by the European System of Central Banks (ESCB), involving the European Central Bank (ECB) with a monopoly of monetary policy determination and participation by the NCBs to implement that policy.

In principle a monetary union need not necessarily have a single currency, and this was acknowledged by the Delors Report (European Commission, 1989). However a single currency has a number of advantages: it is a symbol of the intended durability of the monetary union and of the commitment of the member states, which will have sacrificed their national currency symbol; it reduces the cost of transactions between different countries by eliminating the need for currency conversion; and it is politically neutral – before the Maastricht Treaty there was some concern that the Deutschmark would become the *de facto* single currency. These issues were stressed in a report for the Association for the Monetary Union of Europe (AMUE) (1990), which had some influence on the Commission's submission to the intergovernmental conference (IGC) that led to the Maastricht Treaty. The treaty recommended the introduction of the single currency as soon as possible after the start of stage three.

The single currency would ideally have been introduced through a 'big bang' approach. But it was logistically impossible to introduce it simultaneously for every means of payment, as an accounting unit, and for the denomination of all financial assets (Association for the Monetary Union of Europe, 1994). In the circumstances the Bundesbank and numerous small German banks were believed to favour starting the final stage of EMU by locking national currencies and using national central bank intervention to preserve the lock. The single currency would then be introduced some years later. But markets may have taken this as indicating that the authorities themselves had doubts about the durability of monetary union, and therefore private sector organisations such as banks would have been reluctant to commit the large expenditure needed to convert their computer systems, train their staff and so on. The Commission and the European Monetary Institute (EMI) were thus persuaded that the single currency had to be used in some form or other from day one. They proposed that it should immediately be used for the denomination of government bond issues; for money and foreign exchange market interventions by the ECB; and for the denomination of commercial bank settlement accounts at nation central banks. Its compulsory use in retail payments and accounting would follow later, as would the introduction of notes and coin. This phased introduction of the single currency was adopted by the Madrid European Council of December 1995. The key point is that both in the run-up to the Maastricht Treaty and subsequently there was no logical necessity or political certainty that EMU would be accompanied by a single currency from the very start. It did so because of a need for private sector preparations and to prevent German backsliding.

Although separate national notes and coins will continue to exist during the transition period, legally they are just denominations of the euro, with an irrevocably fixed conversion rate to the single currency. According to the relevant regulation, 'the euro shall be divided into the national currency units according to the conversion rates' (Council Regulation EC974/98 on the Introduction of the Euro). An analogy might be the relationship between the pfennig and the Deutschmark. There is no reason to suppose that 100 pfennigs are worth any more or any less than one Deutschmark. When the conversion rates between the participating currencies and the euro were fixed on 1 January 1999 and monetary union came into existence, people should have been indifferent about holding deposits in one currency denomination rather then another – unless they feared that a participant might leave.

So in a legal sense the monetary union has had a single currency called the euro since 1 January 1999. Between 1 January 1999 and 1 January 2002 the euro will be used by the ECB for all money and foreign exchange market interventions, transactions between banks and transactions between large firms. Individuals may be able to use the euro when making payments by credit card and possibly by cheque (depending on the country in question and its banking arrangements). But to the ordinary person it will not *seem* as though there is a single currency until euro notes and coins have been introduced and national ones withdrawn.

In conclusion, the creation of monetary union in Europe is a unique and unprecedented event. On the one hand it is arguably the first significant example of sovereign states with separate national central banks forming a monetary union without first forming a full political union. On the other it will be a monetary union with a single currency, the Delors Report having rejected a mere locking of national exchange rates in order to eliminate any perception that countries might leave (European Commission, 1989).

Benefits, costs and risks of a single currency

Completion of the single market

It is argued that Europe is fragmented by monetary differences, despite the single market programme to remove obstacles to the free movement of goods, services, people and capital. Cross-border European business and personal travellers face currency fluctuations and risk together with the costs of converting one currency to another. The latter include not only charges imposed by banks or bureaux de change – companies also have to pay for departments and staff to administer different currencies. Consequently, it is argued, firms – especially small and medium-sized ones – are impeded from undertaking cross-border trade and investment in Europe. This results in a less efficient allocation of resources across Europe than in a single currency area such as the United States. The cost of having to do business in different currencies has been put at 0.4 per cent of EU GDP (European Commission, 1990).

In theory a regime of freely floating exchange rates is fully compatible with a single market so long as the exchange rates vary to correct movement in relative rates of inflation. (If inflation is 10 per cent higher per year in A than in B, then B's currency should fall by 10 per cent per annum to maintain the relative real prices of their imports and exports.) In practice life is more complicated: if all internal prices, including wages, were wholly flexible and adjusted virtually instantaneously and fully to changes in the exchange rate – and *vice versa* – the intellectual case for monetary union might be weaker, although the pressure from industrialists might be stronger because of the frequency and cost of accounting changes. Another problem is that exchange rates tend to 'overshoot': appreciations or depreciations go further than required by differences in inflation rates (and are often the result of speculative movements), sometimes for relatively long periods. Moreover the potential benefits to individual firms of being able to undertake all their European business in one currency are not available in a floating exchange rate regime. Additionally, the risk of devaluation, especially against the Deutschmark, has meant that interest rates have to be higher in countries thought to be at risk of devaluation. Within a monetary union interest rates would therefore be lower in such countries and investment higher. Increased cross-border trade and investment as a result of EMU would boost economic growth in the European single market (provided that interest rates in traditionally low-inflation countries, such as Germany, are not higher as a result of participating in a monetary union with the rest).

Although positive, the scale of these effects is debatable and they have to be weighed against the cost of participating in monetary union, notably the loss of monetary autonomy, a theme to which we return below. At the same time it is worth noting that the single market is incomplete for reasons other than the absence of monetary integration: implementation of the directives into national legislation and their enforcement is patchy; the working of a competitive single market is distorted through the existence of state aid (subsidies) and differences in taxation; and in certain industrial sectors where nationalisation and/or 'national champions' are prevalent (for example electricity and gas, telecommunications, civil aviation, defence procurement) the single market process has been very slow to get off the ground. Indeed it is ironical that some of the most fervent supporters of monetary union – on the ground that it will complete the single market – are governments with a poor record in implementing or enforcing the single market legislation. On the other hand EMU might indirectly accelerate the development of the single market in the protected sectors because the budgetary constraints needed to enter and subsequently comply with monetary union are encouraging a number of countries to privatise their protected sectors and, in consequence, open them up to greater competition.

A very different line of reasoning from the suggestion that the single market cannot be completed without monetary union is the claim that it cannot survive without it. This is best summarised by Thomasso Padoa-Schioppa's (1990) argument that the following form an unstable combination, or in his words an 'inconsistent quartet': the free movement of goods and services, national sovereignty over monetary policy, freedom of capital movements and a regime of floating exchange rates. The single market may also be endangered by pressure on governments to protect firms and jobs exposed to any unfair competitive advantage conferred by the devaluation or sustained undershooting of the currencies of other member states.

European economic integration, efficiency and growth

Although it is an objective of the single market to rationalise industry by allowing it to operate at a pan-European level and reap the economies of scale associated with a borderless market of 350 million consumers, the monetary fragmentation of Europe is said to impede the process. According to this view, the single currency is the missing piece in a jig-saw of dynamic integration of markets across frontiers: 'our view is that the Euro is the tool by which we will make a global player out of the middle-sized nations such as Germany, France, the UK and other European countries to be able to compete with the US or in the future with far East Asia' (Wolfgang Stofer of BMW, *Financial Times*, 7 October 1997). The scale of this 'dynamic' boost to European integration is impossible to quantify but is not necessarily trivial. Were it, however, to lead to the greater regional concentration of industries, economic shocks specific to particular industries would tend to become shocks specific to regions or countries. As explained below, monetary union may be institutionally ill-equipped to deal with such an eventuality.

An improved trade-off between inflation and growth

A complementary argument stressed by the European Commission (1990) is that monetary union will permit greater and less inflation-prone growth in Europe. Growth, it is argued, will be stimulated by the combined effects of:

- A stimulus to cross-border trade induced by the elimination of currency risk and the lowering of cross-border transaction costs.
- The encouragement of greater investment once countries previously at risk of devaluing against the Deutschmark no longer have to pay interest premiums.

At the same time, it is argued, price and wage expectations will be much more constrained under monetary union, as companies and workers adjust to two developments that respectively make it less likely that inflation will be accommodated by monetary expansion or devaluation: the first is the creation of a European Central Bank that is wholly committed to the control of inflation, independent of political interference and determined to inherit the credibility of the Bundesbank; the second is the drastic narrowing of opportunities to use exchange depreciation to restore competitiveness once the separate national currencies are replaced by a European one. A reduction in wage expectations would reduce the monetary and/or fiscal tightening needed to offset inflationary wage demands and thus increase the growth of demand and output. Economists sometimes describe such a change as a shift in the non-accelerating inflation rate of unemployment (NAIRU), where NAIRU is the rate of unemployment at which the rate of inflation is stationary. The European Commission (1990) has estimated that the benefit to the EU of lower inflation in a monetary union could be 0.3 per cent of GDP. This is an attractive argument but it is subject to qualifications:

- In order to get to monetary union, tight monetary and fiscal policies have constrained growth and exacerbated unemployment.

- Whether and how fast labour market behaviour will change and the non-inflationary growth rate in Europe will improve remains to be seen. In many countries low inflation continues to be associated with high unemployment, suggesting that underlying labour market behaviour and the NAIRU have not yet significantly changed.
- There may be a contradiction between the claim that the European Central Bank can borrow the credibility of the Bundesbank and the ambition of many proponents of monetary union to create a central bank with a focus on the needs of Europe as a whole, rather than Germany alone. The best performer may be replaced by an institution reflecting average performance and conditions.
- If the economic cycles and inflation rates of participating countries differ, tensions may arise between those which want high interest rates to contain inflation, and those which need lower interest rates to reduce unemployment. In short a focus on average monetary conditions ('one size fits all') may not always be appropriate, and the inflation/growth trade-off might become more manageable for the EU as a whole, while deteriorating and becoming less easy to handle in particular parts of the EU. It is impossible to resolve this conundrum from first principles: all will depend on how growth, inflation and inflationary expectations develop under monetary union. But divergent growth prospects and policy tensions have emerged at the time of writing, the duration and severity of which remain to be seen.

Global role for the euro

Just as the EEC grew out of concern that Europe was at risk of being squeezed between Russia and the United States, many proponents of monetary union have wanted to challenge the global role of the dollar, which is the most important single currency in the foreign exchange holdings of countries around the world, and the most important single currency in the denomination of global imports and exports. Whereas the EU and the United States account for 31 per cent and 27 per cent of global GDP respectively, EU currencies only account for 21 per cent of foreign currency reserves in third countries as opposed to 64 per cent held in dollars (Bergsten, 1998).

Although the EU and the United States have comparable shares of global trade in goods (20 per cent and 18 per cent respectively), only 33 per cent of trade is denominated in EU currencies whereas 48 per cent is denominated in the dollar (Portes and Rey, 1998). There is clearly substantial scope for the euro to displace part of the dollar's share of reserves and its use in trade denomination. How quickly the euro will replace the dollar to a degree commensurate with the EU's global economic role is, of course, conjectural. Initially at least, central banks and investors in the rest of the world are likely to adopt a 'wait and see' policy because the euro has no history.

However there is a dilemma here. On the one hand it is hoped that the euro will function as a *hard currency* that is attractive to investors because it is safe and well-managed. On the other hand an argument that is made for displacing the dollar in investors' portfolios is that its 'benign neglect' by the US authorities has repeatedly secured an unfair competitive advantage for American exporters and made penetration of the US market relatively difficult; the logic of this position points to a relatively *weak euro* – one that will be unattractive to investors. In a sense these contradictory ambitions are irrelevant provided it is the ECB, and not politicians, that seeks to influence the external value of the euro in a manner intended to support a strong counterinflationary policy; this might mean a relatively hard euro that is attractive to investors but not strongly favoured by EU exporters.

The speculation as to whether or not the euro will be a 'hard' or 'soft' currency is, in any event, oversimplified. The ECB will strive to maintain price stability within the monetary union, that is, it will be hard internally. However, as the euro has no track record it may take the ECB some years to establish credibility even if inflation is low. Although, for example, France has maintained a rigorous counterinflationary regime since 1987, it was only from about 1997 that the markets and other observers finally acknowledged the credibility of French monetary policy. In between many felt that France would be unable to maintain the almost fixed link between the franc and the Deutschmark, given its previous track record of inflation and devaluation – hence the ERM crises of 1992–93. Drawing on this analogy, an internally hard euro may nonetheless be regarded as a relatively soft currency in foreign exchange markets. The danger is that the ECB will adopt an excessively macho monetary policy to counteract this, thereby exacerbating low growth in Europe. One should not, however, exaggerate this, since an excessively tight monetary policy also lacks credibility if there is doubt that it can be maintained in the face of high or growing unemployment.

The principal economic cost of participation in monetary union is that the countries in question sacrifice the freedom to set their own exchange rates and interest rates. However in a world of global financial markets where well over $1000 billion of currency is exchanged daily, the currency of any small or medium-sized country – in other words a European country – may be buffeted beyond the control of its central bank. Even a massive sacrifice of gold and foreign exchange reserves may not suffice.

So one may question whether monetary independence truly exists. Moreover any attempt to revive competitiveness and growth through devaluation is subject to severe erosion if not total failure in the long run, as higher import costs create inflation and wage pressures. The general consensus in the economic literature is that the long-term effect of devaluation is typically close to zero. However the ability to depreciate one's currency may provide an important safety valve in times of crisis, allowing time for other adjustments to improve the long-term position of an economy.

Optimum currency areas

If a group of countries – such as the members of the EU – have *similar economic structures,* they will tend to react to economic shocks in the same way. It follows that there is no point in any of them trying to devalue against the others and they should consider forming a monetary union (Mundell, 1961).

The other side of the coin is that countries with different market structures and behaviour are exposed to *asymmetric shocks*: external economic events may affect them in different ways (Bayoumi, 1994; Bayoumi and Eichengreen, 1996, 1997; Buti and Sapir, 1998; Gross, 1996). In these circumstances the loss of the ability to alter their own interest or exchange rates could impose serious costs in the short to medium term, even where there are no long-term benefits from devaluation. Where the exchange rate cannot be devalued, the whole burden of adjustment to an external shock or other loss of competitiveness will fall on labour markets, either in the form of reductions in real wages (for example money wages will fall or rise more slowly than prices) or higher unemployment (Eichengreen, 1993).

A contrast is often drawn in the academic economic literature between Europe and the United States, which is also composed of many states and regions with differing economic structures (Bayoumi and Eichengreen, 1977; Bini-Smaghi and Vori, 1993; De Grauwe and Vanhaverbeke, 1993; Eichengreen, 1990, 1991; Greenwood, 1975; Gros, 1996). Research by the OECD suggests that wage earners are more likely to maintain real wage rates than in the case of the United States: reductions in real wages are more difficult to achieve in Europe than in the United States. Moreover there is greater mobility of labour between the different states or regions of the United States than is the case in Europe, where movement between areas of recession and those experiencing economic growth is impeded by differences in language, customs, tax and social security systems, access to housing and so on. (Migration in France between departments or in Germany between Länder is only between a third and a half of migration between states in the United States, although Gros, 1996, disputes this.)

Also, in the United States there are federal budgetary mechanisms which have the effect of dampening down differences in economic growth among the states. This is not so much the result of specific regional transfers as the effect of the normal tax and social security system. The progressive structure of income tax means that post-tax incomes tend to rise and fall more slowly than pre-tax ones, so the difference between boom regions and recessionary ones is less than it would be in the absence of a common fiscal structure. At the same time the growth of social security contributions will be greater than the growth of unemployment benefits in booming regions while the opposite will be true of those in recession. But there is no common tax/social security structure across the EU. The consequence of lower labour mobility and the absence of a sizeable EU budget means that asymmetric economic shocks pose greater problems in Europe than is the case in the United States.

The question, therefore, is *whether* the member states of the EU represent an optimum currency area. Empirical studies (Bayoumi, 1994; Bayoumi and Eichengreen, 1994, 1996, 1997; Bini-Smaghi and Vori, 1993; Boltho, 1994; de la Dehesa and Krugman, 1992; de Grauwe and Vanhaverbeke, 1993; Eichengreen, 1990, 1993; Greenwood, 1975; Gros, 1996) suggest that a small monetary union among a subset of the EU composed of, say, Austria, Benelux and Germany would come close to an optimum currency area; but they differ in their estimates of cyclical similarity even between France and Germany; several suggest that the Mediterranean countries (Greece, Italy, Portugal and Spain) could face particular difficulties in adopting the same monetary policy as Germany; and they generally suggest relatively low correlation between the British/Irish and German economic cycles.

In short the precise boundary of a European optimum currency area is extremely difficult to draw, perhaps impossible. But the optimum currency area theory does imply that economies with differing responses to economic shocks will find it difficult to adjust to a single monetary policy regime. This is not to say that countries with greater exposure to asymmetric shocks should not participate in EMU, only that they will face greater problems in adjusting to shocks that affect them and the core in different ways A single monetary policy, combined with tight constraints on the use of fiscal policy to expand deficits and stimulate demand, could therefore create unemployment, with attendant social and political stresses. Such difficulties might come as something of a surprise to countries that have never had a full debate on the risks as well as the benefits of monetary union.

Another way of achieving adjustments might be to allow the relaxation of national fiscal constraints. The Stability Pact (Chapter 8) does allow budget deficits to rise above 3 per cent of GDP in 'exceptional' circumstances, defined as a fall in GDP of at least 2 per cent a year (a relatively rare occurrence in practice). Provided that budgets have been in balance or even surplus prior to the onset of a recession, this allows a 3 per cent deficit to emerge before penalties are applied. If in practice countries enter monetary union with fiscal deficits it follows that the margin for manoeuvre will be extremely limited, calling into question the credibility of the Stability Pact should fiscal expansion be implemented in order to avoid the risk of political/social upheaval.

The macroeconomic criteria adopted at Maastricht for determining membership of the monetary union do not include a requirement that participants should have similar economic structures or employment–inflation relations if they are to form a sustainable monetary union. This means that some combination of the following is needed: greater labour market flexibility; a common contracyclical

EU budget; and more leeway for member states to determine their own fiscal policy, for example countries in recession must be allowed to run budget deficits to maintain the level of demand and employment, provided that such deficits are subject to strict limits, surveillance and sanction if necessary. Nonetheless academics differ both in their assessment of the problem and their proposed solutions. Gros (1996), for example, argues that the contrast between Europe and the United States with regard to interregional labour mobility is flawed. But Obstfeld and Peri (1998) express considerable concern about low labour mobility across frontiers, which is politically unacceptable in Europe anyway, and about the prospects for increased fiscal transfers; they propose a relaxation of fiscal constraints at the national level.

It may be objected that much of the analysis in the foregoing paragraphs has tended to exaggerate the likely difficulties because it fails to anticipate how economic behaviour will itself be changed by the arrival of monetary union. The empirical studies of correlations between the economic cycles of European countries are based on historical data and *it may be that monetary union will produce greater similarity of behaviour.* Price and wage fixers will know that monetary policy will be determined by a single, politically independent central bank, and not several NCBs, each of them open to different degrees of political influence and many of them working to different electoral cycles. Likewise fiscal policy will be subject to legally binding constraints and peer group vetting, at least reducing the impact of differing political influences over the degree of fiscal stimulus or contraction in member states (Buti and Sapir, 1998). One source of cyclical difference between countries is the extent to which households and firms are dependent on short-term borrowing at variable interest rates: countries such as Italy (where long-term borrowing has been difficult, given the reluctance of lenders) and the UK (where long-term borrowing and lending at fixed interest rates has been unpopular, given the UK's inflationary track record over many years) may be particularly sensitive to movements in interest rates. On the other hand, participation in monetary union might produce a convergence of borrowing (and lending) behaviour among the various member states, thereby producing more closely correlated cyclical behaviour.

However, significant increases in cross-border labour mobility and the development of a contracyclical budget do not appear to be a prospect, so the ability of Europe to adjust to asymmetric shocks will remain weaker than that of the United States. The combination of a single market with a monetary union could even make the situation worse: with geographical specialisation, shocks specific to industries translate into shocks specific to regions or countries. It is difficult to determine, on the basis of logic or evidence, how serious the costs and risks of monetary union are likely to be, and how they may be weighed against the undoubted benefits. But the significant point may be that the difficulties have been insufficiently debated in many EU countries.

The required economic environment: economic union

A monetary union with a single monetary policy, managed by a common central bank and acceptable to countries with a track record of low inflation, needs the following elements in the economic environment of all the prospective participating countries if it is to go ahead and remain sustainable:

- Low rates of inflation are needed to convince countries such as Germany that the other candidates are acceptable partners. Low inflation is also necessary (although not always sufficient) if a single monetary policy, especially the interest rate, is to be agreed and remain appropriate for all participants.
- Low government deficits are needed to avoid pressure on the common central bank to raise interest rates in order to offset inflationary pressure caused by deficits. Again this is an important test that must be passed if countries with a track record of fiscal prudence are to accept other participants.
- Stable exchange rates are needed to sustain the common interest rate and avoid the risk of last-minute competitive devaluation.

These conditions should be satisfied over a sustained period prior to full monetary union and the first two should continue after it has started. However the message of the previous section is that these criteria may be necessary but insufficient unless:

- the cyclical behaviour of participating countries is sufficiently similar to sustain acceptance of a single monetary policy without serious disagreement;

- and/or labour markets are fully flexible with respect to wages and labour mobility;
- and/or a common contracyclical budget is in place;
- and/or there is sufficient flexibility for individual member states to adopt different fiscal positions in order to stimulate or restrict domestic demand without disrupting the successful adoption and implementation of the single monetary policy;
- a common public accounting system exists to provide transparency and ensure that all member states define and measure their fiscal position in an identical manner.

As noted, a major economic driver of monetary union was the concern to eliminate the monetary fragmentation – in the sense of currency differences and fluctuations – which impeded the completion of the single market. It was, however, acknowledged that although a 'single market for goods, services, capital and labour' would need to be 'complemented by common policies and co-ordination in several structural, micro- and macro-economic domains, an efficient economic union requires much less centralisation of policy competencies than monetary union' (European Commission, 1990). A degree of economic policy coordination is needed to constrain fiscal deficits within EMU in order to reduce pressure on the ECB to raise interest rates, with damaging effects both to investment and to trading competitiveness via any appreciation of the euro in foreign exchange markets. Without fiscal policy constraints and coordination there is a risk that countries with growing deficits will harm other economies in the monetary union: on the one hand the other countries will benefit from extra demand for their exports; on the other they will share in any ECB interest rate increases, with the adverse effects noted above (Buti and Sapir, 1998). The question arises of precisely how much policy coordination is required.

In principle there is a need for mutually agreed quantitative ceilings of deficit and debt, institutional arrangements to ensure their achievement and common public accounting rules to reduce the risk of 'creative accounting' to camouflage fiscal imprudence. Key issues include:

- What those quantitative ceilings should be. Those chosen for the Maastricht Treaty are summarised below and discussed in greater depth in Chapter 8.

- How to ensure there is sufficient flexibility to enable a speedy and effective response to adverse economic shocks. This is likewise discussed in Chapter 8, together with the Stability and Growth Pact.
- The extent to which the coordination of fiscal policy requires *tax harmonisation*. This is not discussed in the present book, since the focus of fiscal policy in support of monetary union is on the aggregate deficit, rather than the precise microstructure of taxation and public expenditure. Distortions created by differences in tax structures and state aid are more the concern of that part of economic union formed by the single market. It should merely be noted here that differences in tax rates alone are an insufficient indicator of any tax 'distortion'. For example Germany applies a relatively high rate of corporation tax to a relatively narrow tax base (and *a fortiori*, one based on a narrow definition of corporate profit), whereas the UK applies a lower rate to a much wider tax base, measured according to a much more comprehensive definition of corporate profit (Chennells and Griffiths, 1997).

The required institutional arrangements

In order to develop and implement the common policies that characterise a monetary union, it is necessary to create and maintain appropriate institutions. Clearly an essential institution is the common central bank, tasked with managing the single monetary policy. In constructing that institution a number of issues need to be addressed:

- The extent to which it should be politically independent in determining its objectives and implementing its policy; how any independence should be assured; the institutional arrangements needed for its political supervision if it is not to be wholly independent; and such accountability as can be combined with independence.
- What objectives it should be required to meet, in particular whether it should focus solely on price stability or (like the US Federal Reserve Bank) take account of growth and employment prospects.

- What operational targets it should set in order to meet its primary objectives, including the rate of inflation or the rate of monetary growth.
- Which policy instruments it should use to achieve its operational targets, including market intervention or the administrative control of both commercial bank assets and liabilities.

Procedures and other institutional arrangements are needed to monitor and assess the monetary and fiscal performance of participants in order to ensure that these are compatible with low inflation and the common monetary policy. If not, thought needs to be given to the form of possible deterrents and sanctions. Likewise consideration needs to be given to the extent of any coordination between the central bank and the ministers responsible for fiscal policy in order to minimise the risk of their pulling in opposite directions or, acting independently, exacerbating unemployment in Europe.

Finally, a monetary union cannot be implemented unless the great mass of ordinary people in each participating country accept and understand what is involved, and the private sector understands what it needs to do and has sufficient time to do it. The new currency has to be substituted efficiently and effectively for the national currencies that it is intended to replace.

Conclusions

EMU has a potential to create a zone of low inflation, low interest rates, increased cross-border trade, increased investment, a more integrated European economy and a currency with a major global role. The achievement and subsequent sustenance of EMU requires substantial convergence of economic behaviour both at the macrolevel among participating economies and at the microlevel in terms of economic structures and market behaviour. However economies and their internal structures do differ across the single monetary zone in Europe, as they do across the United States, but with the difference that in Europe the safety valves for coping with asymmetric economic shocks – labour market flexibility, geographical contracyclical fiscal transfers – are largely absent. Expert opinion is divided on the seriousness of the risk of asymmetric shocks and the ability of the EMU participants to handle any which do arise within the fiscal constraints embodied in the Maastricht Treaty and the subsequent Stability and Growth Pact. Any solution will require a substantial degree of economic cooperation, within a common institutional framework. A key issue for the coming years will be how far this process of cooperation and institution strengthening needs to go in order to sustain EMU itself, quite apart from the achievement of the more ambitious goal of political union – towards which, in the minds of some, EMU is simply a stepping stone.

Chapter 3

Conceiving Monetary Union, 1957–88

The next three chapters examine the political history of European monetary integration. Although they break down the story into three phases, they are thematic studies rather than chronologies. This chapter covers the period 1957–88 and looks at the changing political economy of Western Europe: the relationship between market integration and monetary integration, the nature of political preferences for currency stability and of dissatisfaction with alternatives to full monetary union. Chapter 4, which covers the climacteric years 1988–91, looks at two exclusively political influences on monetary union: the impact of dramatic change in the international political system, and of the institutional peculiarities of the European Community's internal political arena, particularly its arrangements for setting the agenda of integration and bargaining the interests of its member states. Chapter 5 covers the years 1991–98 and examines the interaction between the implementation of monetary union and the changing politics of European integration at both national and EU level.

The early political history of monetary integration

Movement towards greater economic interdependence has been a constant feature in the reshaping of Western Europe since 1945. Trade in goods and services has developed steadily throughout the period. Financial flows have grown exponentially since the 1960s. In combination, these two factors mean that the selection of the right kind of monetary regime for Western Europe is a matter of prime political importance, affecting the level and shape of any cross-border integration in trade and investment, and, not least, the capacity of governments to pursue the economic policies of their choice. A regional policy regime, intermediate between national and international solutions, has long been one option for European governments. The founding members of the European Community agreed to consider their monetary policies as a matter of common concern when they signed the Treaty of Rome in 1957 (European Commission, 1957, Article 104), and the first Commission proposals for a measure of monetary integration date from as early as 1962 (European Commission, 1962).

Yet until the 1980s the European Community often seemed to have an uncertain grip on the economic governance of Western Europe. Some students of international political economy presented the new interdependence as largely ungoverned. Others believed that it was conditioned by the changing character of US hegemony, with only a limited role for European influences (Calleo, 1982; Gilpin, 1987; Odell, 1982; Keohane, 1984; Strange, 1988). Still others believed that the states had adjusted to interdependence, rather than being overwhelmed by it (Hoffmann, 1966), and that economic integration at the European level was more of an instrument of state policy than a challenge to it, since it had been consciously deployed by governments to free themselves from domestic constraints and enlarge their internal resources (Milward, 1992; Helleiner, 1995).

The limited relevance of the EC seemed to be confirmed by the confounding of its ambitions and the failure of some of its relaunches. By the 1980s the goal of creating a common market under the Treaty of Rome (1957) had been frustrated as governments merely substituted an ingenious array of 'non-tariff barriers' (subsidies, nationalistic purchasing by public bodies, unreasonable product standards) for conventional tariffs. According to some estimates, the level of protection was just as high as it had been twenty years earlier, in spite of export growth (Ceccini, 1988).

Monetary integration had meanwhile been the subject of still more spectacular policy failure. With the erosion of the Bretton Woods system of internationally fixed exchange rates after 1967, the original six member states of the EC agreed to the formation of a European monetary union at the Hague summit of 1969. The Luxembourg prime minister, Pierre Werner, was appointed to chair an expert group to develop the proposal. When the Werner Report appeared in 1970 it recommended the creation of monetary union by 1980, with a phased approach to include the coordination and convergence of national monetary and fiscal policies; the adoption of common policy guidelines; and the gradual reduction of exchange rate fluctuations between participating countries and their eventual elimination. It also proposed short-term balance of payments support to participants in difficulty (European Commission, 1970).

The Werner Plan differed from the later Delors Report and the Maastricht Treaty in two ways. First, it emphasised the need for common fiscal policies and an enlarged EC budget to dampen economic fluctuations and differences in the cyclical behaviour of member states. Second, it did not provide a prescriptive model for a central bank. The March 1971 Council of Finance Ministers (Ecofin) accepted the plan. Amongst subsequent efforts to implement it were:

- The Snake in the Tunnel (1972). This limited bilateral currency movements among EC members to a 2.25 per cent band, just half the 4.5 per cent band within which they would all fluctuate against the US dollar under the Smithsonian agreement of 1971.
- The European Monetary Compensation Fund (1973).
- Policy guidelines to promote convergence (1974).

Yet the attempted monetary union of the 1970s was a tender plant in a harsh environment. The Snake began to disintegrate after the collapse of the Smithsonian agreement in 1973 and fell apart altogether as a result of the 1973–74 oil shock, which also demolished efforts to promote convergence. Under these conditions a monetary union could only have been achieved with a more substantial loss of policy autonomy than most member governments were prepared to accept, and quite probably with a degree of short-term sacrifice that would have been incompatible with their electoral survival (Tsoukalis, 1977). The EC duly broke into two currency blocs: the 'hard currency' countries arranged around West Germany, which were able to keep to the disciplines of the 'snake'; and the 'soft currency' countries organised around France, which for the most part had to float freely.

Monetary questions and the revival of European integration, 1979–86

The EC began to reassert itself as an arena for the management of the region's political economy from the end of the 1970s; significantly, this occurred in the monetary field before it did in trading relations. In place of full monetary union, the EC introduced the more modest European Monetary System (EMS) from 1979, following a joint initiative by German Chancellor Helmut Schmidt and French President Valéry Giscard d'Estaing at the Bremen European Council of June 1978 to promote a zone of monetary stability in Europe (European Commission, 1978; Ludlow, 1982; Jenkins, 1989; Moravcsik, 1999, pp. 238–313). The principal feature of the EMS was an Exchange Rate Mechanism (ERM) of 'fixed but adjustable exchange rates'. The rules and performance of the ERM are fully reviewed below. For the moment it is enough to note that it established the following:

- A grid or matrix of central parities (exchange rates) between participating countries.
- Bands within which the above could fluctuate against one another: plus or minus 2.25 per cent (narrow band) or 6 per cent (broad band).
- A new currency, the ECU. This was formed as a 'basket' or 'average' of EC currencies, weighted according to their relative share of EC GNP.

In practice, however, the *bilateral* spread between the weakest and the strongest (the Deutschmark) national currencies continued to dominate policy, rather than the symmetry implied by a *multilateral* relationship to the average, the ECU. Nonetheless the ECU acquired a role as the currency denomination in which private companies with a pan-European spread of business raised funds by issuing bonds (as did some governments). By 1993 there were almost 200 billion ECU's worth of bonds outstanding. In addition the ECU was actively used in cross-border banking activity. Yet it never became a major feature of commercial transactions in goods and services.

Although considered by many to be one more initiative that would surely fail, the EMS had stabilised by the mid 1980s into a significant policy regime for the narrowing of exchange rate fluctuations in Western Europe. Indeed it is often suggested that it moved through three distinct phases (1979–83, 1983–87, 1987–1992/3), each representing a tightening over the last in the coordination of monetary and currency policies (Gros and Thygessen, 1992). Modest though they were, the ERM and the EMS constituted a partial monetary union. National currencies were far more interchangeable, and while national decisions on the management of the money supply continued to be of vital importance, they were guided and constrained by European level rules, and intermittently coordinated by the EC committees responsible for the ERM.

Just as the EMS was establishing itself in the early 1980s, pressure was building to use the EC institutions to restructure trade relations in Western Europe. The 'national champion strategy' was in tatters as leading companies came to believe that their performance would be better served by a single framework of European rules than by each government attempting to support its own producers. Governments realised that they would have to coordinate more of their rule making if they were to generate the economic growth needed to meet the performance expectations of those who had voted them into office. The single market programme of 1986–92 accordingly launched a wide-ranging assault on non-tariff barriers with a view to making it almost as easy to trade across political boundaries as within them (Cecchini, 1988; Pelkmans and Winters, 1988; Jacquémin and Sapir, 1989). The Single European Act (SEA) also recalled the commitment to monetary union made in 1972, and urged member states to intensify their monetary cooperation.

Without wishing to suggest any deterministic relationship, the principal initiatives in trade and monetary integration – the EMS, the single market and, later, monetary union – do seem to have developed interactively from the early 1980s. The EMS promoted a measure of convergence in the nominal or inflationary performance of the member states, without which the removal of trade barriers under the single market programme would have been politically more stressful. The single market and Single European Act of 1986 then changed the EC's political system in a manner that influenced the subsequent bid for monetary union. In the limited but significant area of market regulation, two kinds of authority – national and European – now enjoyed cojurisdiction. This had important implications for the subsequent monetary union initiative. The Commission was freed from political dependence on the strict unanimity of member states, and, to the extent that governments now needed it to make the single market work, the Commission was able to show a new boldness in its political entrepreneurship. The single market programme also mobilised Europe's largest corporations into the EC political arena (Cowles, 1995), creating a ready source of allies for any further initiative that would, in Delors' words, put a 'second tiger in the tank' of European economic integration once the '1992 programme' had completed its course. Many of the leading companies that had formed the European Round Table to argue for the rationalisation of trading conditions in the EC, now joined the Association for Monetary Union in Europe (AMUE) (Greenwood, 1997, p. 117).

In both academic and political circles, the relationship between the single market and money integration rekindled an old debate about the nature of European integration: would policy innovations at the European level be self-contained, or would they tend to create 'spillover pressures' in which interdependency between public policies would repeatedly force governments to expand the scope of integration or abandon established gains (Haas, 1958; Lindberg, 1963; Tranholm-Mikkelsen, 1991)? One person who thought that the single market would create a precise and important spillover pressure was senior Commission economist, Thomasso Padoa-Schioppa, who predicted that the following would form an 'impossible quartet': the single market, the removal of all capital controls, exchange rate stability under the ERM, and national autonomy in the management of the supply of and demand for money (Padoa-Schioppa, 1987). As it stood, this was just a framework for clarifying the choices available to European governments: either the single market programme would have to stop short of liberalising all capital flows (which would have drastically reduced its impact); or the ERM would have to be relaxed through the use of wider bands or more frequent realignments; or member governments would have to allow the ERM to evolve into a system in which monetary policy was fully integrated at the European level and the scope for national discretion largely removed. Given that the latter solution was the only one which preserved previous achievements (tight currency bands) and present commitments (liberalisation of capital markets), the origins of monetary union seem at first sight to provide dramatic confirmation of the spillover theory.

But it would be a mistake to suggest that governments had little alternative to full monetary union. On the one hand 'spill back' to a looser ERM was a serious option. On the other, full monetary union was not the only means of using spillover to consolidate existing policies: several economists suggested that intensification of the disciplines of the ERM would do just as well (Kenen, 1995, p. 10). In short, full monetary union only came on to the agenda in response to the political preferences of key member governments, and not through economic necessity (Eichengreen and Frieden, 1994, pp. 5–9). Those preferences were of two kinds: aversion to exchange rate variability and discontent with the operation of the ERM. The next two sections ask why key actors held them with such a force that they were prepared to contemplate all the risks and loss of national sovereignty associated with full monetary union.

Political preferences for exchange rate stability

Since the Second World War, fixed exchange rate systems have exercised a gravitational pull on government policy in several EC member states (McNamara, 1998, p. 98). For most of the period, these countries have been signed up to one international currency regime or another, or have hurried to invent new ones when exposed to the risk of unconstrained floating. Amongst the structural factors that may have conditioned this abiding preference for some element of exchange rate stability are the following.

Sensitivity of domestic economic and social models to currency fluctuation

Small and open economies may find that currency volatility produces large fluctuations in the tax receipts and social security outlays associated with generous welfare models. Even in large economies the commercial banking sector may align with exporters to promote currency stability. This is more likely where producers are financed by domestic bank loans, rather than by international equity finance (Henning, 1994).

The structure of political risk

Exchange rate politics have often been a high-wire game for European governments anxious to maintain domestic electoral coalitions or preserve their governing credibility. Whether governments feel that the balance of risk lies with exchange rate fluctuation or rigidity is likely to depend on two factors: (1) the structure of domestic political systems, particularly the economic interests of voters or parties who are marginal to the formation of winning coalitions; and (2) the type of economic interests whose prosperity and active cooperation are likely to affect good governing performance. A recent article hypothesises that 'incentives over the exchange rate regime reflect the configuration of domestic political institutions, particularly electoral and legislative institutions': governments in majoritarian systems like that of the UK are more likely to want to retain their discretion to vary the exchange rate, as the political cost of failing to align the electoral and economic cycles may be high; those in coalition systems may, conversely, find that a fixed exchange rate system buys market credibility, since it allows coherent policy strategies to be entrenched and thus protected against interparty wrangling (Bernhard and Leblang, 1999). Where the preference is for fixed rates, monetary union reduces the risks associated with currency politics by eliminating several parities within Europe and transferring responsibility for the remaining exposure to instability from national governments to an EU framework.

The nature of pay-offs from European integration

The balance between the benefits and costs that a country receives from European integration may be sensitive to exchange rate variability. The Common Agricultural Policy (CAP) is the example that is normally cited. But a far more important illustration may be provided by the integration of markets in general. According to an argument that has frequently been put, freely floating currencies tend to overshoot equilibrium values for long periods and by substantial amounts. This in itself has the same effect in refragmenting a single market – and in misallocating resources – as any tariff barrier. As French economist Pierre Jacquet has put it: 'under flexible exchange rates, the European single market would be the theatre of exchange rate overvaluations and undervaluations' (Jacquet, 1998, pp. 58–63). Political reactions to rapid and dramatic changes in the exchange rate might then compound direct economic costs.

Political systems may have a limited capacity to resist demands for protectionism in periods of recession or sudden dislocation. This would create special problems for the single market programme, dependent as it is on the decentralised enforcement of complex rules by the member states themselves. The single market programme has always been dependent on trust between states: there are reasons to fear that member states might respond to the stress of exchange instability by slipping into a game of prisoners' dilemma – reverting to protectionism for fear that others might be about to do the same. Paradoxically this argument in favour of monetary union may have been less persuasive if a single market had been institutionalised in a European Community that had already been granted more supranational powers over its member states.

The international distribution of power over exchange rates

A powerful argument for unconstrained foreign exchange (forex) markets in a world of high capital mobility is that this allows markets to discipline unsustainable government policies. But this presupposes that forex markets are politically neutral and technically optimal in their judgements (Gilpin, 1987). The counter-argument to this has been put by Willem Buiter, a member of the Bank of England's monetary policy committee:

> where forex are driven by the fancies of asset markets rather than economic fundamentals they may be more cause than cure of shocks and instability and, as such, they do not so much oil the process of change as inflict the need for adjustment and associated costs on the real economy (Buiter, 1999b).

Some of the governments that have been keenest on monetary union have questioned the role of the forex markets for the following reasons. They are overwhelmingly concentrated in particular centres – New York, London, Tokyo and Frankfurt – with the result that their understanding of particular countries and their policies seems variable. The forex markets are often accused of privileging particular views of how economies work, while enjoying the capacity to turn their judgements into self-fulfilling prophecies, with the result that their assumptions are often inadequately tested; and even when their judgements are fair, they may be unequal in their consequences, since in any world in which some moneys function as global currencies, governments will differ in their capacity to shift the burden of adjusting to market pressures onto someone else.

Political discontent with the ERM

Although the previous section explained why many governments had such a preference for exchange rate stability that they were not prepared to loosen the ERM in response to the liberalisation of capital markets, it left unanswered the question of why they rejected the alternative of intensifying the mechanism short of full monetary union. Several economists suggested that this would be a technical possibility: so long as member states were prepared to intensify the discipline of the ERM to the point at which their money supplies were effectively run as a single bloc, they would not need to abandon their national currencies or surrender powers to a new institution. An attraction of the ERM was precisely that it avoided the visible transfer of sovereignty to supranational institutions, since it relied for the most part on a system of self-enforced rules. The most important of these are set out in Box 3.1.

Few governments though were completely content with the functioning of the ERM. Since the rules of the system had never been enough on their own to ensure its solidity, the credibility of the ERM came to depend on the policy leadership of the German central bank. Although designed as a neutral rule-based mechanism, the ERM developed into a hierarchial relationship in which both leaders and followers had their discontents. The price which the markets consistently demanded for maintaining the exchange rate peg was that other countries should better any interest rates set by the Bundesbank, regardless of whether the latter were appropriate to their own domestic conditions. Some economists even suggested that political inequality between EC countries would persist as long as those in the ERM had separate yet semi-fixed exchange rates: since markets would be irrational to accept a fixed price between a 'poor reputation' currency and a 'good reputation' currency without being offered an interest rate premium, the authorities in the latter country would always end up by setting policy for both (Barro and Gordon, 1983).

Asymmetric exchange rate systems could, however, destabilise the economic cycle, deepening recessions and exaggerating booms, for all countries apart from the policy leader (De Grauwe, 1996, pp. 98–9). A further difficulty was that inequality between member states could scarcely have been further from the original technical and political design of the system. The ECU had been created to give

Box 3.1 The rules of the Exchange Rate Mechanism

1. A grid of participating currencies would be established. Each currency would be assigned a 'central rate' around which it could only vary within fixed bands, initially of plus or minus 2.25 per cent for most countries and 6 per cent for those who were still adapting to the full rigours of the system.
2. In addition to staying within the permitted distance from their central rates, no two currencies would be allowed to deviate from one another by more than their permitted band (2.25 per cent or 6 per cent).
3. The central rates would be established with reference to an average – or basket – of all EU currencies, the European Currency Unit (ECU).
4. The central rate of any one currency could only be changed by the 'mutual agreement' of all participating governments and the Commission.
5. When a currency reached 75 per cent of its permitted divergence it would take corrective action by:
    a) intervening to buy or sell currencies;
    b) changing its monetary policy;
    c) altering its fiscal policy;
    d) requesting a change in its central rate.
6. If two currencies approached the limits of their divergence from one another, their national authorities would intervene in each other's currency. Exchange rate stability would thus be delivered with neutral effects on the overall amount of money in circulation in the ERM zone (De Grauwe, 1996, p. 96)
7. Countries would continue to manage all their own currency reserves. But their central banks would be able to support their own exchange rate by borrowing from others and then selling that money to buy back their own currency. They would, however, have to repay all credits in the currency in which they had been borrowed after fixed periods varying from 45 days to six months. This served two purposes: it allowed the system as a whole to distinguish temporary exchange rate volatility from fundamental disequilibria, and it gave member states a strong incentive to take corrective action. To repay a credit in another currency after one's own has depreciated, is effectively a fine.
8. In so far as national authorities needed to consult one another to keep to these rules they would do so through 'Community bodies, including the Council of Ministers'.

Source: Resolution of the Brussels European Council on the establishment of the European Monetary System, 5 December 1978.

the ERM a neutral reference point: participants would follow a basket of currencies and not the currency of any single member state. Both the French and German governments had, in addition, seen the ERM as a means of preventing a strong Deutschmark from under-cutting European integration as a means of multilateralising German power. By institutionalising German policy leadership, it had the opposite effect to that intended. As the Bundesbank president, Karl-Otto Pöhl, would later remark, 'the Bundesbank turned the original concept on its head by making the strongest currency the yardstick for the system' (quoted in Marsh, 1992, p. 233).

Yet the Bundesbank was a reluctant leader. To the extent that it probably took some decisions that it would not have taken in the absence of the system, its policy ceased to be exclusively geared to the management of the German domestic economy (Frattiani and von Hagen, 1992). On the other hand its unilateral actions completed the break with the original design of the system. While it had been anticipated that effective intervention would take the form of selling currencies that were doing well and buying those that were in trouble, the Bundesbank was unwilling to loose control of its own monetary creation in such a way. It tended to buy back Deutsch-marks sold by other countries. The result was fourfold: it was far more difficult to stop the Deutschmark from bouncing up against its ceiling and correspondingly harder to defend other currencies; the buying of the German currency was made even more of a one-way bet for speculators; the overall system had a deflationary bias; and the burden of policy adjustment was thrown back even more heavily on the weaker currencies, rather than being distributed equally between national authorities.

Not the least of the paradoxes of the situation was that other national authorities became increasingly complicit in the West German leadership of the ERM, even while railing against its consequences. To understand this it is necessary to appreciate that monetary integration in Europe was taking place against the back-ground of a 'paradigm shift' in the economics discipline. Changing theoretical understanding of how economies work became a power-ful independent variable in both the operation of the ERM and the subsequent drive for full monetary union (Goodhart, 1995).

While it had been common in the 1960s to believe that govern-ments could choose between many different combinations of inflation and unemployment, the new orthodoxy was that the only lasting effect of attempts to push unemployment beneath its natural rate was to embed a higher level of inflation in the system as the base line for future rounds of price and wage fixing. This created a double conflict of interests: between governments and those they were supposed to represent; and between the long- and short-term goals of any monetary policy undertaken by an elected body. By temporarily stimulating the economy, governments could improve their chance of winning elections. But the public would be worse off thereafter. On the other hand full employment with constant prices would be unobtainable, even when this was sincerely desired. Wherever it seemed to conflict with the short-term interests of governments in political survival, the public and markets would generate inflationary expectations that defeated the longer-term purpose (Kydland and Prescott, 1977).

There were apparently only two ways out: either to hand over monetary policy to an independent authority unconcerned with the fighting of elections; or to enter into international commitments that would convince labour and financial markets that governments had tied themselves to the mast of financial rectitude (Begg and Wyplosz, 1987). The ERM was something of a mix between the two: it delegated policy to someone else's independent central bank – the Bundesbank – and its rules could only be broken by casting doubt on a country's wider commitment to European integration.

Conclusion

An important motive for monetary union was the wish to escape from some of the problems of the EMS. Yet the very asymmetry of the existing monetary relationships shaped the distribution of bargaining in the search for an alternative: it ensured that countries such as France and Italy would be demandeurs in any negotiation, while West Germany would be the critical veto holder: the one country in a position to grant or withhold consent to any regime change. A further consideration was that any substitute for the ERM would have to allow member countries to secure and extend the perceived benefits of the mechanism: reduced exchange rate volatility and the improved credibility of economic management.

Beyond this there were at least five other ways in which the EMS shaped the monetary union that came after it:

- A progressive tightening of the ERM was originally conceived as providing a 'glide path' to monetary union.
- For those countries that participated, the ERM may have shaped private market expectations in a manner that was eventually to make monetary union more attainable.
- The ERM provided important policy lessons for those public authorities which would be involved in any future monetary union: indeed it formed those who were professionally responsible for monetary matters into a tightly knit 'policy community' in which there was a good deal of analytical agreement on how best to conduct policy (Dyson, 1994).
- Because the ERM did so much to build up the Bundesbank as the policy leader in European monetary policy, it made it even more likely that any successor regime would have at least to command the cooperation of Frankfurt.
- However the foregoing effects operated differentially. There were always two bands to the ERM, the narrow (plus or minus 2.25 per cent) and the broad (plus or minus 6 per cent). Some countries spent most of the period 1979–93 in the broad band. Others either joined late, or joined for only brief periods or not at all. Still others availed themselves of the right to realign more frequently than the rest. These differences meant that each country would face different political and economic adjustments to reach full monetary union. This structured the dispersion of interests in the Maastricht negotiations.

Chapter 4

Bargaining Monetary Union, 1988–91

The previous chapter showed that there was no automatic connection between the single market and a single currency. Yet once the first was agreed, the second was an understandable political preference for those who disliked both exchange rate instability and some of the political inequalities inherent in the ERM. Even this conclusion, however, fails to provide a full understanding of why monetary union was ultimately a political decision. Accordingly this chapter will introduce two further themes: the powerful link between change in the international political system and the consolidation of a winning coalition in favour of monetary union; and evidence that the detail of monetary union was significantly influenced by the institutional structures through which it was mediated – by the distinctive arrangements that the EU makes for the framing of options (agenda setting) and the bargaining of interests.

Setting the agenda for monetary union

Getting an issue considered at all – or in the desired form – is half the battle of EU bargaining. A decision-making process that tends towards overload can only handle a limited number of new initiatives at any one time; and as coalitions cluster around a handful of agreed constructions of problems, decision makers are keenly aware that the key political battles are won or lost when options are selected and framed, and not just when final decisions are made (Peters, 1996; Richardson, 1996). Monetary union provides a striking example. As seen, the earliest proposals that led to the present initiative for monetary union came from the French and Italian governments at the beginning of 1988. The drift of the argument was that the money supplies of participating countries should be aggregated and managed according to a mutually agreed set of rules. This was to be preferred to the existing arrangements for three reasons: policy judgements would be based on economic conditions in all member states, and not skewed, as in the Bundesbank-led ERM, towards those in just one member state; for most member states an intensification of European cooperation would therefore lead to an *increase* in political autonomy; and finally, the ERM was regarded as having a bias towards deflation and the overvaluation of Europe's currencies, since it put the burden of adjustment on weaker currencies to raise their interest rates (Balladur, 1988; Amato, 1988).

In attempting to raise monetary integration to the top of the EC agenda in early 1988, the French and Italian governments enjoyed important political resources: the authority of existing treaty commitments, and the support of the presidencies of both the Commission and the Council. Although seen by others as too vague to amount to very much, the French and Italian governments felt that the Single European Act contained a serious commitment to further monetary integration, and they now intended to hold their partners to it. In pursuing this goal they had the support of Jacques Delors, who had always wanted to make monetary union the focus of his Commission presidency, and had, in part, only been persuaded to bide his time on the ground that it would be easier to follow a single market with a monetary union than *vice versa* (Grant, 1994; Ross, 1995).

The support of the Commission would be an indispensable asset. Over the next three years it would devote a large part of its energies to working out the means by which monetary union could be realised, with the result that the monetary union IGC would be far better structured than its counterpart on political union (Dyson, 1994, p. 146). The Commission also used its power of initiative to maximise support for EMU and minimise the chance of any counter-coalition. By pushing ahead aggressively with proposals for the liberalisation of financial markets, Delors forced the member states to recognise the unsustainability of the *status quo*: they would have to accept either greater currency volatility or some measure of further monetary integration (ibid., pp. 120–1). According to Andrew Moravcsik (1999), the Commission president even advised the French government that France should leave the ERM unless the latter was replaced by a policy regime equally sensitive to economic conditions in all member states. This in turn had the effect of decisively shifting the trade-off faced by the German government: the 'default' position in the event of failure to agree on monetary union would no longer be continuation with the ERM but a return to floating with a greater risk of Deutschmark overvaluation (ibid., p. 414). By signalling at an early stage that the cohesion funds might be increased and used to support policies of convergence towards monetary union, Delors also reduced the risk that the southern countries and Ireland would align with the UK to oppose the initiative.

In some ways the most remarkable role in the first half of 1988 was, however, played by the German presidency of the Council. The Franco-Italian proposals had only called for common management of the European money supply. Given the unusual structure of West German interests in any policy change, it was striking that it should have been a paper drawn up by Foreign Minister Hans-Dietrich Genscher that first took the position that, if monetary union was to happen at all, it should be fully institutionalised around a single currency and a European central bank (Gros and Thygessen, 1992, p. 313). The Genscher paper began the all-important process of steering the Franco-Italian initiative across the reefs of German domestic politics. Key to this were two forms of issue linkage that would dominate the negotiations all the way through to the Maastricht European Council at the end of 1991: (1) monetary union would be far more acceptable to German opinion if it represented an externalisation of Bundesbank disciplines to the whole of the European economic area, rather than the infection of domestic German economic management by the laxer practices of others (Szukala and Wessels, 1997); and (2) monetary union could be a price worth paying for the further development of the EC in the direction of political union (Gaddum, 1994; Schönfelder and Thiel, 1994).

For the moment, however, any grand political trade-off was a distant prospect, and the supporters of monetary integration had to limit themselves to the far more modest objective of keeping the project in play. Potentially there were at least three different areas of significant opposition to full monetary union:

• First it risked alienating the British government. One of the foremost achievements during the period 1984–88 had been to settle the long-standing dispute with the UK over the fundamental financial terms of its membership of the EC, and this was in turn considered to be a principal reason for the marked improvement in the capacity of the EC institutions to take effective decisions. In contrast it was clear that the Thatcher government would either veto monetary union or, if it felt unable to do that, revert to a position of hostility to the *acquis communautaire*, with adverse consequences for the overall performance of the EC.

- Second, the German Bundesbank likewise required careful handling. Its exact powers and preferences are considered below. For the moment it is enough to anticipate the general conclusion that the German central bank had a conditional veto on monetary union. Although constrained from outright hostility, there were various conditions under which it could greatly complicate the initiative in relation both to German public opinion and to the international financial markets. Kohl was also keenly aware that Bundesbank opposition to the formation of the ERM had contributed to the erosion of his predecessor's coalition in the early 1980s. He did not want to suffer a like fate in relation to monetary union.

- Third, Ireland and three of the Mediterranean countries (Greece, Portugal and Spain) were far less convergent than the 'core countries' in both monetary terms (inflation and interest rates) and real performance (GNP and employment levels). Because these countries were between 20 per cent and 50 per cent behind the average EC level of development, some economists argued that they had to be given far more flexibility to grow quickly: 'a one size fits all' monetary policy would be peculiarly inappropriate to their needs and retention of a variable exchange rate instrument would be important to align them smoothly with the rest of the European economy. There was also some discussion of the extent to which the public finances of these countries (and those of Italy) were dependent on 'seigniorage': interest-free loans from issuing a national currency. Any such dependence would limit their ability to make a rapid transition to monetary union without the painful restructuring of their taxation systems and public services (Dornbusch, 1988, pp. 24–30). At the political level, at least three of these countries – Spain, Portugal and Greece – were new entrants to the EC. By appearing to create an 'inner core' from which they would be excluded, monetary union could easily be perceived as an attempt to reverse the verdict of enlargement.

Given these potential sources of opposition, it is understandable that the German presidency took a cautious approach at the Hannover European Council in June 1988. In exchange for French and Italian agreement to move ahead with the liberalisation of financial markets, the question of monetary union was remitted to a committee of experts consisting of the president of the Commission and the governors of all twelve central banks. This allowed consideration of monetary union to get off the starting block without provoking too much hostility in either British or German circles. Those two countries had the strongest interest in rapid movement towards financial liberalisation, and the deal was a logical form of issue linkage to the extent that increased cross-border financial flows would have implications for currency stability.

At the time, some believed that Hannover would bury the issue of monetary union. According to Pöhl, even Chancellor Kohl gave the impression that the Delors committee would either produce a report that was not followed through, or one that was winnowed down to incremental change to the ERM by the logic of lowest common denominator bargaining (Grant, 1994, p. 120). In the event Hannover kept the initiative alive, and most important of all it began the process of neutralising potential opposition from national central bankers by giving them the opportunity to design the monetary union of their choice. Later in this chapter it will be shown that a decisive political coalition in favour of monetary union was not finally consolidated until some way into 1990. However the battle over the form that any monetary union would take, if it were to happen at all, was decided far earlier. The report which emerged from the Delors committee in March 1989 determined all the main issues of principle, and a good deal of the detail too. Amongst its most important outcomes were the following:

- First, a single currency was confirmed as the preferred option for monetary union, on the ground that any other approach would produce the costs and risks without the full benefits. Without a single currency the transaction costs of converting between currencies would remain. Above all the risk of monetary union breaking apart at a later date would be greater if national currencies were not physically replaced by a single currency from which it would be difficult for member states to disentangle themselves. A multicurrency monetary union would thus have lower credibility with the public and the markets (European Commission, 1989, para. 23). By worrying about 'reversibility', the Delors Report contained the paradoxical subtext that the very fragility of the EU political system argued for the most complete form of monetary union available.

- Second, a European central bank was thought to provide the best management structure for monetary union. The report pointed out that complete liberalisation of financial flows would combine with a single currency to break any link between the 'jurisdiction of national central banks and the area in which their banking systems operate'; and that, accordingly they would only be able to achieve their goals through a single monetary policy agreed at the European level. For reasons it was too tactful to mention, the report implied that it would not be enough to assign such a task to a board of national central bankers without taking the further measure of creating a new European institution (European Commission, 1989, paras 24, 31). In this regard it was following the Bundesbank's position that it would be necessary to institutionalise a permanent executive of centrally appointed bankers, majoritarian decision rules, adequate powers to oversee implementation by national central banks, and clear lines of responsibility for the performance of monetary policy.

- Third, as with the Werner Report twenty years earlier, monetary union was thought to require a three-stage transition. As seen in Chapter 3, all member states would join the ERM during the first phase, capital movements would be fully liberalised and mutual surveillance of national economic policies would be introduced to the Council. The second stage would involve the introduction of limits on government borrowing in member states and the establishment of the new institutions. It would be a 'training process leading to collective decision' and there would be a gradual 'transfer of operational functions' (though, as will be seen, this last point was one on which the Delors Report did differ from the eventual outcome in the TEU). The third stage would see the irrevocable locking of national currencies and the introduction of a single currency. The central bankers on the committee thus effectively forced Delors to concede that if monetary union were to happen at all, it would be a long haul. This contrasted with the belief of some in the Commission that it should follow on directly from the completion of the single market at the end of 1992. Indeed the committee rejected all commitment to a firm timetable, preferring to insist that only the qualitative satisfaction of convergence criteria should count.

The Delors Report thus narrowed down the alternatives and focused the debate. From now on a preference for a single currency and a central bank would provide the dominant conception of monetary union, ensuring the stability and coherence of the coalition in favour of a new initiative, in spite of real differences of interest and some attempts to play on those divergences by launching counter-proposals.

In contrast the Delors committee brought out the principal incompatibilities between the potential opponents of monetary union. While the joint opposition of the UK and the southern countries would have signalled that monetary union could only be pursued at the risk of a full-scale schism in the EC's membership, Thatcher instead chose to rely on the Bundesbank to oppose the initiative. In agreeing to the Delors committee, she had expected the governor of the Bank of England, Robin Leigh-Pemberton, to work with Karl-Otto Pöhl to pull the teeth of any monetary union (Thatcher, 1993, p. 708). The difficulty with this was that even insofar as the German central bank shared the preference of the British government for the *status quo*, it was politically constrained from engaging in any coordinated opposition to further monetary integration. As a non-state actor that had no interest in subverting its own reputation for political independence, the Bundesbank was disinclined to insert itself into the intergovernmental diplomacy of the European Council, especially if this meant aligning with another member state against its own government. Nor could it necessarily be expected to oppose monetary union on its own initiative. Since it was a technocratic body that only had a mandate to concern itself with inflation inside West Germany, it had no justification for pushing any opposition to monetary union beyond the point at which it received reasonable reassurance on price stability. This meant that proponents of monetary union could, as has been seen, lessen the force of any Bundesbank opposition by the simple tactical device of getting it to state its own terms.

Pöhl's own retrospective assessment, provided in articles and interviews after his retirement, provides some helpful insights. First, he took the view that the Bundesbank could only slow down the process and not stop it, and even that option was made more difficult by his inclusion in the Delors committee (Grant, 1994, p. 121). Second, the Bundesbank's own preference was for a small monetary union of Benelux, France and West Germany (ibid., p. 147). But this was an unlikely outcome once discussions came to be nested in the EC, with all its commitment to maximising solidarity between members.

Once the agenda moved on from the principle of monetary union to the means by which it might be realised, an alignment between the Bundesbank and the UK became even more implausible, since the two were only alike in sharing a first preference for the *status quo*. They could not have been further apart in their second preferences – in their views of the form that any monetary initiative should take, were it to happen at all. The institutional conditions under which the Bundesbank might be reconciled to the creation of a European central bank were precisely those that would confirm British hostility, and *vice versa*. This was brought out first by Pöhl's insistence to the Delors committee that any monetary union had to have a properly centralised management structure under a European central bank with a secure legal base in the treaties, and second by the UK's attempts to make counterproposals, to which the analysis now turns.

Counterproposals

Having failed to keep a monetary union constructed around a single currency and a European central bank off the agenda, the British government now made counterproposals in the hope of challenging the assumption that the Delors Report was the only route to further monetary integration. In November 1989 it promoted a scheme of competing currencies, whereby any national currency could be freely used throughout the EC (HM Treasury, 1989; Lawson, 1992). Since people would choose to hold the national moneys with the fewest inflation risks, the British government argued that its scheme would produce an 'unforced' convergence between the currencies – and economic performance – of the member states.

When the other governments showed little interest in competing currencies, the British government adopted a plan for a parallel

European currency. Under the 'hard ECU' plan of June 1990, the ECU would cease to be little more than an accounting device and become a real currency. Although it would not replace national currencies, it would be managed in such a way that it would always be the strongest currency in the ERM. It would also contain the anti-inflationary guarantee that it would only be issued in exchange for the withdrawal of national currency (Bank of England, 1990).

The hard ECU was more shrewdly calculated than the competing currencies approach. By demonstrating how a neutral EC currency might replace the Deutschmark at the heart of the ERM, it recognised that the only way to trump support for the immediate creation of a monetary union was to show that there was some way of escaping the political inequalities of the ERM without returning to a regime of freely floating currencies. However there were two flaws to the British approach which, in combination, meant that it was widely perceived as a wrecking tactic rather than a helpful counter proposal:

- The plan meant abandoning any timetable for the transition to a single currency, in contrast to the opinion that this was needed for business preparations to be made (AMUE, 1990).
- Members of the British government made contradictory statements on whether they were happy to see the hard ECU evolve towards full monetary union.

In addition the British government now courted the opposition of the Bundesbank. Both the competing currencies idea and the hard ECU were seen by Frankfurt as likely to make it more difficult for national authorities to manage their monetary aggregates without destabilising transnational flows; and as creating circumstances in which there would be no clear lines of responsibility for the overall management of Europe's money (Dyson, 1994, pp. 136–7, 141–2; Gros and Thygessen, 1992, pp. 331–41).

The initiatives were accordingly interpreted as the pursuit of domestic politics by other means, not as serious attempts to devise positions that were negotiable at the European level. The British chancellor of the exchequer at the time, concedes in his memoirs that the competing currency initiative had the 'largely domestic' intent of forcing ERM membership on to the cabinet agenda (Lawson, 1992, p. 943). Likewise the hard ECU proposal was retained as the public position of the British government long after the substance of the negotiations had moved on, since one of its functions was to paper over internal partisan divisions by providing the different wings of the Conservative Party with a shared policy that they could defend for very different reasons (Forster, 1999, p. 52).

Monetary union and change in the international system

The first European Council to be held after the publication of the Delors Report – the Madrid meeting in June 1989 – agreed that there was sufficient interest amongst the member states to justify convening an intergovernmental conference on monetary union. As this was also the last European Council meeting before the collapse of the communist regimes in Eastern Europe changed the whole context of negotiations on the future of the EC, it is important to take stock of just how far the twelve had advanced towards agreement on monetary union under the influence of considerations of *internal* political economy, and in the absence of *external* geopolitical incentives to reconsider the shape of the EC. As Kenneth Dyson (1994) observes, a close reading of the presidency conclusions from the Madrid European Council reveals that there were still grounds for caution: no date had been fixed for the intergovernmental conference to open or conclude, and the idea of a three-stage transition to monetary union had been accepted without any understanding that participation in the first stage committed countries to proceed to subsequent ones.

The missing element was the absence of a strong German interest in monetary union. Several commentators have argued that West Germany never had any interest in substituting a single currency and central bank based on some average European performance for the Deutschmark and Bundesbank (De Grauwe, 1996, p. 150). In reality, Germany's interests in further monetary integration were complex. Against the foregoing objection had to be set a series of attractions: the hope that monetary union might be used to export German economic disciplines to the rest of the European 'co-prosperity sphere' (Szukala and Wessels, 1997); the fear that a strong Deutschmark could make West Germany uncompetitive; and a general interest in advancing the cause of European integration, so that it might one day facilitate the normalisation of relationships between the two Germanies (Garton-Ash, 1993).

Andrew Moravcsik uses the fact that the West German government was moving firmly in the direction of monetary union well before geopolitical change in Europe to argue that even for Germany the main attraction of a single currency was commercial. The possibility that the ERM might collapse as a result of the liberalisation of capital markets or frustration with its political inequalities, left German exporters heavily exposed to the danger of currency overvaluation (Moravcsik, 1999). But this may be an 'over-correction' of conventional wisdom. Many Germans considered that loss of the Deutschmark would be tantamount to sacrificing one of the principal achievements of postwar West Germany, a potential loss of identity that only became easy to handle in the context of the Federal Republic being traded in for a newly reunified German state. In addition the Federal Republic is a consensus-based political system. A situation in which considerations of monetary stability and those of commercial interest pulled in different directions may well have prompted the Kohl administration to scale down its plans for monetary integration, given the need to balance electoral survival, the unity of its three-way coalition, the continuous struggle to maintain support in the Bundestag and Bundesrat, and the policy coherence of an executive based on a system of semi-autonomous ministries. Indeed it was precisely because it would, in normal circumstances, have been able to rely on the constraining effects of this consensus system that the Bundesbank felt it was enough to hint at 'misgivings', while avoiding opposition (Marsh, 1992, pp. 235–47). The argument that monetary union was needed to adjust the overall pattern of Germany's external relations to geopolitical change was thus a welcome reinforcement of the process of consensus formation. It was probably also a genuine additional motive, even for those who had already been convinced by commercial arguments alone. The following paragraphs explain why.

Faced with the disintegration of the East German state, Kohl laid down two guiding principles. On the one hand the German people had to be accorded the same right as any other to live in a single national community. There could not, as Kohl put it, be any second Versailles (Kohl, 1991, p. 524), in which Germans laboured under discriminatory restrictions unreciprocated by others in Europe. Yet it was equally important that any new Germany should take a form that was acceptable to its eleven neighbours and the superpowers. This was the classic German problem, described by one author as the seeming impossibility of creating a German state that satisfied both the Germans and their neighbours (Ritter, 1962, p. 11). Long the most intractable tension in European politics, the German problem had defined the rhythms of regional conflict since the middle of the nineteenth century, and eventually contributed to the division of the international system itself. There was no guarantee that it would be any easier to solve in the 1990s than in the 1940s.

If mishandled, reunification had the potential to ruin the external relationships by which the postwar Federal Republic had been reintegrated into international society, as well as the values upon which its domestic state and society had been constructed. A divided Germany was, as one author put it, the 'foundation stone on which the entire European order had existed since the 1940s' (Fritsch-Brumazel, 1991, p. 58). There were a number of fears about what might follow any attempt to reverse this arrangement. One notion was that a reunified Germany would be tempted to pivot between Eastern and Western Europe, magnifying its own power position while reducing neighbours to insecurity and nervous exhaustion. A second idea was that Germany would look beyond the region to relations with the superpowers. Some predicted a German–Soviet alignment; others a 'unique and privileged partnership' with the United States (Delors, 1994, p. 258). A third possibility was that a reunified Germany would come to be preoccupied with its own internal affairs. Lulled by the creature comforts of its own economy and society it would neglect responsibility for the wider international systems upon which the security and prosperity of others depended (Kohl, 1991, p. 524).

Cross-cutting these speculative hypotheses was one certainty: reunification had already overturned the central assumption of an 'asymmetric Franco-German relationship' upon which French attitudes towards European integration had been premised since 1950 (Cole, 1997). According to this idea, West German economic strength would be offset by French political leadership; or as de Gaulle had famously put it, West Germany would provide the horses, and France the coachman of European integration. A further anxiety was that German reunification could only be made possible by sacrificing the arguably still larger prize of peace and tranquillity in the international system as a whole. The hope that the Soviet Union would make a peaceful transition to postcommunism was replaced by a real fear of an authoritarian reaction. Mitterrand's view was recorded by an aide as follows: 'only Gorbachev can stop reunification. If he does not do this, he will lose his position and we will have a general in the Kremlin' (Attali, 1995, p. 490).

During the early months, Mitterrand's own thinking crossed the range of possible reactions to reunification (Cole, 1997), seeming at one moment to welcome it and at another to oppose it, most notably when he probed the possibility of a joint Franco-Soviet veto, or shared his fear with the leadership of the dying East German state that 'the European order might collapse and become unstable if events moves to quickly' (*Der Spiegel*, 29 April 1996; *Le Monde*, 4 May 1996). By early 1990 it was, however, already clear that opposition to reunification was impractical, as West Germany was sucked into the management of East Germany by the need to prevent social collapse and uncontrollable migration flows (Bark and Gress, 1992, pp. 1183–9). Meanwhile Washington signalled that it would align with Bonn to push for an early move towards reunification before the creation of a single German state could be linked to proposals for the demilitarisation or wholesale denuclearisation of central Europe, which would have overturned the security infrastructure of the Atlantic Alliance.

Yet it was still in the gift of statecraft to give reunification a form that commanded the consent and reassurance of other states. Not the least country with an interest in this was Germany itself. The idea that states could seek to limit their own power in their rational self-interest had come to be a mantra of the postwar politics of the Federal Republic. Whereas the unilateral cultivation of power was thought to have a self-negating tendency to provoke countercoalitions, multilateral institutions reassured neighbours and allowed societies to realise collective goods. For West German governments, the development of key international institutions such as the EC had ceased to be a means to other ends. It had become the objective of foreign policy itself (Anderson and Goodman, 1993, p. 60). In spring 1990 Kohl and Mitterrand agreed a strategy to adjust the Franco-German relationship to reunification, and ensure its continued centrality to the politics of European integration. By calling for two intergovernmental conferences, one on monetary union, the other on political union, Mitterrand and Kohl aimed to use European integration to create a double multilateralisation of the powers of the new Germany (Kohl and Mitterrand, joint letter to the Irish presidency of the Council, 19 April 1990). But why exactly was monetary union chosen for such a role? The following are possible answers:

- First, monetary union would make it 'materially difficult' for Germany to opt for anything other than a cooperative pattern of interstate relations within a well-functioning European Community: once national moneys had been withdrawn, a country would only be able to unbundle itself from the single currency at the risk of considerable economic disruption over an extended period; and as long as Germany was constrained in this way to be a part of the monetary union, the much cherished goal of currency stability could only be delivered by careful attention to the overall credibility and performance of the EC institutions.

- Second, monetary union was a solution to hand. It would have been a major failure of West Germany's entire postwar foreign policy if the process of European integration had not been available to help manage the politics of reunification. Unable to predict when they might have an opportunity to bridge the divide between the two Germanies, successive federal governments had built up the EC in the hope that it would offer a ready-made framework of constraints into which a reunified Germany might be slotted (Garton-Ash, 1993). A situation in which reunification became a *fait accompli* in just four months as a result of events on the ground (Bark and Gress, 1992, pp. 1183–9) contained a danger that a new German state might become irreversible *before* there was any chance of linking it to an intensified process of European integration. On the other hand there was one proposal for further European integration that had coincidentally been worked out in considerable detail in the months preceding reunification – monetary union.

- Third, monetary union was the price named by the French government. As a primary goal was to ensure that the Franco-German relationship survived geopolitical change in Europe, it was largely up to the French government to name its price by indicating what would reconcile it to reunification, and prevent the shape of the new German state from becoming controversial in French domestic politics.

As the French government was forced by reunification to abandon
its Gaullist notions of using European integration to institutionalise
an asymmetrical relationship with Germany, it became newly
forceful in pressing for political equality and open, collaborative
behaviour in all matters of common concern: monetary union would
end German policy leadership in a significant area of economic
policy making; political union would make the foreign policies of all
member states more transparent to the others, a matter of
considerable importance to the French now that Germany had
more scope to develop as an influential international actor. But the
French government did not want foreign policy cooperation to be
highly institutionalised in its own right, thus it was useful, as has
been seen, to look to parallel initiatives on the economic and
monetary front to ensure continued German attentiveness to the
overall credibility and performance of the EC. If correct, this
interpretation means that monetary union and political union were
logically linked multilateralisations of German power, rather than
two issues that were coincidentally pasted together to gain a
bargaining consensus.

The intergovernmental conference: the bargaining phase

While France and Germany 'up-graded their common interest' in
change by linking monetary union and political union, such an
exchange only sharpened the alienation of the British government by
increasing the level of political integration that would be associated
with the introduction of a single currency. However an IGC could be
called on a simple majority of the EC members, with the implication
that the UK would have to wait until the 'end-game', when other
member states had negotiated a detailed agreement between
themselves, before exercising any veto. Moreover the obvious
response to any British veto would simply be to pursue a like
initiative outside the formal framework of the EC. This meant that
provided it was not itself forced into a monetary union, the UK was
always likely to prefer a single currency developed within the EC to
one established outside it. The latter would provide the UK with no
influence over subsequent developments and no automatic right to
join, should it ever want to do so.

Not only were the other member states emboldened to make a surprise proposal at a special European Council in Rome in October 1990 to proceed to stage two of monetary union from the beginning of 1994, the Italian presidency also broke with formal protocol by asking all the other member states to express their positions before turning to the British prime minister. In this way Andreotti was able to demonstrate that all other member states were prepared to join in the necessary majority for proceeding with the IGCs, even before Thatcher had expressed her position. The sense that an outright veto of monetary union would be somewhere between hopeless and dangerous contributed to her removal a month later. Although it remained possible up to the last moment, anticipation of a British veto on monetary union had already given way to detailed discussion of the precise nature of a UK opt-out when Thatcher's successor, John Major, had his first dealings with Kohl and Mitterrand in early 1991 (Selsdon, 1997). While all the foregoing meant that eventual agreement was likely from the start of the negotiations, important details remained to be bargained, including the following.

Choice of timetable

The attempt to create a monetary union in the 1970s had sparked a debate between the 'economists' and the 'monetarists': the economists thought that the EC countries should wait for all the conditions for monetary union to fall into place before indissolubly locking in their currencies. As no-one could possibly know when this would happen, a fixed timetable had to be avoided. To the monetarists, on the other hand, such a strategy could mean waiting for ever, since in their view public policies and private market behaviour would only converge in *response* to a precise and credible commitment to form a monetary union by a certain date (Tsoukalis, 1977). When the idea of monetary union was relaunched in the 1980s, the economist view remained the preferred position of the Bundesbank: there should be no fixed timetable, as monetary union should not happen at all until the conditions were right.

However all but two of the member governments – Denmark and the UK – were determined that they should not only have a fixed timetable before embarking on such a hazardous adventure, they should also have an irreversible one. It is significant that this was the main point upon which the European Council was prepared to go firmly against the Bundesbank. Because the economic analysis suggested that much of the cost and risk of monetary union would be 'up-front', most members wanted some protection against the possibility that they would make the necessary sacrifices only to find that partners had had second thoughts about proceeding (Winkler, 1999). The eventual outcome was an agreement that the third stage of monetary union would go ahead in 1997 if a majority of member states had fulfilled the criteria, otherwise it would start automatically at the beginning of 1999 among whichever countries had qualified. Given that the latter arrangement significantly increased the probability of monetary union proceeding, the British government might have been expected to oppose it. However it was introduced to the negotiations after the UK had been conceded its opt-out, and the other members were accordingly inclined to see the obligation as something that concerned them alone (Forster, 1999, p. 69; Hogg and Hill, 1995, p. 149).

The nature of stage two

To recap, stage one of monetary union had already started by the time the IGC convened. Following the Delors Report of April 1989 there was widespread agreement that stage three should consist of a central bank and a single currency. Therefore, only stage two needed to be determined. Here there were two contending positions. One was that a European monetary institute should be created and that this should gradually assume the functions of a European central bank during the second phase of monetary union, due to begin on 1 January 1994. This would allow for a running-in period and it would make the collapse of the initiative increasingly unlikely, as governments and markets progressively locked their financial arrangements into the new currency and its institutions. However the Bundesbank objected that such a strategy would mean a period of divided control in the management of Europe's money: there would be a phase during which it could be in the interests of particular national authorities to behave irresponsibly and create excessive monetary expansion. The profits of years of counter-inflationary discipline could be dissipated.

In the event the Bundesbank's position prevailed. It was agreed that any European monetary institute established in stage two would make the technical preparations for the creation of the new central bank but not exercise any of its powers. In many ways, stage two would be a period of adjustment at the national rather than the European level: its principal activities would be continued efforts by national authorities to meet the qualifying criteria and to undertake to make their own national central banks independent, so that these could in turn be federated as a strictly independent European Central Bank.

Qualifying criteria

There is room for much disagreement on whether monetary union really does require constraints on the borrowing and indebtedness of member states; and if so, whether those limits should be rigid or flexible, qualitative or quantitative (Buiter *et al.*, 1993). However the Bundesbank insisted on permanent constraints on borrowing by national governments, on the ground that monetary union could otherwise encourage irresponsible fiscal behaviour that would make it difficult for the European central bank to control monetary expansion. The German government agreed with this position, seeing the parallel development of fiscal controls as a means of using monetary union to advance its own ambition of creating a comprehensive zone of economic stability in Western Europe (*Ordnungspolitik*). Most of the other governments aligned themselves predictably. The Netherlands sympathised with the German approach. Italy and some others opposed deficit limits because of the enormous adjustment costs they would impose, and a suspicion that the criteria were being designed to ensure that some countries were almost certain to fail to enter monetary union. France objected because it was eager to create a wide monetary union in which there would be several counterpoints to the Bundesbank approach. There were however two curiosities. The first was Spain, which supported tight fiscal criteria on the ground that this would help it bring its own public finances into order (Dyson, 1994, p. 149). The second was the UK, which supported the criteria for largely tactical reasons: it thought they would split the coalition in favour of monetary union. However the countries opposed to the criteria eventually had to concede the point in order to get what they wanted on a fixed timetable. The eventual outcome was a 3 per cent limit on borrowing and a 60 per cent constraint on total indebtedness, subject to the 'in-built' flexibility that allowance would be made where deficits were 'exceptional and temporary' or had been declining 'substantially and continuously' (European Commission, 1992, Article 104c).

Coping with the British and Danish problems

The ideal position of the majority of governments was that all members should agree to the 'preprogrammed' approach, which would make monetary union an obligation of EC membership to be satisfied according to clear criteria and a fixed timetable once a new treaty had been democratically ratified. However the British and Danish governments indicated that this was either intrinsically unacceptable to them or certain to ensure the rejection of the treaty by their parliaments or public. For these two governments the ideal was that *all* members should abandon the obligatory transition and opt in to the monetary union at a moment of their own choosing. This would avoid any suspicion that some governments were less committed than others, so diminishing their influence over the detailed construction of monetary union, and avoiding the risk that market expectations would be less convergent in the case of their economies, a factor that could complicate their ability to join the monetary union at a later date. Although an early draft of the treaty came close to conceding the UK–Danish position, the other member states were eventually only prepared to concede options that specifically named the UK and Denmark. This was the inevitable consequence of the priority given to the Franco-German compromise, since 'tough convergence criteria in exchange for automatic transition' was clearly incompatible with allowing too many member states to opt in at the moment of their choice.

Conclusion

There would seem to be a very strong case for the following conclusion: the plan for monetary union had its origins in the changing political economy of European integration, but it was only carried to a successful conclusion because of a shift in the external geopolitical environment of European integration. Until the end of 1989 the proposal for monetary union stood or fell on whether it responded to the pressing economic needs of the member governments: the need for a currency regime that would allow escape from the asymmetries of the ERM and continue to deliver exchange rate stability upon the completion of the single market. But it was by no means clear whether this was enough to deliver the required consensus in West German politics. Chancellor Kohl was, however, able to consolidate a coalition in favour of monetary union, and to prevent it from becoming a deeply divisive and contested issue in domestic politics by linking the single currency to the widely held view that it would help reconcile Germany's neighbours to its reunification.

Chapter 5

Implementing Monetary Union, 1991–98

In the study of European integration, the politics of implementation are often as important as those of bargaining the initial deal. This chapter examines the political fragility of the monetary union project for much of the period 1991–98; the strategies of domestic political adjustment pursued by those governments seeking to qualify for membership; the contention that the identity of the founding membership was significantly affected by the decision to pursue currency union through the institutions of the European Union, rather than some other forum; and explanations of why the transition ultimately succeeded, with a founding membership of eleven.

The attainability of monetary union aroused considerable scepticism. One argument was that it was based on an unstable coalition: the Bundesbank was thought to be unreconciled to the Treaty of European Union, and key actors in the French and German governments to have incompatible objectives, as well as rather different understandings of what had been agreed at Maastricht (Connelly, 1995). Another argument was that the means chosen to attain monetary union were likely to conflict with the end itself: that the convergence criteria would undermine public support and depress economic activity, so plunging monetary union into a downward spiral of political and economic failure (De Grauwe, 1995). A third suggestion, often heard in more rarefied contributions to the French referendum campaign, was that monetary union would soon be abandoned as an anachronism, more suited to the early stages of the Cold War than to its end game: supranational structures were apparently no longer needed to bind states into codes of good behaviour, since markets and democracy would ensure the same outcome without suspending healthy forms of competition between national policy regimes, or circumscribing the right of national communities to make important choices for themselves. A fourth point of view was that it was unclear whether the EU had the political coherence and institutional resources needed to hold a project such as monetary union together during the long transition to a single currency: that it was politically too weak to tame the anarchy of international currency markets.

The ratification and currency crises of 1992–93

Some writers have seen the agreement of new EU treaties as a two-level game: the same set of solutions has to work in the 'bargaining game', where the goal is to arrive at a text that all the governments can sign, and in the 'ratification game', where the aim is to ensure that no national parliament or public rejects the treaty. But because bargaining precedes ratification – sometimes with a lag of several years – governments may systematically miscalculate the chance of obtaining consent for their agreements. Because the Treaty of European Union (TEU) provoked just such a 'ratification crisis' the whole project of monetary union was thrown into doubt during 1992–93. In June 1992 the Danish public voted against the treaty. The British government, which had at one stage intended to prove its European credentials by being the first to ratify the TEU, now suspended passage of the enabling legislation, pending its approval by all other member states. President Mitterrand responded by calling a referendum in France, hoping both to divide the French right and to shore up the authority of the treaty. However the campaign divided all mainstream forces in French politics, and provided only ambiguous political legitimation for the treaty and monetary union: in an outcome that came to be known as 'le petit oui', France voted by just 51 to 49 to proceed (Moravcsik, 1993b).

The Maastricht ratification crisis of 1992–93 was to have lasting effects on the politics of the transition to monetary union. In spite of the treaty clause committing most member states to move to stage three without further reference to their parliaments or publics once the TEU had been ratified, there were always going to be limits to the willingness of governments to press ahead without a domestic consensus, not least because the new currency would have to command the acceptance of its users. This problem was particularly acute in Germany. As the clause on automatic transition to stage three had been introduced to the Maastricht European Council at the last minute by Mitterrand and Andreotti, Kohl had accepted it on his own authority and without reference to his cabinet. With the ratification crisis, German opponents of the TEU felt emboldened to launch a legal challenge in the Constitutional Court, which ruled, *inter alia*, that the Bundestag could not be denied the opportunity to hold a vote on whether the convergence criteria had in fact been satisfied (Bundesverfassungsgericht, 1993). Meanwhile the Bundesbank made it clear that it would be issuing its own report on the satisfaction of the criteria, before any Bundestag vote.

The political problems of 1992–93 interacted with a developing crisis within the ERM, though the precise causal connections between the two are a matter for some debate. Between 1987 and 1992 the ERM seemed to settle down to a period of stability, without any realignments. This reinforced an orthodoxy in EU thinking that a progressive hardening of the ERM would ease the way to full monetary union. However the old ERM collapsed in a two-stage crisis between September 1992 and August 1993. The first wave attacked the 'soft underbelly of the system': that is, the countries that had still not achieved full nominal convergence – the UK, Italy, Spain and Portugal. The second afflicted the core itself, notably the Franco-German parity. Although the two crises overlapped, it was not until August 1993 that the EU's finance ministers finally abandoned the fight. In what was a *de facto* suspension of the old ERM, they agreed to widen the margins of fluctuation to plus or minus 15 per cent.

This is not the place to review the various explanations that have been offered for the collapse of the old ERM (see Cobham, 1994, pp. 3–5). Of greater concern to this analysis is the debate that developed between those who thought it would make monetary union more or less attainable. In one corner were those who argued that the average interest rates in Europe could now fall. Together with a more realistic set of exchange rates, this would aid economic recovery and make the convergence criteria easier to attain. In the other corner were those who continued to believe that a strong ERM was a necessary glide path to stage three: in addition to its place amongst the qualifying criteria for entry, the discipline of the currency mechanism was thought to be a powerful tool of 'nominal convergence' on low rates of inflation, and thus a helpful means of preparing the EU for a 'one size fits all' interest rate. It was also considered to be a useful means of coordinating macroeconomic policy without having to set up interim institutional mechanisms which would have alarmed the Bundesbank and tested the capacity of the EU to handle such decisions intergovernmentally (Currie and Whitley, in Cobham, 1994, p. 167).

The main impact of the crisis may, however, have been political. In the short term there was a noticeable soft-peddling on monetary union, and a serious loss of confidence that the EU had the institutional capacity to consummate a monetary union in the face of the massive financial power of the currency markets. The British prime minister felt emboldened to mock the project as having 'all the potency of a rain dance'. In the longer term the main effect may, however, have been to weaken the position of those who still hankered after a 'half-way house' and to concentrate the coalition in favour of monetary integration behind the option of full monetary union.

The politics of convergence

Even if governments succeeded in maintaining winning domestic coalitions for the principle of monetary union, they could not be sure of obtaining agreement for the austerity measures needed to meet the qualifying criteria. One of the reasons why the TEU set the convergence criteria at 3 per cent for annual government borrowing and 60 per cent for accumulated debt was that those levels were close to the average national performance at the time the treaty was signed. The EU was, however, in the mature phase of an economic upturn during 1990–91. In reality the average underlying structural deficit in member states (adjusted for the economic cycle) was between 5 per cent and 6 per cent. Various one-off measures were used to reduce deficits for 1997 only. But the need to maintain broad political and market credibility in the bid for monetary union limited the scope for accounting tricks, and the application of the criteria entailed sacrifices that were real enough. Between 1993 and 1997 the average structural deficits of member states narrowed from 6 per cent to 2 per cent.

In each country the domestic politics of convergence were slightly different, depending on the coalitional structure of governments, and the likely electoral sanctions and rewards associated with either implementing the criteria or failing to make the test of monetary union. Yet everywhere they represented a distinctive break with the previous politics of domestic adjustment to European integration. In the past the acceptability of EU decisions had often been depended on the citizen only experiencing them indirectly, as national policies or as market responses not immediately associated in the public mind with new European policy frameworks (Beetham and Lord, 1998). In the case of the convergence criteria things were, arguably, the other way round: national governments used the authority of an EU project to achieve a fiscal restructuring that they would have had to undertake anyway, and a new European policy regime was constructed on the back of tax increases and public expenditure cuts, rather than intangible market forces. A further problem was that the politics of adjustment were interactive between the different domestic arenas. To some extent this produced some deft collusion: governments helped each other out of domestic difficulties that might have stopped any one of them from qualifying. But it also produced some real competition to shift political costs and risks from one member state to another.

The cases of France, Germany and Italy illustrate these various themes. Whereas Helmut Kohl was present throughout the seven-year steeplechase to satisfy the Maastricht criteria, the durability of the deal that he had negotiated with François Mitterrand was tested by three changes of political leadership in France. In 1993 the Parti Socialiste government was replaced by an administration of the centre-right (the Balladur government 1993–95). In 1995 Jacques Chirac succeeded Mitterrand as president and promptly substituted a new centre-right administration (the Juppé government, 1995–97). In June 1997 the centre-right was replaced by a government of the left under Lionel Jospin. At several points it looked as though monetary union would take second place to internal political alternation or other domestic objectives. Fiscal restructuring was slowed down by competition between Balladur and Chirac for the presidential nomination between 1993 and 1995. During the 1995 presidential race, Chirac suggested that he might hold a referendum on the single currency. He also campaigned on a programme that was ambiguous between promising reflation and qualifying for monetary union. The result was to reduce the public acceptability of the programme of fiscal retrenchment that was eventually introduced. Two winters of public protest brought the Juppé administration to the point where it felt unable to carry on implementing the convergence criteria without fresh electoral authority.

However the surprise election of Jospin in June 1997 provided the severest test to date of the continued commitment of a French government to monetary union. The incoming coalition of the left had campaigned on the demand that four conditions should be added to the single currency project: renegotiation of the Stability Pact; a European economic government to act as a counterweight to the ECB; the inclusion of the southern countries in stage three; and avoidance of a euro overvaluation against external currencies. These conditions can be seen as the price that monetary union had to pay for the two-round voting system by which French governments are elected. Because success is determined by the ability of large parties to persuade smaller ones to transfer votes between the two rounds, the multiparty coalition of the left had to campaign on a programme that made significant concessions to the Communists and the Greens on the single currency project. Another suggestion is that the four conditions were part of a programme that was not designed for implementation, but to minimise the extent of an expected electoral defeat.

On winning the election Jospin therefore found himself in a bind. On the one hand he only had a slender majority in the assembly and the PS was unable to rule without the votes of the Communists and Greens. On the other the four conditions were directly contrary to the basis upon which Kohl had spent the last years shoring up his own domestic coalition on the issue of monetary union. For a moment it looked as though the single currency was caught in a political contradiction: the conditions that would allow it to proceed in German domestic politics were precisely those that would make it politically unsustainable in France, and *vice versa*.

From September 1994 Kohl had a majority of just ten in the Bundestag, made up of a three-way coalition of his own Christian Democrats (CDU), the Bavarian Christian Democrats (CSU) and the Liberals (FDP). Almost all the regional governments (*Länder*), upon which the German federal system is based, were in the hands of the opposition, which accordingly enjoyed a blocking majority in the upper house of the German parliament, the Bundesrat. This conjuncture presented Kohl with tough challenges of political management. As seen, the Constitutional Court had ruled that the treaty commitment to an automatic transition to monetary union could not extinguish the right of the Bundestag to hold a vote on whether it felt the convergence criteria had been satisfied. In addition it was by no means a foregone conclusion that Germany would itself satisfy the convergence criteria. To ensure that it did, Kohl would have to negotiate measures acceptable to all three components of his coalition and then usher them through the Bundesrat, which was controlled by the Social Democrat opposition.

Not only did different members of the coalition have different preferences as to how the criteria should be met, but also the two smaller parties had difficult electoral positions to protect. After reunification the FDP faced the threat of falling beneath the 5 per cent threshold of electoral support, without which a party receives no representation in the German political system. The CSU, on the other hand, looked as though it might lose overall control of its power base in the Bavarian state government for the first time since the war. While the FDP attempted to fight for its political survival by carving out a political niche as a low-tax party, the CSU sought to protect its flank against more conservative forces in Bavaria by assuming a sceptical line towards the replacement of the Deutsch-mark by a single currency. This combination threatened to create a political gridlock around the convergence criteria. The left of the CDU baulked at spending cuts which would have eroded social protection, the FDP opposed tax increases, and the CSU made it clear that it would not accept a relaxation of the 3 per cent target for government borrowing. At one point, in December 1996, Kohl had to threaten to resign to secure a budget that all three parties in the coalition were ready to back.

Meanwhile the SPD saw electoral advantage in suggesting the postponement of full monetary union, and in placing the governing coalition under the further strain of having to negotiate its budgets with the opposition if they were to secure Bundesrat approval. Doubts about a headlong rush towards monetary union allowed the SPD to play both sides of the political street, at once appealing to those conservatives who were concerned about the abandonment of the Deutschemark, and to more left-wing constituencies anxious about unemployment and austerity. However a critical turning point came in the Hamburg state elections of 1997 when the SPD failed to turn the monetary union issue to its advantage in spite of its candidate's support for a delay in the start of stage three. Ultimately there were three constraints on the mobilisation of opposition by the SPD. First, the SPD could only cohere around a call for a delay to the start of stage three, not outright opposition to the single currency.

Second, anxiety about the demise of the Deutschmark continued to be counterbalanced by strong public support for European integration in general. Third, the unpopularity of the single currency in the polls did not necessarily mean that it would be a sufficiently salient issue to influence voting behaviour. From Kohl's point of view, the best course was therefore to remove all pretexts for delay; to preserve 'issue linkages' that made it clear that monetary union was part of a wider package of European integration, and to work for refinements to the project that pre-empted domestic criticisms. Before returning to an examination of how he attempted this, it is necessary to introduce the case of Italy to our reconstruction of the interactive (domestic and European) game faced by governments seeking a successful launch of stage three of monetary union.

Italy provided a quite different example of the politics of domestic adjustment. Until the end of 1996 it looked as though everyone would be best satisfied if Italy aimed to qualify on the basis of its public accounts for 1999 or 2000. This would allow it to 'save face' by joining in time for the introduction of the single currency, while giving it between four and five years – rather than the seemingly impossible two years – to reduce its public deficit from 7 per cent to 3 per cent of GNP. Meanwhile Germany could be brought safely inside stage three, before Italy was a full member of the group. Three factors combined to undermine this incremental strategy. First, it began to look as though Spain and Portugal would qualify for stage three in 1997, thus highlighting Italy's political failure to be a founding member of monetary union. Second, the Italian government found that it had a one-off opportunity to put itself in a virtuous circle of deficit reduction by making a dash to qualify. Third, the formation of the centre-left Olive Tree Coalition was important. With a political power base in the north, it was exposed to challenge from the regionalist Lega Nord, which could be expected to gain support if the 'feckless' south was blamed for Italy's failure to qualify for monetary union.

On the other hand, qualification would require a minority coalition to push through an unprecedented restructuring of public finances in just two years, and to do this at the same time as it was attempting further constitutional adjustments to the political system itself. If the government looked to the right for extra votes it risked having to make concessions to Silvio Berlusconi on constitutional issues, such as the independence of the judiciary. If it looked to the left it risked dependence on the Reconstructed Communist Party (RC), from which the most important component of the governing coalition – the Democratic Left (PDS) – was anxious to differentiate itself. During the final lap to qualify the Prodi administration had briefly to resign when the RC refused to vote for the 1997 budget. Ultimately, Prodi's greatest asset turned out to be the strength of domestic consensus in favour of monetary union. The income tax surcharge actually gained legitimacy by being labelled the 'euro tax' and the RC had to drop its opposition to fiscal retrenchment when trade unions turned out on the streets of Florence and Bologna to protest *against* obstruction of the austerity measures needed to qualify for stage three!

Whatever their particular difficulties, all governments seeking to qualify shared one advantage: they had access to the European policy framework, and therefore an opportunity to use it to ease their domestic difficulties. As seen, however, this was as much a competitive game as a collusive one. The cases of France and Germany illustrate the point. Faced with the domestic political gridlock described above, Kohl's finance minister, Theo Waigel, anticipated conservative opposition to monetary union by proposing a Stability Pact of enforceable constraints on public borrowing in countries adopting the euro. Although there was little support in the Council of Ministers for his initial suggestion that the limit on government borrowing should tighten from 3 per cent to 1 per cent of GNP, he was able to gain useful room for domestic political manoeuvre by negotiating a pact in which fines would be levied on those countries which persistently broke the 3 per cent borrowing limit. The importance of the Stability Pact to the neutralisation of German domestic opposition rose in proportion to the probability that Spain, Portugal and Italy would qualify for stage three. It allowed Kohl to give the following answer to the criticism that the convergence criteria were just 'one-off tests': a country that insisted on qualifying before it was ready would do so at its own risk, and not that of the EU as a whole. Well before there was even the slightest possibility of a default, a government with excessive borrowing would pass under the tight supervision of the Stability Pact. In a memorable showdown with Chirac at the Dublin European Council of December 1996, Kohl made it clear that the Stability Pact had such an important place in his domestic political strategy that he could not proceed to full monetary union without it (Milesi, 1998).

The problem was that when the French government looked to the European framework to ease its domestic difficulties, it did so in a manner that brought it into direct conflict with Kohl's efforts at domestic political management. Kohl would later quip that it took two years for Mitterrand to 'accept Europe', Chirac six months and Jospin two weeks. However the politics of French adjustment to monetary union had reached a genuine impasse by the summer of 1997. For some months the new French government gave up on any unconditional guarantee that it would meet the criteria: its position was that it was still committed to the single currency and that it would try its best to reduce borrowing to 3 per cent, but any further austerity measures would be politically impossible and economically harmful. For its part the German government had little choice but to recognise that the Jospin administration was probably the only remaining force in French politics which could sustain the single currency project: with the defeat of the Juppé government the mainstream right had turned to the long-standing critic of the single currency, Philippe Séguin, and beyond the weakened parties of the centre lay no one except the Front National.

All of this meant that there was little choice but to attempt the seemingly impossible task of integrating elements of Jospin's four conditions into the final arrangements for monetary union without disturbing the integrity of the Stability Pact, which was so important to German opinion. The Stability Pact was thus renamed the Stability and Growth pact. The creation of a new Employment Council was included in the Amsterdam Treaty (Duff, 1997). Above all the German government gave ground on the creation of a special Euro Council, which would be confined to the countries that were full members of the monetary union. The French finance minister, Dominique Strauss-Kahn, argued that monetary union could not enjoy legitimacy if elected governments seemed only to be concerned to shuffle off their share of political responsibility for economic welfare. The independence of governments and central banks did not, therefore, remove the need for both to be equally organised at the European level (*Financial Times*, 27 November 1997).

The politics of membership

The politics of convergence overlapped those of determining the initial membership. But the two issues were never identical. First, the objections to the inclusion of some countries were of a kind that could not be removed by their satisfying the membership criteria. Indeed the criteria often seemed to function as camouflage for things that could not be stated publicly about the economic governability of some member states. Second, there was the problem of what to do with countries that were judged not to have satisfied the criteria even though their governments very much wanted to participate. Third, there was the converse problem of those who did not want to take part in the first wave even if they satisfied the criteria. It was in relation to these last two points that the severest tensions looked like developing between the economics and politics of the project. As seen, economic considerations pointed to the importance of forming an optimal currency area, even if this required the involuntary exclusion of some countries. For this reason the Bundesbank was thought to be eager to steer monetary union towards the formation of a narrow grouping of Germany, France and the Benelux countries (plus Austria after 1995). Former Bundesbank President Pohl, for example, responded to the gathering crisis in the ERM during 1992–93 by calling for the immediate formation of a 'small' monetary union, which would effectively have pre-empted the Maastricht Treaty.

On the other hand there were good political reasons to fear the divisive implications of any differential application of EU policy regimes. Those who were involuntarily excluded from monetary union might refuse to lend their full cooperation to other EU policies and decision-making processes. The 'outs' might come to fear that the single currency 'ins' would tend to form a voting bloc on those other EU questions, so locking them into a permanent minority and removing the fluidity of alignments which had in the past promoted the cohesion of the EU by ensuring that those who lost on some issues won on others. The economic positions of the 'ins' and the 'outs' could also be cumulatively divergent, thus increasing the political difficulty of any subsequent effort to bridge the divide. Economic and political tensions could affect the sustainability of the single market, particularly if countries sought to compensate for their exclusion from stage three by running a soft currency policy.

Volatility in the wake of the ERM crises of 1992–93 had already strained trading relations between France, Italy and the UK. The effects of involuntary exclusion on the domestic politics of particular member states also had to be considered, as did likely implications for elite and public attitudes towards EU membership in those countries. In Spain and Portugal the possibility of a small monetary union was often presented as a partial reversal of the 1986 enlargement of the EU that defined their identity as European countries. In Italy exclusion would have been still more traumatic. Not only was Italy a founding member of the EU, but its participation in EU policy regimes was considered indispensable to good domestic governance. Failure to qualify would almost certainly have discredited the new leaders and groups who were struggling into existence following the collapse of the first republic in the early 1990s. It could even have threatened the cohesion of the state itself, with the prosperous north blaming the subsidy culture of the south for its exclusion from the mainstream of European economic opportunities.

A kind of 'domino effect' also operated: the likely inclusion of some countries often reduced the feasibility of excluding others. There was almost universal agreement that there was no point in going ahead without France and Germany. A monetary union which did not include at least one other major European power looked like magnifying Germany's leading position in the European political economy, rather than multilateralising it. Yet France and Germany could not form a single currency without dislocating the Benelux economies. Belgium could not be brought into the monetary union without introducing an interpretation of the debt criterion which would allow Italy to qualify if it also satisfied the 3 per cent borrowing limit. French governments often supported a wide monetary union to reduce the weight of Germany in its decision making and to ensure that its southern producers were not vulnerable to the volatile currencies of excluded Mediterranean neighbours. Once it looked as though Spain and Portugal might qualify, the effects of excluding Italy from the founding membership were clearly going to be still more devastating for the Prodi government. As various actors manoeuvred to secure the founding membership of their choice, there was one factor that sometimes slipped from view: the final choice of members would not be played out in any one domestic political arena, it would be governed by EU procedures. Governments would have to justify excluding others in the European Council – and possibly in the face of a Commission recommendation that reflected the opposite conclusion. Whatever interpretation of the criteria was eventually adopted, it would have to be applied fairly and consistently.

But what of those countries which might choose not to participate? Four fell into this group: Denmark, Greece, Sweden and the

UK. Greece showed no wish to qualify for the first round. In Denmark and Sweden, referendums on European integration in the early 1990s had divided domestic politics, not least the ruling Social Democratic parties. The governments of both countries were therefore anxious to avoid decisions that would further strain internal cohesion. They already faced the challenge of ratifying the treaty changes set to emerge from the Amsterdam IGC, and in Sweden's case a general election was scheduled for the autumn after the European Council was due to make its decision on the start of stage three. There was, however, one crucial difference: Denmark had secured an opt-out from automatic and obligatory transition to stage three on satisfaction of the criteria; Sweden had not. Nonetheless, the Swedish government announced at the end of 1996 that it would not be seeking membership and it effectively disqualified itself by not rejoining the ERM before that date. Although this provoked a letter from the presidency of the Council reminding Sweden of its formal obligations, the other members did not press the matter. The voluntaristic aspect of the politics of membership was underlined as much by the folly of including 'reluctant partners' as by the difficulty of excluding any country that was set on joining. Member states had to be left to make their own judgement on the manner and timing of seeking domestic consent for adhesion to stage three. For both Denmark and Sweden, there was a case for waiting until the single currency was up and running elsewhere in the EU before putting the question to popular vote.

As domestic constraints tightened around the UK's Conservative government between 1993 and 1997, it became evident that it would be in no position to exercise its option to participate in the first wave of monetary union. This raised the problem of how it should respond to the possibility that other countries might form a single currency from which the UK had excluded itself. Whatever answer was given to this question would have to satisfy an awkward two-level game. Faced by a divided cabinet, a split party, a disappearing parliamentary majority and meltdown in the opinion polls, domestic political management was paramount to the Major government. On the other hand it remained the policy of the British government to participate in the shaping of a single currency that it might have to join at a later date. As the UK knew to its cost, enlargements of EU policy regimes are governed by the doctrine of the *acquis communautaire*: in order to prevent the destabilisation of compromises between existing members, late entrants are only permitted to negotiate the speed and modalities of adopting established policies and institutions, not their content.

Under pressure of political competition, the Labour opposition was unwilling to allow itself to be outflanked on monetary union by the Conservatives. Both parties accordingly entered the 1997 election under the cover of a promise to hold a referendum before exercising the UK's option to join the single currency. Nonetheless the change of government provoked speculation as to whether the UK would aim to join in time for the introduction of the single currency in 2002. In spite of strong pleas from the CBI to consider this option very seriously, the Blair cabinet rejected it in the autumn of 1997. One set of reasons was economic: the economic cycles of the UK and the euro zone would have to be aligned to the point at which the UK could be safely accommodated in a 'one size fits all' interest rate policy; sterling was currently overvalued relative to the euro zone; and structural factors made the UK economy unusually sensitive to interest rates, with the implication that it would have to carry a disproportionate share of any 'burden of adjustment' to the monetary policy pursued by the European central bank. Other factors were political. The Blair administration calculated that after years of Euroscepticism, it would be unwise to hold a referendum on joining the single currency before British opinion was more confident about the UK's position in the EU. Nor was it prepared to take risks with its governing credibility at the start of what it hoped would be at least two terms of office. These factors illustrated the 'path-dependent' character of the UK's relationship with the monetary union project: the options of any one government are necessarily limited by the investment of previous administrations in economic convergence and political commitment.

Franco-German compromise on the creation of a new Sectoral Council of Ministers confined to members of the euro (The Euro-11 Council) highlighted the institutional dilemma of 'outs' such as the UK: if the agenda for the main Council of Finance Ministers (Ecofin) was to be discussed beforehand in a forum confined to the euro countries, most agreements would, *de facto*, be made before the 'outs' had an opportunity to take part. The 'outs' responded with the demand that they should be invited to all sessions of the Euro-11 Council and that they should only be required to withdraw when the meeting turned to a predefined list of issues that only affected the 'ins'. The British government claimed that anything else could even put the Euro-11 Council in breach of the TEU, which committed all members to regard monetary policy as a question of common concern. The French government, on the other hand, insisted that the 'outs' could not expect the privileges of membership without its obligations: they could only expect to be kept informed and to be invited to meetings at the discretion of the 'ins'.

The negotiating dynamics on this question contained several ambivalences that were highly revealing of the politics of monetary union. While the French and German governments needed to defend a 'members only' Euro Council as this was the basis upon which they had agreed the Stability Pact, they both kept a line open to the UK. The Kohl administration – which was coming under attack from the Bundesbank for agreeing to the Euro-11 Council in the first place – saw the UK as a likely supporter of its view that such a body should complement and not challenge the decisions of the European central bank. The French government, on the other hand, indicated that it would support graduated access to the Euro-11 Council in proportion to the commitment of any 'out' to work towards full membership. In other words it sought to use it as an opportunity to lever the new British government closer to monetary union. This reflected a general belief that monetary union should eventually embrace all member countries if the political and economic cohesion of the EU was to be ensured, and a particular preoccupation that sterling should be included in the euro to improve the prospects of it developing as an international currency. As for the UK itself, it both set itself up as leader of the 'outs' and seemed at one point to be ready to cut a separate deal in which the UK would have special access to the Euro-X on account of its size (*Financial Times*, 1–15 December 1997).

The end game

Market estimates of which countries were likely to participate if monetary union went ahead could be gauged at any moment by looking at the spread of bond prices. For most of time the best guess seemed to be that the founding membership would consist of between seven and nine countries, so how did the EU get to the finishing line with eleven countries ready to qualify for stage three?

One argument is that the eleven just got lucky. The economic cycle turned in their favour just at the right moment and a substantial depreciation of the euro-zone currencies against the dollar and sterling allowed the continental economy to be floated off the rocks. Once they had a lucky break, the vicious circle of the early years of the transition rapidly turned into a virtuous one: with economic recovery it became easier to satisfy the criteria, and each country that moved closer to satisfying the criteria found that its bond prices converged on German levels, thus further reducing current borrowing and increasing their chance of qualifying. This was especially important for Italy. Another suggestion is that political leadership was important. By working on detailed changeover plans presented as a green paper to the Madrid European Council in 1995, the Commission kept the initiative alive – and revived its market credibility.

However a further explanation relates to the 'lock-in' effects that governments may experience once they sign up to European policy initiatives (Pierson, 1996). These are of two kinds. First, the very act of entering a binding political commitment changes the pay-off matrix of either adopting or abandoning a new policy. National political leaders find that they cannot accept failure without severe damage to the overall reputation of the EU and to their own credibility as a reliable partner of other member states. The power of this 'lock-in' effect is proportional to the felt need of governing elites for a well functioning EU if they are to achieve their objectives, and to domestic perceptions that the smooth management of EU issues is an important test of governing competence. A second lock-in effect has to do with the increasing importance of the relationship between political leaderships and international financial markets. The instinct of politicians may be to keep their options open, rather than tie the fate of their careers to initiatives that might fail. But international capital and currency markets impose a contrary logic: if politicians want to achieve their objectives they have to prove their commitment by taking risks and paying costs in the currency of tough political choices. By 1997–98 the markets had extracted a substantial sunk investment of political credibility from Europe's leaders: to fail at such a point would be to confront the public with the ghastly reality that all sacrifices entailed in meeting the convergence criteria in a manner that was credible to the markets had been vain.

Lock-in effects which followed from nesting the monetary union initiative into the EU institutions may also explain a further feature of the final outcome. As has been seen throughout this analysis, the optimum currency area for the core countries that were in a position to push ahead on their own probably consisted of just six or so participants. Anyone attempting to explain monetary union on the basis of monetary economics alone would therefore be hard pressed to give a convincing account of why a founding membership of eleven eventually emerged. It is, however, relatively easy to explain as the effect of mediating monetary union through the EU institutions: countries could only be involuntarily excluded at the price of rancour and discord spilling over into other areas of EU policy making; and once the qualifying criteria became EU norms they would, as seen, have to be applied fairly between member states, with full 'face-to-face' explanations for all decisions made. In other words, qualification for monetary union was a classic 'nested game', in which common membership of the EU institutions produced a different outcome in terms of the composition of stage three from any that would have been likely under a consideration of monetary interests alone (Tsebelis, 1990; Sandholtz, 1996): the 'core' countries were prepared to accept a suboptimal outcome in terms of their monetary interests (they could have done better by going for a small monetary union) in order to avoid political and economic costs in a series of linked games (the single market, the overall process of integration and so on).

Chapter 6

The Economics of the Maastricht Treaty

This chapter examines the practical arrangements for introducing the single currency set out in the Treaty on European Union (TEU) including the phased approach, the convergence criteria for determining membership of EMU, and the Danish and UK protocols concerning their membership. It then considers some of the key policy issues outlined in the treaty: monetary policy in stage three, economic and fiscal policy surveillance, exchange rate policy, the relationship between monetary and fiscal policy, and the fixing of exchange rates for the start of stage three. It concludes that many important issues central to the introduction of the new currency were inadequately set out in the treaty.

The TEU, negotiated at Maastricht, sets the framework for economic and monetary union in Europe. It describes in very broad terms how the transition to the single currency should progress: criteria according to which a member state's participation will be assessed; a framework of objectives, rules and procedures for the central banking institutions; the common objectives and the rules by which member states should determine their monetary, fiscal and exchange rate policies; and the legal basis for the introduction of the single currency. The TEU contains protocols which enable Denmark and the UK to choose whether or not to participate. In parallel with monetary union, the treaty extends the competence and institutional arrangements of the EU on a 'three pillar' basis (the institutions of the European Community, Common Foreign and Security Policy, and Justice and Home Affairs). But these matters are beyond our scope.

A phased transition

The treaty followed the Werner and Delors Reports in laying down a three-stage transition to EMU, though each document differed in the purposes it assigned to each stage. The TEU version was as follows.

Stage one

Following the Madrid European Council of June 1989, stage one was deemed to have begun on 1 July 1990. It involved the completion of the single market, economic convergence and closer cooperation on economic and monetary policy between the member states. In practice the single market has not been completed: the league tables so far published by the European Commission reveal a very mixed record on the part of member states in translating single market directives and regulations into national law; single market rules are far from complete in a number of key sectors, including utilities such as electricity and gas; application of the single market programme in other sectors, such as civil aviation and telecommunications, has been slow; numerous distortions associated with state aid remain; and differences in the structure and rates of taxation largely remain in place in the case of direct taxation, reflecting differences in national priorities and social philosophies with regard to such matters as incentives and income redistribution.

Stage two

Stage two commenced on 1 January 1994. It involved the establishment of the European Monetary Institute (EMI), with responsibility for the technical preparations for stage three, especially the development of the procedures and instruments of economic policy needed for a single monetary policy. Article 109f(2) of the treaty states that the EMI would:

- Strengthen cooperation between the central banks of the member states.
- Strengthen the coordination of the monetary policies of the member states with the aim of ensuring price stability.
- Monitor the functioning of the European Monetary System.
- Hold consultations on issues falling within the competence of the central banks and affecting the stability of financial markets.
- Take over the tasks of the European Monetary Cooperation Fund, which would cease to exist.
- Facilitate the use of the ECU and oversee its development, including the smooth functioning of the ECU clearing system.

For the preparation of stage three the EMI would:

- Prepare the instruments and procedures necessary for carrying out a single monetary policy in stage three.
- Promote the harmonisation, where necessary, of the conditions governing the collection, compilation and distribution of statistics.
- Prepare the rules for operations to be undertaken by the national central banks within the framework of the European System of Central Banks (ESCB).
- Promote the efficiency of EU cross-border payments.
- Supervise the technical preparation of ECU bank notes (European Commission, 1992).

The EMI was established in Frankfurt on 1 January 1994. Member states began to submit their economic convergence plans to the Commission and the EMI for assessment and comment. New rules came into force under Article 109e, including a ban on the monetisation of government debt (Articles 104, 104a) and a 'no bail out clause', which prohibited financial support to governments or public bodies of other member states (Article 104b). Governments were directed to avoid excessive deficits (Article 104c) and member states were required to start making their central banks independent (Article 109e.5).

Stage three

Stage three completes economic and monetary union. It includes the irrevocable locking of exchange rates amongst the participating countries, the establishment of a European Central Bank (ECB) and a European System of Central Banks (ESCB), to be followed by the rapid introduction of a single currency and close coordination and mutual surveillance of economic and fiscal policies.

Convergence and timetables

The treaty enabled stage three to start on 1 January 1997 if 'a majority of the member states fulfil the necessary conditions for the adoption of a single currency' (Article 109j.3). The decision to go ahead would be made as follows. The European Commission and the European Monetary Institute (EMI) would assess each member state to see whether it had achieved 'sustainable convergence' according to the qualifying criteria. The Commission would then make a recommendation on the basis of which the Council would decide by 'qualified majority whether each member state had met the necessary conditions for the adoption of a single currency', and 'whether a majority of the member states' had done so (Article 109j.2). The criteria are:

- The achievement of a high degree of price stability, apparent from a rate of inflation which is close to that of the three best performing member states.
- Sustainable government finances, as measured by the limits on government borrowing and debt in Article 104c (6).
- Observance of the normal fluctuation margins provided by the Exchange Rate Mechanism of the European Monetary System for at least two years, without devaluing against the currency of any other member state.
- Durable convergence, as reflected in long-term interest rates.

Protocols to the treaty spell out the criteria in more detail:

- *Price stability* is defined as an annual rate of inflation that is no more than 1.5 per cent higher than the average in the three lowest-inflation member countries.
- The fiscal criteria are defined as an *annual budget deficit* not exceeding 3 per cent of gross domestic product (GDP) and total outstanding government debt not exceeding 60 per cent of GDP. These fiscal criteria are the most difficult to meet and the most open to political judgement, since the treaty allows the Council some discretion. The limit on annual government deficits need not apply where 'the ratio has declined substantially and continuously' and comes close to 3 per cent, or where 'the excess is exceptional and temporary and the ratio remains close' to 3 per cent. Likewise the 60 per cent limit on debt may not apply where 'the ratio is sufficiently diminishing at a satisfactory pace' (Article 104c.2).
- *Long-term interest rates* must not exceed 2 per cent above the average of those in the three member countries with the lowest inflation rates, interest rates being measured on the basis of long-term government bonds.

- *Exchange rate stability* is defined as being within the normal band of the ERM for at least two years. Following subsequent currency crises, it was unclear whether the 'normal bands' meant the original narrow band (plus or minus 2.25 per cent) or the 15 per cent band introduced in August 1993. UK officials in particular argued that formal membership of the ERM was no longer a meaningful test of eligibility, *de facto* currency stability being the only relevant criterion.

As noted above, the criteria were combined with a fixed timetable to achieve a political compromise between the Germans, who were concerned about the risk of participating in a monetary union with countries that had a poor record of controlling inflation and budget deficits, and the French, who were concerned about the risk of EMU not going ahead at all. Right up until the European Council took its decision in May 1998 on which member states would participate in the first wave of membership, conflict between observance of the timetable and respect for the convergence criteria was a major concern. There has been considerable debate among economists as to whether the convergence criteria were necessary for any other reason than to convince German public opinion (Gros and Thygesen, 1998; Kenen, 1995). It is worth noting that while it adopted the three-stage approach recommended in the Werner Report, Maastricht went much further in emphasising the need for prior convergence. In contrast many commentators suggested that convergence should and would *follow* rapid transition to monetary union, whereas a lengthy stage two would be hazardous, exposing Europe to the risk of currency instability and speculative attack. Likewise economists have debated the rationales for the specific criteria adopted at Maastricht. The following is a summary of possible justifications:

- Prior convergence in inflation makes it less likely that the ECB will have to set common interest rates at a level which will depress output in low-inflation countries.
- The fiscal condition may be needed if the deficits of the profligate are not to push up interest rates in the monetary union as a whole. Some dispute this on the grounds that most of the extra interest rate costs will fall on the indebted themselves and that market discipline will therefore be a sufficient deterrent without

the need for fiscal rules. But this ignores the 'externality'– the cost of higher interest rates to borrowers in other member states.

- In addition to its continued relevance now that the ERM bands have been broadened, some have taken the position that the exchange rate criterion is superfluous (Thygesen, 1996); that the other criteria are essential in determining whether a country should enter a monetary union, after which it would not have an exchange rate of its own anyway. Against this, a commitment to exchange rate stability may reduce the scope for last minute realignments, in particular efforts by member states to engineer a competitive devaluation – although the evidence for this being a serious risk is far from apparent. A more powerful argument is that currency stability in the run-up to stage three would provide credibility for the subsequent locked exchange rate regime.

- As to the long-term interest rate criterion, differences in long-term interest rates reflect market views on future rates of inflation, short-term interest rates, devaluation and debt default risk. The first three of these will diminish if not vanish once a country has joined EMU, and if one takes the view that it is most unlikely that an EU country will ever default on its debt, the long-term interest rate criterion is arguably redundant. Countries perceived by the markets as being likely to join EMU because of their performance against the other criteria benefit from reductions in long-term interest rates anyway. Nonetheless markets may have doubts about the ability of particular countries to maintain low inflation or strict fiscal discipline once admitted to monetary union. Countries may also be more likely to default once deprived of the opportunity to print their own currency to pay off debt. In any event, long-term interest rates reflect the confidence of global financial markets in the candidature of a particular country, and their inclusion as a criterion may be justifiable for that reason alone, especially if the high rates and low credibility of one member have adverse effects on others.

As a majority of member states did not meet the required criteria for EMU to proceed in January 1997, the fall-back position in the treaty became operative: 'if by the end of 1997 the date for the beginning of the third stage has not been set, the third stage shall start on 1 January 1999. On 1 July 1998, the Council, meeting in the composition of Heads of State or of Government, after a repetition of the [procedure referred to above – that is, assessment of economic convergence] shall, acting by qualified majority ... confirm which Member States fulfil the necessary conditions for the adoption of a single currency' (Article 109j.4). Member states that did not fulfil the convergence conditions would have a derogation. The following articles of the treaty would not apply to them: those imposing obligations under the excessive deficit procedure (such as penalties in the event of failure to take corrective action); those covering participation in the governing council of the ECB; and those concerned with the implementation of a single monetary policy, including open market operations, foreign exchange reserves and the issue of notes and coins. Where such matters were involved, the voting rights of member states with derogations would be suspended (Articles 109k.3 and 4).

It is worth concluding by noting that the timetable for the introduction of stage three was never as fixed as it appeared at first sight. Alternative starting dates were provided because of the need to meet the convergence criteria, and tensions between the timetable and the need for convergence meant that it was always likely that there would be a multispeed EMU, with the prospect of different countries participating at different times into the future.

Danish and UK options

Denmark and the UK negotiated protocols which gave them the right to choose whether or not to participate in EMU even if they met the convergence criteria. Denmark was given the right to notify the Council whether it wished to participate in stage three: 'in the event of notification that Denmark will not participate in the third stage, Denmark shall have an exemption. The effect of this exemption shall be that all Articles and provisions of this Treaty and the Statute of the ESCB referring to a derogation shall be applicable to Denmark.' Although Denmark was given the right under its protocol to abrogate its exemption at a later date, it decided to opt out following the referendum of June 1992. Under Article 109k.2 the assessment of Denmark's economic performance against the convergence criteria – or that of any country with a derogation – would then be decided by qualified majority vote.

The UK negotiated an opt-in, giving it the right to notify the Council of any intention to move to the third stage before 1 January 1998, but it could change its notification at any time after the beginning of stage three provided it satisfied the necessary conditions. In the event of a decision not to participate, it could take no part in the decisions of the governing council of the ECB, in the appointment of its executives, or in relevant votes in the Council of Ministers. It would be exempt from the implementation of the ESCB monetary policy and would not be bound by the policy decisions of the ESCB or subject to sanctions under the excessive deficit procedure.

In practice all the member states, including those with opt-outs, put in place monetary and fiscal policies that would give them freedom of action to participate if they so chose (Denmark and the UK), or to join as soon as possible after 1999. Remarkable progress was made towards reducing rates of inflation, fiscal deficits and long-term interest rates, particularly amongst the Mediterranean countries.

The Maastricht model of central banking

A key feature of the Maastricht Treaty was the creation of a politically independent European Central Bank, with independence guaranteed by primary law and through the length of tenure of its executive. In view of the concerns of traditionally low-inflation countries, it was essential that the ECB should be able to borrow the credibility of the Bundesbank if the Dutch and German governments, voters and banks were to be persuaded to accept monetary union with other countries.

At the start of stage three a European System of Central Banks (ESCB) would be created, composed of a European Central Bank (ECB) and national central banks (Article 106). Article 105 specifies that 'the primary objectives of the ESCB shall be to maintain price stability'. Its basic tasks are:

- to define and implement the monetary policy of the EU.
- to conduct foreign exchange operations consistent with the provisions of Article 109.

- to hold and manage the official foreign reserves for the member states.
- to promote the smooth operations of payment systems.

The independence of the ECB is guaranteed by Article 107, which states that 'neither the ECB, nor a national central bank, nor any member of their decision-making bodies shall seek or take instructions from Community institutions or bodies from any government of a member state or from any other body'.

The treaty specifies the institutional structure of the ESCB: a general council, a governing council and an executive board (Articles 109a-f and Protocol on the ESCB). The key decision-making powers of the ESCB lie with the governing council and the executive board, where the governing council includes the executive board and the governors of the national central banks. The executive board is composed of a president, vice-president and four other members, to be appointed 'from among persons of recognised standing and professional experience in monetary or banking matters by common accord of the governments of the members states' (excluding those with a derogation).

Bearing in mind that each member of the governing council has one vote and decisions are reached by simple majority, from the start the executive of the ECB would be outnumbered by the governors of the participating national central banks in any monetary union of more than six members. The executive can be assumed to want to determine monetary policy in accordance with the needs of the monetary union as a whole – on the basis of average circumstances and prospects. In contrast national central bank governors may wish to reflect differences in the economic and monetary circumstances of their own countries, especially if economic cycles are not perfectly correlated (Begg *et al.*, 1998).

It was intended that the independence of executive members would be strengthened by the requirement that their term of office should be eight years and non-renewable (Articles 10, 11, ESCB Protocol). In the event only the vice-president was unambiguously appointed for eight years. The first president, Wim Duisenberg, was selected despite France's preference for Jean Paul Trichet, and it was widely rumoured that a political deal had been struck by which Duisenberg would step down after four years, although he asserted to the European Parliament and in other public statements that he had been appointed for eight years and would leave at a time of his own choosing. Other members of the executive were appointed for periods of as little as four years. French President Chirac said that it was natural that France should wish to see a Frenchman appointed to the presidency of the ECB (and it should be noted that all central bank governors throughout the world are political appointees), but this did not mean that France would wish to interfere in the ECB, the independence of which was guaranteed by the treaty. Chapter 12 returns to this issue of how the politics of the European Council may affect the appointment and credibility of the ECB.

The ECB came into being with the selection of the first wave of participating states and commenced operations on 1 January 1999. It has the sole right to authorise the issue of bank notes – member states are able to issue coins, but only with the ECB's consent. Its initial capital – up to 5000 million euros – was to be contributed by each national central bank on the basis of member state shares in population and GDP. It has taken over foreign reserves of up to 50 000 million euros from the national central banks, to be supplied on the same basis as their relative contributions to ECB capital. The use of foreign exchange reserves remaining with national central banks is subject to ECB approval.

A number of important issues concerning the ECB/ESCB were left unresolved by the treaty, including the precise division of responsibility between the ECB and ministers in regard to the determination and execution of the euro foreign exchange policy, details of the monetary policy instruments (especially reserve ratios) to be operated by the ECB, and the terms of access to the euro payments system and to euro liquidity by countries with derogations. A further issue touched on in the treaty concerns the role, if any, of the ECB in banking supervision (see Chapter 9).

Treaty provisions for economic and fiscal policy surveillance

Under Article 3a the activities of member states are 'based on the close coordination of economic policies'. They are required to establish 'the irrevocable fixing of exchange rates leading to the introduction of a single currency, and the definition and conduct of a single monetary policy and exchange rate policy, the primary objective of both of which shall be to maintain price stability and without prejudice to this objective, to support the general economic policies in the Community'.

Economic policy will be based on broad guidelines determined by the Council (Article 103.2). Closer coordination and sustained economic convergence will be monitored by reports from the Commission. The performance of each country will be subject to multilateral surveillance (Article 103.3). 'Where it is established ... that the economic policies of a member state are not consistent with the broad guidelines or that they risk jeopardising the proper functioning of economic and monetary union, the Council may, acting by qualified majority on a recommendation from the Commission, make the necessary recommendations to the member state concerned. The Council may ... decide to make its recommendations public' (Article 103.4).

Fiscal policy is the subject of considerable attention in the treaty, both with regard to the criteria for qualifying in the first place, and continuing obligations once a country is a member. In particular member states must avoid excessive government deficits (Article 104c). The 'reference value' for such a deficit is defined as a ratio of 'three per cent of planned or actual government deficit to gross domestic product', subject to the same exceptions as outlined on page 83 for the budget deficits needed to qualify for initial membership (Article 104c.2). If the Commission thinks that a member state has an excessive deficit – or is in danger of having one – it has to address an Opinion to the Council. If the Council agrees that there is a problem, it issues the member state with recommendations and a timetable for correcting the excessive deficit. The Council may make these recommendations public, but only 'where there has been no effective response' (Articles 104c.7 and 8). If a member state 'persists in failing' to act on the Council's recommendations it may be asked to 'submit reports on what it proposes to do to put the situation right' (Articles 104c.9 and 11) and the 'Council may apply ... one or more of the following measures:

- To require the member state ... to publish additional information, to be specified by the Council, before issuing bonds and securities.
- To invite the EIB to reconsider its lending policy towards the member state.

- To require the member state to make a non-interest-bearing deposit of an appropriate size with the Community until the excessive deficit has, in the view of the Council, been corrected.
- To impose fines of an appropriate size.

Exchange rate policy

The treaty allows the Council of Ministers to reach formal agreements on exchange rates between the euro and other currencies (Article 109), so long as it has received a recommendation from the ECB or from the Commission after consulting the ECB, and the agreement is consistent with price stability (Article 109.1). Under the same conditions it can also formulate general orientations, short of formal agreements, for exchange-rate policy towards other currencies (Article 109.2). On the other hand the ESCB is required to conduct foreign exchange operations 'consistent with the provisions of Article 109 ... and to hold and manage the official foreign reserves of the member states' (Article 105). In short the ECB and government ministers appear to have some overlapping responsibilities with regard to the external value of the euro. Concern has been expressed that this could give rise to conflicts, with the ECB preferring a harder euro to dampen inflationary pressures, and Ministers preferring a relatively soft euro in order to boost exports, restrict imports and boost employment and growth. The French government brought these matters to a head at the Dublin and Amsterdam European Councils (December 1996 and June 1997). The informal Ecofin at Mondor Les Bains in September 1997 then agreed that ministers should initially refrain from giving guidance to the ECB on exchange rates, and that any subsequent guidance should only be temporary and on the basis of evidence that the external value of the euro had deviated substantially from that implied by economic fundamentals. How this will work remains to be seen.

In late 1998, the directors of the ECB stressed that they would not favour a hardening of the euro against other international currencies under the conditions of low inflation and high unemployment then current in the EMU zone. Following the start of stage three the German finance minister pressed for 'target zones' for the exchange rate between the euro and other major currencies. The ECB publicly rejected this suggestion, stressing that its objective was internal price stability. The debate on responsibility for exchange rate policy touched on a more fundamental political and academic concern: the coordination of monetary and fiscal policy, to which we now turn.

Monetary and fiscal policy relationships

The Maastricht framework gave the ECB a monopoly over monetary policy, free from political interference, but economic and fiscal policy would remain the responsibility of ministers from the participating states. The treaty created a monetary committee to review the monetary and financial situation and report to the Council and the European Commission (Article 109c), but in practice central bankers have also attended. At the start of stage three

> The Monetary Committee ... shall be dissolved ... and replaced by an Economic and Financial Committee ... to which the member states, Commission and ECB shall each appoint no more than two members ... The Committee will have the following tasks: to deliver Opinions at the request of the Council or of the Commission or on its own initiative ... to keep the economic and financial situation under review ... and to report regularly thereon to the Council and to the Commission, in particular on financial relations with third countries and international institutions (Article 109c).

The committee would have an important role in the excessive deficit procedure, where it would be required to formulate its own report on any Commission Opinion that a member state was at risk of running an excessive deficit (Article 104c). It would also 'review the monetary and financial situation in member states with a derogation' (Article 109c.2).

However the French government argued that these arrangements would be inadequate if the ECB was to take account of the broader political and economic situation within the monetary union. At the Dublin and Amsterdam European Councils of December 1996 and June 1997, France appeared to press for a ministerial body that could influence or, at the very least, propose policy guidelines to the ECB. This position and any suggestion that Ecofin might be turned into a European 'economic government' was firmly rejected by other member states, especially Germany and the Netherlands. What emerged from the Luxembourg European Council (December 1997) was agreement to create a 'Euro-X committee' to provide a forum for discussing economic and fiscal policies among the participants in stage three ('X' at the time because the 11 founding members had not been chosen). Those not expecting to participate at the start of stage three were concerned about being excluded from a body which could formulate economic policies with implications for their own countries. A compromise was reached that stage three participants would meet in the Euro-11 committee to discuss matters of concern among themselves, but they would not exclude other member states from consideration of matters of common concern; and Ecofin would remain the decision-making body. But it was unclear who would decide which matters were of common concern or according to which criteria. Nor did the arrangement exclude the possibility that the Euro-11 members would vote *en bloc* in Ecofin. As the Commission had been worried that its role might diminish if Euro-11 somehow superseded Ecofin, it was also agreed that the Commission – in practice DG II and its responsible commissioner – would attend and provide papers for Euro-11, in effect acting as its central secretariat and economics staff. There can be little doubt that the supporters of the Euro-11 concept hoped that it would evolve into a forum for the coordination of economic and fiscal policy among the 'ins' and that it would form an effective and powerful counter-party to the ECB. They pointed out that within any member state the national central bank had a powerful and effective interlocutor in the form of the Ministry of Finance but no equivalent existed under the Maastricht framework for monetary union.

How this will work remains to be seen, but a number of independent academic commentators (Allsopp and Vines, 1996; Arrowsmith and Taylor, 1996; Meade and Weale, 1995) have expressed concern that the Maastricht Treaty provides an inadequate basis for monetary–fiscal policy coordination. Tension between the ECB and the new German administration did emerge shortly after the start of stage three, in view of adverse conditions in Germany, which favoured a relaxation of interest rates set by the

ECB for the euro zone as a whole. In the extreme, Europe could face the worst of all worlds: an independent ECB focused solely on achieving near zero inflation and a Stability Pact that inhibits an active contra cyclical budgetary policy – the two combining to deepen or prolong European recession. On the other hand the flexibility built into the fiscal constraints – permitting budget deficits of more than 3 per cent in exceptional circumstances – might be offset by an ECB determined to neutralise any expansion of demand. However the ECB will not necessarily interpret its objective of maintaining price stability as meaning zero inflation, and it will need to take account of the wider state of the economy of the 11.

Fixing exchange rates at the start of stage three

The treaty provided for the irrevocable fixing of parities (Article 109l.4), the decision on conversion of parities being taken on the basis of (1) unanimity among the member states proceeding to stage three and (2) a proposal from the Commission. At the start of stage three the treaty required the Council to adopt the conversion rates at which participating currencies would be irrevocably locked and their currencies converted into euro. The fixing of parities 'shall not by itself modify the external value of the ECU' (Article 109l.4). In December 1995 the Madrid European Council confirmed these provisions and stated, 'unequivocally that (the third) stage will begin on 1 January 1999'. It also confirmed that, 'in the case of contracts denominated by reference to the official ECU basket of the European Community ... substitution by the euro will be at the rate of 1:1, unless otherwise provided by the contract'. A number of problems associated with this approach were identified (Begg *et al.*, 1997; Levitt 1997):

- There would be a gap of several months between the identification of states proceeding to stage three and the locking of their exchange rates. This presented the risk of speculation and market turbulence during the intervening period.
- Some countries might try to use the gap to manipulate their currency by devaluing it to gain competitive advantage.
- It did not address the requirement that rates should be locked at parities which represented stable equilibria.

There were a number of proposals to address the problem. One, associated with the former president of the EMI (Lamfalussy) was that when the countries were chosen an announcement should be made that the rates would be locked on 1 January on the basis of the average of their market rates over the previous two or three years, thereby dampening the effect of any late currency turbulence or manipulation. Another was that an announcement should be made that rates would be locked at ERM central parities, which were widely understood, with the assurance that any divergence between the market rates and the ERM central rates on 31 December 1998 would be corrected by last minute central bank intervention – the promise of which should ensure that the market rates would quickly jump to ERM central parity, thereby avoiding speculation, manipulation and the need for intervention. A third proposal was that at the moment the countries were chosen their parities should be locked, requiring the coordination of monetary policy and a promise of unlimited central bank intervention to support those rates. But this would be the less attractive the greater the number of member states participating. In the event an agreement was reached 'with a view to guiding markets in the run-up to stage three' between the member states adopting the euro, the governors of the central banks of these member states, the European Commission and the European Monetary Institute. A joint communiqué on 2 May 1998 stated:

> the current ERM bilateral central rates of the currencies of the member states adopting the euro on the first date of stage three . . . will be used in determining the irrevocable conversation rates for the euro. These rates are consistent with economic fundamentals and are compatible with sustainable convergence. [This] procedure . . . will not modify the external value of the ECU which will be replaced on a 1:1 basis by the euro.

An annex to the communiqué set out the relevant arithmetic and procedures. In short, all the authorities concerned agreed on the need to guide markets in order to reduce the risk of currency speculation or competitive devaluations in the seven month period prior to the start of stage three. As things turned out, the bilateral exchange rates between the countries selected for stage three were stable, including the lira, despite the fall of the Italian government in September 1998.

Practicalities: the transition to the single currency

The treaty largely focused on the macroeconomic and broad policy
framework for establishing EMU and almost wholly neglected the
practicalities of introducing the single currency into everyday
commercial and personal life. Having determined the framework
for establishing a common monetary policy, including fixed
exchange rates, the basis for the powers and operations of the
European Central Bank and the obligations of member states once
they joined the monetary union, the treaty simply stated that after
irrevocably locking the exchange rates the Council should 'take the
other measures necessary for the rapid introduction of the ...
the single currency in those member states' (Article 109l.4). There
was a widespread expectation that this would be a relatively
simple matter and could be achieved very quickly. As things turned
out, the final transition to the single currency in the form of notes
and coins would not occur until three years after the locking of
exchange rates.

A number of bankers, especially those from the UK (Levitt, 1994),
emphasised that the introduction of a new currency would involve
massive and lengthy investment in new hardware: vending machines,
ticket machines at railway stations, telephone boxes and so on. Bank
computer systems, involving possibly hundreds of millions of lines of
code, would need to be scrutinised and changed, and the changes
would then need to be tested. Such was the scale of the outlay (about
2 per cent of annual running costs for about 3 years) that nobody
would be prepared to go ahead until it was certain when stage three
would start and which countries would be included.

Likewise public bodies (especially the tax and social security
authorities) would have to make massive changes to their own
computer systems (requiring up to three years to implement), as
would retailers and, to a lesser extent, the manufacturing and
commercial sectors. To avoid uncertainty about the status of
financial contracts denominated in currencies due to be eliminated
by the single currency, there were also calls for the EU to guarantee
continuity of contracts.

The initial response of a number of governments, Commission
officials and even senior figures in the private sector was that these
concerns were exaggerated and probably represented efforts by
those hostile to EMU to frustrate its implementation. Eventually
the Commission and the EMI acknowledged the scale of the task

and a phased approach to the introduction of the single currency was proposed in separate reports from those institutions during 1995. These drew on earlier work initiated in the private sector by the Association for the Monetary Union of Europe (1994). The basic options for the introduction of the single currency were as follows:

- A 'big bang', where there would be a near-simultaneous switch from national currencies to the single currency in a very short period, perhaps a long weekend. While this was recognised to be the theoretical ideal, it was rejected because of the sheer scale of the task of converting all the necessary machinery. Although it might have been possible to plan for such a 'big bang' several years in advance by building duplicate machinery and computer systems to handle the new currency, the uncertainty about precisely when EMU would start (bearing in mind the options of 1997 and 1999) and which countries would participate, meant that neither the private sector nor public administrations were prepared to bear the costs involved.
- An alternative option, favoured by the Bundesbank, was a 'delayed big bang' whereby stage three would start with the locking of exchange rates but the single currency would not be introduced in any form at all until some years later, the participating national central banks using domestic currency operations to preserve the exchange rate lock. This was rejected on the ground that it would look as if governments and the monetary authorities did not have sufficient confidence in the durability of stage three to introduce the single currency.
- An intermediate option proposed by some (including one of the present authors) was for the central bank to start using the single currency from the first day of stage three for its money market and foreign exchange interventions, and for governments to denominate their bonds in the single currency in order to demonstrate their commitment and that of the monetary authorities. The introduction of the single currency for personal transactions would follow some time later, thereby giving banks, retailers and public administrations sufficient time to manage the transition in an efficient and effective manner. Something along the lines of this proposal (favoured by the Association for the Monetary Union of Europe) was incorporated into the reports by the European Commission (1995) and the EMI on the transition to the single currency during 1995.

In December 1995 the Madrid European Council agreed that the single currency would be called the euro and that stage three would commence with the locking of participating currencies on 1 January 1999, to be followed by the introduction of euro notes and coin no later than 1 January 2002, with national notes and coin being withdrawn no later than 30 June 2002. In the intervening period the ruling principle was to be one of 'no compulsion, no prohibition': nobody would be compelled to use the single currency but they could do so if they found a willing counter party. The exception was that all new sovereign (that is, state-issued) bonds would be denominated in euro and the ECB would undertake all its monetary policy and foreign exchange market operations in euro from day one.

Conclusions

The treaty set out a deadline for the introduction of the single currency. It also established economic convergence criteria as the basis for determining participation, though the rationales for the individual criteria were open to dispute. The establishment of a timetable on the one hand and of convergence criteria on the other inevitably created tension, though this was eased by the fact that the criteria – especially those relating to fiscal sustainability – allowed significant scope for flexible interpretation.

Although the treaty stated that the single currency was to be introduced as soon as possible, it provided no guidance on what that meant or how the single currency was to be made reality through the immense practical and legal tasks involved in replacing national currencies. Stage three was to commence with the fixing of exchange rates among the participating currencies, but again, the treaty was silent on how that was to be brought about.

The Treaty stressed the need for a politically independent central bank. But this did not end the debate on the role and accountability of the ECB, nor on the level of coordination that would be needed between a centralised monetary policy and fiscal policies that would remain under national control. The next chapter discusses the manner in which these matters were resolved in the years between the ratification of the treaty and the start of stage three.

The drafters of the treaty may well have been conscious of potential tensions between monetary and fiscal policy but they were unable to resolve all the issues at the time. However in the case of such practical matters as determination of the fixed conversion rates among the participating currencies, and especially the enormous scale, complexity and cost of introducing the single currency, there is little evidence that the nature of the task was debated or even recognised in the Maastricht negotiations.

Chapter 7

The Economics of the Transition

Several key elements of the transition from national currencies to the single currency were not resolved by the Maastricht Treaty. This chapter reviews these elements and analyses the decisions and compromises that enabled stage three to start in 1999. It also shows how agreement was reached on the phased introduction of the single currency.

The convergence criteria set out in the treaty left a good deal of scope for interpretation, especially with regard to the fiscal criteria. The treaty provided for the introduction of the single currency as soon as possible after the start of stage three without clarifying what that meant, and it skirted around the huge logistical task of introducing the new currency. It was also silent on how irrevocable locking of the exchange rates was to be achieved. Fiscal policy was to be tightly constrained in order to achieve the deficit and debt targets. On the one hand this caused concern that the promise that monetary union would create extra growth would be negated; on the other the treaty seemed insufficiently rigorous to commit member states to maintain fiscal prudence once they entered into monetary union. Although the treaty gave the ECB responsibility for achieving price stability, it did not define that goal, which did not necessarily mean zero inflation, nor did it specify the precise monetary policy or monetary instruments which the ECB should adopt. In the meantime those tasks were assigned to the EMI. Finally, the treaty caused uncertainty about the continuity of financial contracts that were denominated in national currencies and still outstanding beyond the start of stage three: could contracting parties claim that the elimination of the national currency meant that their obligations no longer held?

To some extent these considerations were apparent to governments and officials when the treaty was signed, especially with regard to interpretation of the convergence criteria, the mechanism for fixing exchange rates and the requirements of fiscal policy. But the others only got onto the agenda of official debate as a result of the efforts of the private sector.

Convergence in practice

Once the Dublin European Council of 13 December 1996 decided that a majority of member states did not fulfil the necessary conditions, Article 109j(4) provided that an assessment should be made as early as possible in 1998 so that stage three could start on 1 January 1999 among whichever countries met the criteria. It was agreed at the 1997 Amsterdam Council that the assessment procedure – involving Ecofin, the European Council and the European Parliament – would operate from 1–3 May 1998 on the basis of assessments published by the European Commission and the EMI as soon as the economic and fiscal data for 1997 were available in March 1997. In the event 11 member states were judged eligible to proceed to stage three. The exceptions were Denmark, which had exercised its opt-out; the UK, which had indicated by the end of 1997 that it did not wish to proceed to stage three in 1999; Greece, which failed to meet most of the criteria; and Sweden, which had no opt-out but did not wish to be among the first wave of entrants, and in the event could not meet the criteria concerning the exchange rate and central bank independence (some suggest that this was deliberate in order avoid selection).

When the treaty was ratified, it seemed out of the question that stage three would start with so many countries. A small EMU of the Deutschmark 'core' seemed more likely. The following sections review the process of convergence which led to the birth of a large EMU (see also Barrell, 1992; Kenen, 1996). For detailed analysis of the relevant data see the European Commission's Convergence Report, 1998b, and EMI, 1998.

Price stability

As seen, Article 1 of Protocol 6 required that inflation in a member state should be no more than 1.5 percentage points above that of the three best performing countries. There was some debate, following the treaty, as to what this meant: did it mean the average rate of inflation among the best three or did it mean the highest rate among the best three, the former interpretation being the stricter of the two? In the event the Commission recommendation made it clear that it was the average which would be used. In 1993 only four countries met the test and the Mediterranean countries were well above the target inflation rate. By 1995, however, 10 countries were within the target. By the end of 1997 – the year used to assess convergence – all member states apart from Greece fulfilled the inflation target. This was a remarkable performance, especially by countries such as Italy, Portugal and Spain, and even Greece looked well on track to meeting the inflation target within a very few years.

Sustainable budget positions

At the time of assessment a member state should not be subject to a Council ruling under Article.104c(6) that it has an excessive deficit. Ireland and Luxembourg are the only member states never to have had a problem in that regard. The procedure takes into account the 3 per cent of GDP limit on annual deficits and the limit on debt to 60 per cent of GDP. But, as seen, neither reference level represented an absolute ceiling. The deficit could exceed 3 per cent of GDP if 'the ratio is declining substantially and continuously and has reached a level that comes close to the reference value or the excess is only exceptional and temporary and the ratio remains close to the reference value'. Likewise, the debt to GDP ratio could exceed 60 per cent if 'the ratio is sufficiently diminishing and approaching the reference value at a satisfactory pace'.

In 1993 only three countries were within the 3 per cent deficit target and this remained the case, with the same three, in 1995. But by 1997 only Greece had a deficit above 3 per cent of GDP and even there remarkable progress had been made. As for the 60 per cent debt criterion, only four countries were below the reference level in 1993. By 1995 only the same four remained within the target, and – with the exception of Luxembourg – even there the debt to GDP ratio was deteriorating. By 1997 only three countries were within the 60 per cent target, Germany having risen above it, while the French debt ratio was also rising.

In view of the flexibility and political judgement (exercised by qualified majority voting) involved in the application of the excessive deficit procedure in June 1996, the Council abrogated its previous decision that Denmark had such a deficit; it did the same for the Netherlands and Finland in June 1997; and for Austria, Belgium, France, Germany, Italy, Portugal, Spain, Sweden and the UK in the crucial meeting of May 1998. In 1993 it was clear that the Mediterranean countries in particular were well above the deficit and debt targets and by 1996 it was even uncertain whether France and Germany would convincingly meet the 3 per cent deficit criterion. Spain and Italy had deficits well above 3 per cent of GDP and Belgium and Italy had outstanding government debt greatly in excess of total GDP. Ireland had started the 1990s with a very high debt to GDP position, but because of the steady fall in the ratio it was never subject to an excessive deficit decision.

By 1997 the debt to GDP ratio was falling in every country apart from Germany. Although it was accepted that the German ratio was set to fall, concern was expressed, especially in Dutch and German circles, about whether outstanding debt was falling fast enough in Belgium and Italy. Many commentators were highly suspicious of the remarkable reduction of the government deficit in a number of countries, since one-off measures were adopted to get below the 3 per cent target. The Italian budget for 1997 included a special 'euro tax', to be repaid in future years; in France the government organised a one-off payment from France Telecom in exchange for taking over the pension obligations of employees with civil service status; exceptional payments were also made into government coffers by TeleDanmark, by the Postsparkasse in Austria and the Banco Nacional Ultramarino in Portugal; and in a number of countries it was suspected that public expenditure, especially on infrastructure programmes, had been moved out of the 1997 accounts. Where it was put into the 1996 accounts it strengthened the appearance of deficit reduction between 1996 and 1997, otherwise it was postponed but not necessarily annulled. The credibility of German fiscal rectitude suffered a severe shock in 1997 when the Ministry of Finance was accused of trying to force the Bundesbank to revalue its gold and foreign exchange reserve holdings and to transfer the proceeds to the government.

Eurostat, the official guardian of EU accounting conventions, ruled that receipts such as those from France Telecom did reduce the deficit. It also determined that one-off new taxes such as the Italian euro tax represented a genuine tax receipt and did reduce the deficit. On the other hand it ruled that proceeds from the revaluation of gold and foreign exchange reserves could not enter into the calculation of deficits.

Unlike the European Commission, which was required to make a recommendation on the countries eligible for proceeding to stage three, the EMI was simply called upon to produce a convergence assessment. Its report (EMI, 1998) stated that 'compliance with the convergence criteria is essential, not only at a specific point in time, but also on a sustained basis ... the decline in deficit ratios below the reference value and the fall in debt ratios in many countries have only recently been realised. Furthermore, the recent reductions in deficit and debt ratios have partly been related to one-off measures.' It went on to say that 'The case for sustained consolidation over an extended period of time, requiring substantial fiscal surpluses, is particularly strong for those countries with debt ratios above 100 per cent (Belgium, Greece and Italy).' With regard to Italy, 'The patterns observed during the early 1990's may be seen as indicative of the risks to public finances which can arise when macroeconomic conditions deteriorate and the primary surplus is insufficient to counter-balance such effect ... high levels of debt increase the vulnerability of fiscal positions in unfavourable circumstances, heightening the risk of a serious worsening of public finances' (ibid). The evidence suggested that measures with a temporary effect reduced the deficit ratio in 1997 by around 1 per cent of GDP, and that they were mostly of a 'one-off' nature. The EMI also drew attention to budget expenditure carry-overs (*Residui Passivi*) amounting to around 8 per cent of GDP.

Convergence assessments from the Bundesbank and the Nederlandsche Bank were even more emphatic in expressing concern about one-off measures and the threat to fiscal positions which would follow from any deterioration in economic conditions, including interest rate rises which the ECB might wish to introduce if the high debt to GDP ratios persisted in the three countries in question. For example the Nederlandsche Bank said in a press release on 25 March 1998 that

> Inflation and interest rates, notably in the southern European Member States only declined in 1997 to near the significantly lower interest rates in Germany, France, the Benelux countries and Austria. Likewise, of very recent date, and in some respects

also less convincing, is the convergence in the field of public finance in a number of member states ... On the basis of current fiscal plans, the fiscal deficit in most member states will only decrease marginally in 1998 ... current medium-term fiscal deficit and debt objectives are not yet commensurate with a fiscal position close to balance or in surplus as required by the Pact for Stability and Growth.

Government deficits and their relationship to GDP reflect macro-economic circumstances, domestic politics and market expectations. At the time of the May 1998 decisions the macroeconomic growth prospects were favourable, thereby providing a basis for forecasting reductions in deficits and the debt to GDP ratios. Domestic politics were such that governments of countries with a history of fiscal laxitude were generally committed, with opposition support, to avoiding increases in their deficits or to reducing them further, as required by the Stability and Growth Pact.

Market expectations are crucial to fiscal consolidation in countries with a high debt to GDP ratio. If financial markets believe that the country concerned is committed to sustaining its reduction in inflation and deficit long-term interest rates fall. This induces a 'virtuous circle' because the reduction in interest rates contributes to further reductions in the deficit. This was a major contributor to the reduction of the Italian deficit, where as a rule of thumb, a 1 per cent reduction in interest rates would reduce the deficit by a like proportion of GDP. It is noteworthy that the spread between Italian and German long-term interest rates had fallen to around a quarter of 1 per cent by May 1998 from around 5 per cent in the earlier 1990s. At the same time the importance of interest rates and interest payments underlay the concern of the central bankers noted above: any increase in the interest rates required by the ECB would automatically push up deficits in highly indebted countries, thereby creating tension between their governments and the ECB over interest rate policy – hence the insistence of central bankers on sustained and intensified fiscal consolidation.

Exchange rate stability

As seen, Article 3 of Protocol 6 required that a member state should respect the normal fluctuation margins in the exchange rate mechanism of the European Monetary System without severe tensions for at least the last two years prior to the assessment; in particular the country should not have devalued the bilateral central rate of its currency against that of any other member state on its own initiative.

In the period running up to the signing of the Maastricht Treaty there had been no realignment within the ERM since 1987 and the normal bands were 2.25 per cent either side of the central rates. But following the uncertainty about the prospects for EMU induced by the Danish and French referendums, and the severe currency turmoils of autumn 1992, a number of currencies devalued or left the ERM. With further crises the bands were widened to plus or minus 15 per cent in August 1993. This raised two questions: what did 'normal bands' now mean? Plus or minus 15 per cent or 2.25 per cent? And was formal membership of the ERM necessary at all? As seen, the British government argued that *de facto* currency stability was what mattered.

The European Commission, the EMI and national authorities deliberately provided little enlightenment. There was concern that the explicit reestablishment of narrow 2.25 per cent bands might induce further speculative attacks. In the event the currency cross-rates within Europe stabilised, apart from the pound sterling, which rose by over 20 per cent against the Deutschmark in the 18 months or so prior to the publication of the March 1998 assessments (partly because strong growth pushed up short-term interest rates in the UK, partly because of an inflow of funds into sterling as a 'safe haven' from continental savers/investors). The Irish pound also rose because of strong links between the Irish and UK economies, but the crucial point is that the Irish did not devalue. The Finnish markka entered the ERM in October 1996 and the Italian lira reentered the following month. Against this background the Commission concluded that

> 12 currencies can be considered not to have experienced severe tension in the past two years under review. The Greek Drachma, the Swedish Crown and the Pound Sterling did not participate in the ERM during the period. However, the Greek Drachma entered the ERM in March 1998 after the close of the review period (European Commission, 1998b).

Of key importance were the statements with regard to Italy:

> For the period under review, the Lira appreciated vis a vis the ERM currencies. Since it re-entered the ERM, the Lira has always traded within the $+/-2.25$ per cent band around the central rate against the median currency in the ERM. Although the Lira has participated in the ERM only since November 1996 it has not experienced severe tensions during the review period and has thus, in the view of the Commission, displayed sufficient stability in the last two years (ibid.).

Broadly similar remarks were made about Finland, but with regard to Sweden the Commission concluded:

> the Swedish Crown has never participated in the ERM; in the two years under review the Crown has fluctuated against the ERM currencies, reflecting, among other things, the absence of an exchange rate target. Sweden does not fulfil the exchange rate criterion (ibid.).

These remarks were crucial but somewhat opaque with regard to the possibility of EMU participation by the UK and Sweden, neither of which were members of the ERM at the time of writing (1999). The Commission's comments on Finland and Italy could be interpreted as confirming the UK's position that *de facto* stability and the absence of devaluation were what mattered. But the comment on Sweden suggests that formal membership of the ERM and an explicit exchange rate target also counted. As for the UK itself, the Commission said that as the UK did not propose to be among the first group of member states to join the single currency, it was not necessary to assess whether the UK met the conditions, so no enlightenment was provided with regard to sterling. In short the matter appears to be open to negotiation. If there is a period of *de facto* stability between sterling and the euro at a long-term equilibrium rate that does not imply serious disruption to the domestic economy, the British government may decide that a short period inside the ERM is unlikely to make much difference, while allowing it to meet a formal requirement should EMU members insist upon it.

Interest rate convergence

Article 4 of Protocol 6 required qualifying states to have a nominal long-term interest rate of no more than 2 percentage points above the average in the countries with the lowest levels of inflation, the comparison being made on the basis of 10-year government bonds. Four Mediterranean countries – Greece, Italy, Portugal and Spain – were above the target in 1993. By 1995 only Greece and Italy were above, the Italian interest rates having risen in the intervening period. By the time of the May 1998 decisions all countries, apart from Greece, had met the target. Quite remarkable reductions in interest rate spreads against the lowest interest country – Germany – were experienced by Italy, Portugal and Spain in particular. By May 1998 the spread over the German rate in that month was no more than about a quarter of a percentage point. These reductions demonstrate the confidence of financial markets that those countries would indeed participate in the first wave of monetary union and that their low inflation and low budget deficit policies would be sustained.

Independent national central banks

The final test required that the statutes of national central banks should be independent in accordance with Articles 107 and 108 of the treaty and the statute of the ESCB. Of the countries subject to the assessment, only Sweden was found to have domestic legislation incompatible with the treaty and the ESCB statute, although a number of countries were in the process of passing the necessary legislation through their national parliaments at the time of the assessment, and Denmark and the UK were not among the countries assessed.

Comment

Assessments at the time of the Maastricht Treaty would have predicted that the foregoing criteria would only have produced a small initial membership. Even so, for a year after the signing of the treaty a January 1997 starting date was expected by many in the Commission and by EMU advocates elsewhere. This changed with the traumas of the 1992 Danish and French referendums, the 1992 and August 1993 ERM crises, and the economic downturn. A 1999 starting date was also thought likely to involve only a few members. From time to time during 1995–96 doubts arose about the qualification of even France and Germany. Nobody could have predicted that the Mediterranean countries would make such remarkable progress in meeting the convergence criteria, though several Dutch and German commentators were sceptical to the last about the sustainability of the counterinflationary and deficit-reducing policies of those countries, especially Italy, on the ground that their conversion to monetary and fiscal prudence was very recent. As the treaty only set quantified reference values for inflation and fiscal policies for one year – 1997 – sustainability was a matter of political judgement. The recommendations and forecasts of the European Commission were that reductions in inflation, budget deficits and debt would continue into the foreseeable future. The central bankers preferred to exhort continued efforts while not going so far as to say that the improvements were not sustainable.

It should be stressed that the financial markets reacted positively when the Italian, Portuguese and Spanish governments showed determination to participate in the first wave. Exchange rates stabilised, interest rate spreads narrowed and government finances improved in a self-reinforcing process. This forced industrialists and financial markets in more sceptical countries such as Germany and the Netherlands (not to mention the UK) to acknowledge that failure to include those Mediterranean countries at the start could produce economic and political turmoil: disappointment of the growing expectation in financial markets that the Mediterranean countries would indeed participate would have caused their currencies to collapse, thereby severely damaging the competitiveness of other EU member states. Interest rates in the Mediterranean countries would have risen sharply, worsening their budget deficits. Furthermore, some of their governments could have fallen, with unpredictable consequences. It was therefore widely accepted that it was in nobody's interests to keep the Mediterranean countries to an inflexible interpretation of the criteria. Nonetheless it is clear from the tone and substance of the convergence assessments produced by the Bundesbank and the Nederlandsche Bank that the doubts about fiscal sustainability were not totally dispelled.

Fiscal constraints in stage three

As it became increasingly likely that a number of countries previously thought unable to meet the convergence criteria in time for the first wave might in fact do so, concern developed in Germany in particular that efforts to meet the fiscal criteria would not be maintained once stage three had started. As seen, Article 104(c) specified a continuing procedure to avoid excessive deficits in stage three, with regular assessments of the economic and fiscal policies of member states by the European Commission, peer group multilateral surveillance by other member states on the basis of the Commission's reports, and the possibility of sanctions, including non-interest bearing deposits and even fines, where excessive deficits were neither corrected in sufficient time nor attributable to cyclical downturns. But the procedure was wholly discretionary, being based on qualified majority voting. It was therefore felt by the German Ministry of Finance in particular that the treaty needed to be supplemented by something much more rigorous.

The German minister of finance, Theo Waigel, proposed a 'Stability Pact' at the Dublin Council. This was finally adopted at the June 1997 Amsterdam Council, but renamed the Stability and Growth Pact because of the emphasis it put on employment creation as well as fiscal discipline. This issue is explored further in Chapter 9.

Fixing conversion rates at the start of EMU

In the previous chapter we saw how the transition to the euro under the Maastricht treaty and the Madrid scenario involved a number of constraints: a gap of seven months between the choice of EMU participants in May 1998 and 1 January 1999, when the treaty allowed the Council to set the conversion rates at which the currencies would be locked; a requirement that the ECU and euro should be exchanged one for one; and a requirement that the external value of the ECU should not change as a result of the conversion to the single currency. This meant that the conversion rate between the euro and any currency had to equal the previous day's exchange rate between that currency and the ECU. But the

ECU basket contained volatile currencies, especially the pound sterling, which would not enter stage three on 1 January 1999. The treaty and the Madrid decisions did not specify precisely how the bilateral conversion rates would be set, and a number economists commented on the risk of turbulence in the currency markets between May and December 1998. A consensus emerged that any process for determining the bilateral rates should meet the following criteria (Begg, 1997; Levitt, 1998):

- It should be credible, that is, it should minimise the risk of market turbulence, especially disruptive attack.
- It should minimise the opportunity for any country, once selected, to engineer a final currency depreciation to gain competitive advantage.
- The mechanism should produce conversion rates consistent with economic fundamentals and market equilibrium.
- Conversion rates should be the market rates prevailing at the time of fixing.
- Because of the tension between an ECU that contained volatile currencies that would not participate in stage three, and the requirement that the ECU should equal one euro at the start of trading, it would be impossible to determine the conversion rates until 31 December 1998.
- On 31 December 1998 the participating national central banks would be responsible for enforcing the bilateral central rate, by means of unlimited intervention in the markets if necessary.

The options

1. *Let the markets decide.* Interpreted literally, this option would have involved abandoning the ERM and the treaty requirement that every member state should treat its currency as a matter of concern. Even if reinterpreted to mean, 'no conversion rate targeting except that implied by the need to remain within the wide-band of the ERM', it would have failed to meet the criteria set out above.
2. *Narrow bands.* The establishment of narrow bands seemed attractive to some because it avoided commitment to a precise set of parities and left some flexible response to market forces.

But the experience of September 1992 and August 1993 had exposed the vulnerability of narrow bands, and the option was not pursued.

3. *Averaging*. Here, an announcement would have been made in May 1998 that bilateral fixings would be determined by a weighted average of market rates over a period stretching from some date prior to the announcement to the end of 1998. The weight for each currency observation would either be identical or biased towards past or future performance. This option was attractive to some in providing a basis for market expectations and dampening the impact of late turbulence or deliberate currency manipulation through the weight of past (and hence unchangeable) exchange rates. However the option did not remove indeterminacy and could even be taken as encouraging any attack or manipulation to be severe, if it was to happen at all.

4. *Central ERM parities*. Many favoured an announcement in May 1998 that the conversion rates on 1 January 1999 would be equal to their central ERM in May 1998. Central parities were widely understood and did not appear to be out of line with economic fundamentals (although Ireland was a special case, albeit relatively small in terms of the weight of the Irish pound). It was argued that if the announcement was credible there would be no need for central bank intervention until perhaps the very last day, to bring spot rates into line with central parities. Credibility would be enhanced if the announcement included an assertion that no further changes to central parities would be made.

A broad consensus emerged that the last of these options was the most attractive, provided that the set of participants was credible – otherwise turbulence could occur anyway (as under any of the above options), and spot rates could move a long way from central parities, severely straining the proposed procedure. Some, however, questioned whether this would be a problem, since speculators would be called to judgement on the final day by massive central bank intervention and this would condition their behaviour in the meantime.

Other options were briefly considered. One was to redefine the ECU basket from May 1998 to contain only those currencies which would convert to the euro. This would leave no ambiguity about conversion rates between 'in' currencies or between the euro and any other currency. But it was dismissed as contrary to Article 109g of the treaty. Another was to fix central parities among the participating currencies from the moment of the announcement of the first wave membership. But this would have required close coordination of the monetary policies of all participating national central banks, including a guarantee of unlimited intervention by the latter. It was regarded as politically difficult if not legally impossible because of the Bundesbank's insistence on the indivisibility of responsibility for monetary policy prior to the start of stage three. Rejection of this option assumed that there would be no coordination of monetary policy between the participating central banks nor any guarantee of unlimited mutual support between May and the end of December 1998. In the event Ecofin and the European Council decided on May 1–3 1998 that ERM central parities would indeed form the basis for locking of conversion rates on 1 January 1999 (joint communiqué, 1998).

The practical implementation of the single currency

Article 109L(4) states that at the start of stage three the ECU would be substituted for the participating currencies and the Council should take 'The other measures needed for the rapid introduction of the single currency to those member states'. Very little debate on the meaning of 'rapid' and how the single currency could be implemented appears to have been undertaken when that clause was drafted. There was a presumption on the part of politicians, officials and many in the private sector who should have known better that, with modern computer systems, the introduction of the new currency could follow the start of stage three in a matter of days or weeks.

The introduction of a completely new currency meant, however, that within individual banks hundreds of millions of lines of computer code supporting possibly tens of thousands of programs would need to be scrutinised, changed and those changes tested. Most computer systems supporting the retail (personal) branches of banks had no multicurrency facility. They had also grown by accretion over the years, with the result that the systems' architecture was often poorly documented, hence the need for any changes to be carefully scrutinised and tested. The task of scrutiny, change and testing would be vast. The substitution of new notes and coin for existing national cash would likewise involve a massive programme of production, distribution and secure storage. Tens of thousands of vending machines (telephone boxes, cigarette machines and so on) would need to be changed, as would all the automatic teller machines (holes in the wall) through which people withdraw cash with the use of a plastic card. A massive programme of staff training, customer information and education would also be required.

Shortly after the treaty was ratified a few individuals in the private sector, especially bankers, started to draw attention to these issues. During 1993–94 a working group with the systems expertise of several banks and corporates across Europe did more work on the matter and concluded that for the average bank the changeover to the computer-base and cash systems could take around three to four years and cost something in the region of 2 per cent of annual running costs each year, amounting to several hundred million ECUs for a large bank (Association for the Monetary Union of Europe, 1994).

Bankers and corporate treasurers also raised the problem of continuity of financial contracts outstanding after the start of stage three. Where these were denominated in a currency which would be eliminated by the euro, would borrowers be able to insist that they would only pay the lower interest rate on the replacement currency, or low-interest lenders demand that the borrower should repay at the higher single currency rate? Chaos would ensue in financial markets if maverick decisions were reached in those centres, including New York, which were most likely to produce litigation. Clear EU regulations were needed to remove legal uncertainty and risk.

Eventually officials of the European Commission, the EMI and member governments acknowledged the scale, complexity and cost of introducing the new currency. The Bundesbank appears to have concluded that after the locking of exchange rates at the start of stage three, nothing should be done to introduce the single currency for a few years, to give time for the system to bed down, gain credibility and for the banks and others to undertake the necessary systems conversions. The German authorities, facing a sceptical population, were worried about introducing the ECU (as the single currency was called at that stage) very early on in the process, largely because this would have meant replacing the existing German government bonds with ECU denominated ones, which many German households regarded with little confidence.

It was stressed to the European Commission and the EMI that if the authorities themselves were not prepared to use the single currency at the start of stage three, this would imply that they had little confidence in the durability of EMU. Some banks likewise stressed the need to introduce the single currency at the start of stage three for the ECB's money market activity, for the denomination of interbank settlements and for the denomination of government bonds. Retail changeover, involving notes and coin, could indeed come later. A number of bankers also stressed that so long as the private sector was uncertain about the timing of stage three and the identity of the qualifying countries it would be unwilling to spend large sums of money in systems changeover or divert scarce skilled IT personnel, hence the conclusion that retail changeover (where the biggest systems and cash logistical problems existed) could only happen some time after the start of stage three.

The European Commission and the EMI responded to these arguments by publishing reports proposing a phased introduction of the single currency, an approach confirmed as follows by the Madrid European Council (December 1995):

- 1 January 1999: the euro (as the single currency was to be named) would become the legal currency of the monetary union, all national currency units being mere fractional representations or tokens of the euro; all new government bonds would be issued in euro and it would be the currency in which the ECB operated in money and exchange markets.
- 1 January 1999–1 January 2002: the principle of 'no compulsion, no prohibition' would apply: nobody could be compelled to use the euro nor anyone prohibited from doing so if they had a willing counterparty.
- 1 January 2002: all financial assets/liabilities to be denominated in euro, all payments other than notes and coin to be in euro; euro notes and coin to be issued.
- 30 June 2002: the latest date for the withdrawal of national notes and coin.

In short the euro was to be introduced in wholesale financial markets first and at the retail/consumer level last. This phased approach was to take into account the time needed by banks and retailers to prepare, and especially the time needed by public authorities (tax and social security administrations for example) to complete the transition to the single currency.

This changeover plan involved the inconvenience and cost of operating two currencies during the transition, with exposure to fraud, error and confusion. The principle of 'no compulsion, no prohibition' was framed for legal purposes. The economic reality, however, is that the use of the euro will spread during the change-over period through commercial pressure and competitive force. A number of large companies will wish to benefit from being able to undertake their transactions and funding in the euro as soon as possible. To this end they will encourage their suppliers to quote prices and take payments in euro and encourage their customers to pay them in the single currency. Consequently the euro is expected to spread through the business 'supply chain' prior to its compulsory use at the end of the transition period. These developments within the supply chain will not be restricted to the EMU zone: other EU countries such as the UK expect the single currency to be used by their exporters to the EMU area, and these may in turn require their suppliers within the UK to take payment in euro.

Although the authorities eventually came to accept the private sector argument that even with modern computer systems it would take some years to introduce the single currency, they were reluctant to acknowledge the risk of legal uncertainty concerning financial contracts denominated in national currencies. Again pressure from the private sector – banks and law firms involved in financial markets – managed to persuade the Commission that a regulation was needed to specify the continuity of contracts: all contract terms, including interest rates, would remain unaltered, even though denominations would change. Officials initially proposed a regulation based on Article 1091 (4). But there was a difficulty: this article did not apply in the UK (under the terms of the British opt-out). A number of monetary authorities argued that it was the UK's problem and not theirs if the opt-out exposed the City of London to uncertainty of financial contracts. Eventually, however, it was accepted that the City of London was not merely the home of British banks but a base for the capital market activities of banks from all EU countries and from around the world. It was accordingly agreed to introduce a regulation under Article 235 which would extend to the UK. A factor contributing to the acceptance of this position was the argument, put by some banks prior to the Madrid Summit, that the credibility of the euro as a global currency would be damaged if laws in major financial centres throughout the world (especially in New York state) were not changed to remove the legal and contractual uncertainties created by the changeover to the single currency. If the UK was not subject to the EU regulation it would be that much harder to persuade the authorities in the United States, Japan and elsewhere to remove legal uncertainty.

In the end two regulations were adopted at the Amsterdam European Council of June 1997. One, based upon Article 235 with immediate effect throughout the EU, specified that the advent of the euro should not allow one party to terminate a contract unilaterally and without mutual agreement; it confirmed the replacement of the ECU by the euro on a one to one basis; and it included rules on rounding off and the use of conversion rates (1103/97). For example conversion rates should have six significant figures and these should not be rounded off when making conversions. The regulation, based on Article 109l (4) and applicable only in the member states of the monetary union, provided for the replacement of national currencies by the euro as their legal currency, at the fixed conversion rate.

Neither the systems and cash logistics of the changeover to the single currency nor the legal provisions were addressed in the Delors Report and the Maastricht Treaty. There is no reason to suppose that governments or the Commission thought about these issues very much at all before they were raised by the private sector, which faced considerable costs in terms of cash and manpower resources, and much uncertainty about when the changeover would happen and in which countries. A contrast has often been drawn with decimalisation in the UK. A three-year Committee of Enquiry under Lord Halsbury reported in 1966 on the principle of introducing decimal coinage in the UK; policy, legislation and the precise day (15 February 1971) were specified early in 1967. A Decimal Currency Board was established and charged with planning the introduction of the new coinage. It worked very closely with private sector agents – especially banks and retailers – and with public administration. Decimalisation was a far easier task than the introduction of the euro, for example only three out of eight coins were changed by decimalisation. Others pointed to the speed with which German monetary unification was completed in 1990 (a matter of months), although it was also stressed that German unification did not involve the invention of a completely new currency but simply the eastward extension of an existing currency and its banking system. What is quite remarkable but rarely noted by governments or the academic literature is that the policy which was eventually adopted – the phased introduction of the euro over a period of three years – was the product of relatively few individuals in the private sector who were concerned about the practicalities of introducing the single currency.

Conclusions

The assessment of convergence, the precise mechanism for fixing conversion rates between participating currencies, the practical implementation of the single currency and the removal of legal uncertainty were key issues which were not resolved until 1997–98. Inevitably the assessment of convergence could not have been made and was not required by the treaty before then. But the other issues received scant attention when the treaty was signed in the first place.

The assessment of convergence left a number of matters unresolved. The Commission's assessments of the sufficiency and sustainability of fiscal convergence were noticeably more optimistic than those published by the EMI and some central banks. However central banks and the Commission agreed that a number of harmful consequences could follow if deficits were not reduced further in the coming years: there would be reduced scope for deficit finance within the 3 per cent Stability and Growth Pact ceiling in the event of an economic downturn; there could be tension between heavily indebted governments and the ECB if the latter saw the need to raise interest rates; and as long as governments continued to have structural deficits, there could be additional market pressure on the ECB, as an institution with no track record, to adopt a tougher monetary stance than would otherwise be the case. A further matter which was left unresolved was the precise requirement for ERM membership on the part of later participants in EMU, notably Sweden and the UK.

Finally, the post-Maastricht process included the emergence of the Stability and Growth Pact. The aim was to reassure the German public and to pressure other member states to maintain fiscal discipline, especially those that had only reduced their deficits in a short sprint prior to the convergence assessment. The Pact is examined in detail in Chapter 9.

Chapter 8

Monetary Policy

The central principle of the new regime is that monetary policy is governed by an independent European Central Bank (ECB), with responsibility for defining a policy appropriate to the euro zone as whole. Before turning to an examination of the ECB's monetary strategy, this chapter introduces the theme of central bank independence by explaining its significance, both for the political consensus that underpins monetary union and for the effectiveness of economic policy making.

Central bank independence

A key theme running through the debate on the creation of the ECB was the stress on independence. Germany was only prepared to sacrifice the Bundesbank on the strict condition that the ECB would be politically independent, as independence was widely regarded as essential to a central bank achieving the goal of price stability, free from political interference. Some EU countries have a history of monetary easing according to the needs of the domestic political cycle, as national central banks have come under political pressure to increase the money supply to fund public spending or otherwise accommodate inflationary pressures. With or without central bank independence, this problem is much less likely to arise in a monetary union, as there is no system of government that is dependent on a single electoral cycle at the European level, and the treaty does not allow the ECB or participating NCBs to fund government borrowing. Nonetheless, an independent ECB can still be expected to add to counterinflationary performance. A number of academic studies have been undertaken into the relationship between central bank independence and inflation (Alesina and Grilli, 1992; Eiffinger and de Haan, 1996). The definition and operational description of central bank independence are not precise but the consensus among researchers has been that independence involves full statutory

120

independence from the state, the political independence of the most senior directors and executives of the central bank following their appointment, and restraints on changes to the statutory basis of the central bank. Taking these characteristics into account, the most independent central banks, such as the Bundesbank, are associated with the lowest rates of inflation, whereas the least politically independent are, on the whole, associated with high rates of inflation. However it can be argued that the Bundesbank has had an easier time than most other European central banks in pursuing a policy of price stability because the goal is shared by a majority of the population, industry and the state itself. In short central bank independence may be a necessary but insufficient condition of price stability. Nonetheless the overwhelming body of evidence demonstrates a consistent link between independence and low inflation, and as the ECB has been created with more institutional and statutory independence than any national central bank in Europe (see Chapter 12), it is likely to stick to the goal of price stability.

From Bundesbank to ECB

One of the principal aims of non-German advocates of EMU was the displacement of the hegemony of the Bundesbank. The Bundesbank set monetary policy according to the prospects and needs of the German economy, focusing on the aim of maintaining price stability. As other EU countries within the ERM aimed to maintain stability between their exchange rates and the Deutschmark, they had to bring their own domestic short-term interest rates into line with German rates set by the Bundesbank, irrespective of whether or not this suited their domestic situations. The problem was most forcibly highlighted after German reunification, when the Bundesbank responded to growing government deficits and inflation in Germany by raising interest rates, even though several other ERM countries were facing recession. The result was the devaluations and departures from the ERM in September 1992 and August 1993. Although matters stabilised thereafter, in part because of the widening of the bands, the underlying aim of replacing the Bundesbank by an ECB that would focus on the needs of Europe as a whole remained at the core of the entire project for countries such as France. For the Bundesbank the *quid pro quo* for giving up its control of German monetary policy was that the ECB should be politically independent and required to pursue a strict policy of price stability (Alesina and Grilli, 1992; Cukierman, 1992).

So monetary policy for much of Europe will be subject to joint decision making with the aim of stabilising prices at a low rate of inflation across the whole area. This will mean examining monetary conditions in the aggregate, taking into account the prospects for inflation and monetary growth in the entire EMU zone, and averaging national data for inflation and money growth. The averaging will need to be weighted to account for differences in the size of the participating countries. For example if EMU consisted of only Germany and Luxembourg and their respective rates of inflation were 4 per cent and 2 per cent, the average inflation rate for the area as a whole would not be 3 per cent but almost 4 per cent. In the case of the 11-country EMU, Germany will account for a third of total GDP (France just over one fifth) so German monetary conditions and prospects will continue to play an important, but no longer dominant, role in the setting of European monetary policy.

Under the Maastricht Treaty the ECB is responsible for the determination of monetary policy and its execution through the structure of the European System of Central Banks (ESCB). The treaty established the key characteristics of the ECB, including its decision-making independence from all other bodies and a prohibition on it seeking or taking instructions from any other institution. All other bodies are required to respect the ECB's independence.

> When exercising the powers and carrying out the tasks and duties conferred upon them by this Treaty and the statute, neither the ECB, nor a national central bank, or any member of their decision-making bodies shall seek or take instructions from any Community institutions or bodies, from any government of a member state or from any other body. The Community institutions and bodies and governments of the member states undertake to respect this principle and not to seek to influence the members of the decision-making bodies of the ECB or of the national central banks in the performance of their tasks (ESCB statute, Article 7).

The treaty established price stability as the key objective of the ECB, although that objective was not defined in precise operational or quantitative terms; for example the treaty did not specify that the aim was to achieve a zero rate of inflation. It was for the ECB to determine what price stability meant as well as the monetary strategy and the policy instruments required to achieve it. The treaty provided only a broad framework for the definition of the monetary policy target and policy instruments. It assigned detailed specification of this task in the first instance to the EMI, subject to a final decision by the ECB. In practice much of the work had to be undertaken by the EMI, in close consultation with national central banks. Otherwise the ECB would have been hard pressed to establish arrangements for an effective monetary policy in the short period between its creation (June 1998) and the commencement of operations at the beginning of January 1999.

Although the ECB's independence is guaranteed by the treaty, it is required to submit an annual report to the European Parliament, European Council, Ecofin and Commission. The president and executive board of the ECB may also appear before the Parliament and its constituent committees. The annual report will cover the prior decisions and activities of the ECB. The ECB is not obliged to discuss future policy with the other EU institutions, nor are there any mechanisms by which limits, sanctions or the threat of dismissal can be imposed upon the president or members of the executive of the ECB by any of the bodies to which it presents reports. There has been criticism that this leaves insufficient room for democratic accountability. We will return to this debate in Chapter 14. For the moment it is sufficient to note that it implies a model of democratic accountability in which the political process is somehow involved in setting the monetary target of the ECB and possibly the instruments and operations it uses to achieve its target. In contrast the only approach to accountability that is compatible with the treaty is for the ECB to give an account of its performance *after the event*, since any formal obligation on it to discuss its intentions *beforehand* would almost certainly be interpreted as exposing it to political direction. Under those conditions the Germans, and probably the Dutch, would never have ratified the treaty in the first place. In short there was always a contradiction in the position of those who wanted to remove the monetary hegemony of the Bundesbank while seeking to achieve a politically supervised ECB.

Nonetheless the ECB will not exist in a political or economic vacuum and some commentators have stressed that one of its implicit goals is the preservation of the monetary union itself.

Consequently it has been argued that the persistence of unemployment or the threat of rising unemployment will not be matters of indifference to the ECB, because it is unlikely to want to tighten its monetary stance in the presence of serious political and social tension. But because the ECB lacks a history and track record of price stability, it can be expected to seek to establish credibility, both in relation to global money markets and price and wage fixers within the EMU zone itself. It will want to remove any doubt that it will tighten monetary policy in the face of expectations of rising inflation or to counteract fiscal loosening by governments. To avoid tensions between governments and the ECB it is important that, in its early years, it should not face some combination of the following: fiscal loosening, rising wage pressures, sluggish economic growth or recession. While the simplest way for the ECB to establish its credentials is to disagree publicly with ministers and stick to its guns, a better course would be to convince governments (and labour markets) that they must be restrained if interest rates are not to be increased.

However, unlike a national central bank, which has to face only a single Ministry of Finance, the ECB had to interact with eleven initially and there will be more later. An early sign of potential tension arose shortly after the birth of the ECB when it became clear that the prospective deficits of several member states were unlikely to decline with sufficient rapidity, in the view of the ECB, towards the zero structural balance required by the Stability and Growth Pact, not least among the countries with the highest debt to GDP ratios. ECB directors responded by warning that the bank might need to raise interest rates beyond the level that would prevail under a more prudent fiscal policy. Any increase in interest rates would, of course, further exacerbate the deficit position of countries with a high debt to GDP ratios because of the heavy burden of interest payments in their national budgets.

In response to concern that the considerable independence awarded to the ECB would give rise to a democratic deficit, President Mitterrand tried to reassure the French during the referendum campaign on Maastricht in 1992 that the ECB would be subject to political oversight by the Council of Ministers, even though his statement was incompatible with the treaty. Subsequently, at the December 1996 Dublin Summit, the French government floated the idea of a new ministerial body to provide policy guidance to the ECB. By the time of the June 1997 Amsterdam Summit this had been transformed into a proposal for a 'Euro-X' body to provide a forum for discussion of economic and fiscal policies among the 'in' countries and, in the view of the French, to act as a counterparty to the ECB in the same manner as national Ministries of Finance have traditionally had a dialogue with their national central banks. Formally at least, decision-making powers would remain with the Ecofin Council, and the 'Euro-X' (now the Euro Eleven) would have no authority over the ECB.

Institutional arrangements

A federal structure broadly modelled on that of the Bundesbank (which has a board, or *Direktorium*, including council members plus governors of the *Länder* central banks) has been created in the form of the ESCB, including all the national central banks (NCBs) and a supreme, single monetary authority, the ECB, located in Frankfurt. Membership of the ESCB and the ECB embraces participating and non-participating NCBs alike but only the participating NCBs are represented in the key decision-making bodies of the ECB: its governing council and executive board.

The governing council is responsible for the formulation of monetary policy and establishing the guidelines for its implementation, which will be largely decentralised via the NCBs. Its responsibilities include the operational interpretation of 'monetary stability' – the prime objective of the ESCB (Article 105) – and decisions on monetary objectives, interest rates and the management of reserves. The governing council is composed of the governors of the participating NCBs and members of the executive board. Each member has one vote, so the Bundesbank president has no more voting power than the head of the Luxembourg Monetary Institute, though, as noted, the larger economies will be arithmetically more important than the smaller ones in the assessment of monetary conditions in the overall euro zone. Apart from a few matters indicated in Article 10.3 of the ESCB statute, decisions will be taken by simple majority. The president of the ECB chairs the governing council and has a casting vote in the event of a tie.

The executive board is responsible for the implementation of monetary policy, including instructions to the participating NCBs.

The executive board is composed of the president and vice-president of the ECB and four other members, each of whom, under the treaty, should serve a non-renewable term of eight years. A third body, the general council, provides a forum for discussion between the NCBs of the 'ins' and the 'outs'. It is composed of the governing council of the ECB and the governors of non-participating NCBs. It will have no role in formulating or executing monetary policy, but it will provide a forum to debate relations between EMU members and other EU member states, including preparations for fixing exchange rates by new entrants to the monetary union. The general council will hear reports from the president of the ECB on decisions of the governing council.

All six members of the ECB executive will serve on the governing council, together with the (initially) 11 governors of the participating NCBs, giving a total membership of 17, rising to 21 if all 15 member states participate. In short the executive of the ECB will be outnumbered by the NCB governors (Eichengreen, 1992). This contrasts with the Open Market committee of the American Federal Reserve Board, where the district Federal Reserve presidents are fewer in number than the central appointees (a ratio of five to seven). In principle the US Federal Reserve focuses on US conditions as a whole, but naturally the district Federal Reserve representatives are concerned about the situation at home, although this does not necessarily mean that they take political instructions. Research into the influence of regional concerns on the monetary policy of the Federal Reserve has nonetheless proved to be inconclusive to date.

In addition to the provisions noted above, the treaty seeks to guarantee the independence of the ECB executive by providing its members with security of tenure. Article 11.1 of the ESCB protocol states that 'Their term of office shall be eight years', but for reasons that are further explored elsewhere in this book, this arrangement may have been thrown into question by the manner in which the first president and executive board were selected in May 1998. It was widely believed that the first president (Wim Duisenberg) would not serve the full term because of France's insistence that a Frenchman should replace him after only four years. The alternative appears to have been to risk a French veto on his appointment at a time when the financial markets were likely to react adversely to anything which called the credibility of the euro and the ECB into question, given that the formal choice of the initial participants and bilateral currency conversion rates were agreed at the same Council meetings. Other members of the executive were appointed at the same time but only one (Otmar Issing of the Bundesbank) was appointed for a full eight years, the other appointments ranging from four to seven years. It remains unclear whether Duisenberg will indeed step down in 2002. Rumours of renewed disagreement reemerged immediately prior to the launch of stage three in December 1998 (*Le Monde*, 29 December 1998).

The treaty requirement that the ECB president should serve for eight years was based on the principle that the term of office should encompass at least one complete economic cycle and be longer than any national political cycle. This was thought important if the ECB was to develop credibility and predictability. Even if EMU and the ESCB did start life in relatively benign circumstances (which is still unclear given the unknown consequences of the Far Eastern economic crisis), the economic cycle has not been abolished. It therefore remains essential for the first president to establish the credibility of the ECB and its devotion to price stability, leaving no doubt that such policies will be continued over the longer term. This is not to say that the ECB will be wholly inflexible: it has an interest in preserving EMU, including its political acceptability, and inevitably the president and executive will not be immune to the 'real-world' consequences of any serious downturn in economic growth and employment. Still, they can be expected to tread a very cautious path.

Looking to the future, two questions arise. Will the executive present a united front in the deliberations of the governing council? And to what extent will participating NCB governors disagree among themselves along national lines? (Eichengreen, 1992; Dornbusch *et al.*, 1998). Although the task of the governing council is to determine monetary policy for the euro area as a whole, it seems unrealistic to expect governors to ignore domestic conditions, insofar as participating states experience different cyclical and monetary conditions. If key monetary policy indicators, whether inflation rates or monetary aggregates, are all moving in the same direction and at not too dissimilar rates, the problem of reaching agreement may not be too severe, but if some countries are experiencing strong inflationary pressure while others face recession, serious tensions seem likely. Econometric research suggests that several countries, including Greece, Italy, Portugal, Spain and the UK, have often experienced significantly different economic cycles from the rest (although differences have also emerged within the 'core' from time to time, and reemerged in early 1999 when the German, but not the French economy, slowed).

The difference between an ECB-based monetary regime and a Bundesbank-led one can be usefully illustrated by considering how policy may have been different had German reunification occurred within EMU. As seen, the Bundesbank responded to the inflationary consequences of reunification by raising interest rates. Economic activity and employment were then depressed as other countries followed suit. Had reunification occurred under EMU, any threat to inflation would have been averaged out over the euro zone as a whole. ECB interest rates would not have had to rise as far as the Bundesbank rates, and economic activity would not have been so depressed. On the other hand, less would have been done to dampen German inflation. This would have called for either greater fiscal tightening in Germany or a more drawn out deceleration of German inflation.

Decentralisation

It has been noted that the governing council places the executive of the ECB in a minority in relation to the NCB governors and that this *will be exacerbated* as more countries participate in EMU. In addition to being in a strong position to determine policy, the NCBs have a considerable role in its operation. According to the ESCB statute: 'To the extent deemed possible and appropriate ... the ECB shall have recourse to the national central banks to carry out operations which form part of the tasks of the ESCB.' Although the executive board is responsible for issuing instructions, implementation will be devolved to the NCBs, which continue to enjoy considerable institutional resources: they draw up their own balance sheets; set their own conditions of employment; and it is they who operate interbank payment systems. Some of them are also responsible for banking supervision in their own countries. Because they have a majority on the governing council it is they who will define where it is appropriate to decentralise operations, and they can be expected, at least initially, to be keen to retain as many functions as possible. These are likely to include open market operations and the detailed implementation of reserve requirements (see below). Decentralisation is sensible to the extent that it is the NCBs which have day-to-day contact and familiarity with the national banking and monetary systems in participating states. But it may also be driven by institutional jealousy, notably the concern of some NCBs that Frankfurt might emerge as the dominant financial centre of the euro zone.

In contrast a number of officials, particularly from the Bundesbank, question the speed, efficiency and long-term sustainability of a decentralised system (Begg *et al.*, 1998). A single monetary policy with a uniform interest rate throughout the EMU zone can only be implemented if there are no 'micro monetary policies' operated by particular NCBs. This requires the ECB to establish a set of procedures for controlling and monitoring the monetary operations of each of the participating NCBs so that the latter are not only above suspicion but also seen to be so. One example is provided by the treaty provision that up to 50 billion euros of foreign exchange reserves may be transferred to the ECB. While neither the treaty nor the ECB protocol sets out what it means for the ECB to manage those reserves, it is clearly essential that any foreign exchange operations by the NCBs should be consistent with ECB policy: the ECB and the NCBs should not buy and sell gold or dollars in a manner that influences the external value of the euro in opposite directions. Likewise it would be inappropriate for an NCB to encourage its national banking system to acquire euro liquidity in anticipation of an ECB clampdown on liquidity. Although it seems extremely unlikely that an individual NCB will operate in a manner contradictory to ECB intentions, clear guidelines and a real-time monitoring system are essential to the effective implementation of monetary policy.

The decentralised system outlined above may be contrasted with that in the United States where Federal Reserve Board policy is undertaken by the New York Federal Reserve Bank, and with the Bundesbank, where market operations are centralised in Frankfurt. The ECB may undertake its operations through a number of or all NCBs, an approach favoured by some NCBs to avoid centralising too much power in Frankfurt and privileging its development as a financial centre. Over time the system is likely either to entrench decentralisation or to promote acceptance of centralisation. At this stage it is impossible to predict which way things will go, given that there are powerful forces pulling in both directions.

Monetary policy strategy

A key task of the ECB is to establish its own credibility for price stability throughout the monetary union and in global financial markets. The European Commission's 'One Market One Money' (1990) predicted that the counterinflationary credibility of the Bundesbank would be extended throughout the monetary union, persuading firms and employees that wage increases not matched by higher productivity would be met with higher interest rates.

As seen, the principal objective of the ECB, according to the Maastricht Treaty, is the maintenance of price stability, although it is also required to 'support the general economic policies in the Community' (European Commission, 1992, Article 105.1). The treaty does not define price stability nor does it specify the strategy the ECB should follow to achieve it, leaving both tasks to be determined by the governing council. It seems unlikely that the ECB will define price stability as narrowly as zero inflation, partly because conventional price indices are believed to exaggerate the rate of inflation (because of inadequate allowance for improvements in the quality or performance of goods as a result of technical progress over time). Moreover it has been suggested that zero inflation leaves insufficient room for changes in relative prices, or for reductions in real wages, where it is difficult to cut money wages. It therefore accentuates the risk of an economic downturn turning into a recession (Buti and Sapir, 1998).

Of more fundamental importance is that the ECB will adopt a *single monetary policy* for the EMU zone as a whole. It will base policy on a view of the inflation prospects for the whole area, even though different countries may experience varying rates of inflation because of differences in cyclical conditions, labour market structures and responsiveness to monetary policy. It will be essential for it to establish how and with what speed this newly constituted EMU zone economy reacts to monetary policy, particularly in its price and wage setting behaviour.

EMU has started with countries in different cyclical conditions, some experiencing strong growth with low or rapidly falling unemployment and strong inflationary pressures relative to the rest, while others are tentatively emerging from recession and are experiencing high or only slowly declining unemployment and weak inflationary pressures. This pattern reflects differences in national economic cycles which may be expected to persist for a while but should diminish as two sources of difference are either removed or substantially dampened: a single monetary policy will replace national monetary policies while fiscal policy will come under the common and tight constraints of the Stability Pact.

Differences in labour market structures across countries are associated with differences in the flexibility with which real wages respond to changes in demand. In countries with relatively flexible wages a reduction in the level or rate of growth of aggregate demand is more likely to induce a greater degree of moderation in wage demands than in countries with more rigid labour market structures. In the latter, the difficulty of cutting wage costs in conditions of falling demand is more likely to give rise to higher unemployment and hence stronger demands for the relaxation of monetary policy than in countries with more labour market flexibility. In conditions of rising aggregate demand, the countries with the least flexible labour market structures are likely to be subject to stronger inflationary pressures and slower reductions in the level of unemployment because employers will be more reluctant to face the relatively high cost of hiring (and possibly later, firing) workers.

Variations in credit structures may also cause differences in the responsiveness of participating states to a common monetary policy, in particular differences in the degree of household and company indebtedness and in the balance between borrowing at long-term fixed rates and short-term variable interest rates. Other things being equal, changes in interest rates affect households and firms with significant short-term variable-rate debt to a greater degree and more quickly than those with lower and more long-term fixed-rate debt (Dornbusch *et al.*, 1998). For example in Italy and the UK, companies have much greater ratios of variable-rate, short-term financing to total debt than in other member countries of EMU. The UK has a much higher degree of household indebtedness than other member states of the EU, while Italian households are net holders of government debt. A rise in the interest rate will therefore have a greater short-term impact on company borrowing in Italy and the UK than in, say, Germany. It will raise household disposable income in Italy and depress it in the UK. In short a tightening of monetary policy by the ECB will have differing effects, in terms of unemployment and output, from country to country.

On the other hand EMU may itself change behaviour and reduce differences in credit structures between member states. Variations in the relative importance of variable-rate, short-term borrowing probably reflect differences in the past credibility of monetary policy: in countries with a relatively poor counterinflationary track record, lenders and borrowers will be relatively more reluctant to take on fixed-rate, long-term credit contracts than in countries where there is greater confidence in the durability of low inflation and current interest rates. Insofar as household indebtedness is associated with house purchase (mortgages), again a greater degree of confidence in the counterinflationary policies of the monetary authorities is likely to induce a greater willingness to take on long-term, fixed-rate mortgages.

A number of econometric studies have been undertaken into the extent to which output changes to a different degree in various European countries in response to a 1 per cent change in the interest rate (Dornbusch *et al.*, 1998). However, to date, research into how far these differences can be explained by variations in national credit structures has proved inconclusive. The governing council of the ECB will have the task of agreeing a single monetary stance, but in the light of the foregoing comments it seems likely that its stance might be too tight for some and too loose for others for some indeterminate time to come. The task facing the ECB, therefore, is to determine a monetary stance which achieves the aim of price stability for the area as a whole, while accepting that different parts of the EMU zone will experience differences in their inflationary pressures and rates of growth in employment and output. As in the United States these differences may be dampened by the effects of interregional migration (which has tended to be lower in Europe than in the United States) and by automatic stabilisers built into the tax and social security structure. But unlike the US budget, the EU budget – at little more than 1 per cent of GDP – has virtually no contracyclical impact, so there is a greater need for national fiscal flexibility in Europe. Yet the latter has been restricted by the Stability and Growth Pact (Chapter 9).

The EMI set out the following requirements for any monetary strategy adopted by the ESCB:

- Public announcement of a quantified definition of the final objective of price stability in order to enhance the transparency and credibility of the ESCB strategy.

- Public announcement of a specific target or targets against which the performance of the ESCB can be assessed by the general public.
- The use of a wide range of indicators.
- Within that set of indicators, a prominent role for monetary aggregates.
- The strategy should be forward looking.

Monetary or inflation target

The choice of strategy focuses on two main alternatives: *monetary targeting* (defined and measured according to the growth of some measure of the money supply) and direct *inflation targeting* (defined and measured according to some indicator of inflation). Different central banks have made different choices but variations in their behaviour are not very great in practice: all central banks forecast the rate of inflation, they all look at the development of monetary aggregates and they all have the same objective of price stability. However the options have different presentational characteristics in terms of objectives and the monitoring of their performance.

A monetary target is based on the belief that inflation is a monetary phenomenon and that in the long run, other things being equal, a given percentage increase in the supply of money will lead to an equal percentage increase in the price level. If a stable relationship between the money supply and the rate of inflation exists, it follows that by controlling the amount of money it is also possible to control the rate of inflation. Consequently the monetary aggregate serves as both the policy target and an indicator of prospective inflation, and a central bank can accordingly influence inflation expectations through its control over monetary aggregates. Key to the success of this strategy is the stability and predictability of the long-term relationship between the monetary aggregate and the rate of inflation. In some countries, notably Germany, such stability has existed for several years and monetary targeting has been claimed as a success. Other countries, such as the United States and the UK, have not experienced the same stability on account of rapid and widespread financial innovation, and changes in the behaviour of firms and households.

There is no agreement as to whether the money–price relationship within the EMU zone will be sufficiently stable to warrant monetary targeting, but research by the EMI has established that aggregate monetary demand appears to be more stable in the EU as a whole than within individual countries. But this does not necessarily demonstrate a firm basis for the use of monetary targeting, for a number of reasons. Stability at the level of Europe as a whole simply averages out differences among the member states; EMU itself, involving the harmonisation of monetary policy instruments, will lead to the creation of a *new* set of monetary relations and responses to policy changes which may not necessarily be predictable from the past because of the major structural break which EMU involves. However monetary targeting does have the advantage of putting a central bank under pressure to explain any divergence between the actual and target behaviour of the chosen monetary aggregate. The use of a monetary aggregate to determine inflationary trends and set interest rates has been the Bundesbank's preferred approach, focusing on M3 (bank notes and coins in circulation plus three-month deposits at banks and certificates of deposit held in the private sector). In the view of the Bundesbank, some other continental central banks and several academic economists, the targeting of a monetary aggregate is necessary if the ECB is to 'borrow the credibility' of the Bundesbank.

In the case of inflation targeting the focus is directly on the expected rate of inflation, which is forecast using a wide range of indicators, including monetary aggregates, monetary policy being adjusted if the forecast suggests that the target will not be met. One trouble with inflation targeting is that the central bank does not have direct or rapid control over the rate of inflation, leaving it open for the central bank to blame unexpected factors beyond its control should it fail to meet the target. On the other hand, it it has been argued, it will be preferable for the ECB to target what it really cares about – the rate of inflation – rather than an intermediate target such as the monetary aggregate, particularly if the latter is open to destabilisation by monetary union itself, should it encourage a great deal of financial capital to flow across national frontiers into new bank accounts and financial assets. As a compromise, it has been suggested that the ECB could experiment with a mixture of both types of targeting.

An overriding task of the ECB, as a central bank with no track record, is to develop credibility as soon as possible. The Bundesbank believes the ESCB can best achieve this by imitating its behaviour.

But because the nature and stability of any relationship between the monetary target and the rate of inflation for the EMU zone as a whole may not be known for some time, the establishment of credibility, including the ability to explain why policy might have failed, may not come quickly. Although the adoption of monetary targeting may not be sufficient to establish credibility, it is probably necessary because of the onus on the ECB to demonstrate that it is as like the Bundesbank as possible in a wide EMU incorporating several countries with a poor long-term record with regard to inflation.

At its meeting on 13 October 1998, the ECB council set out the following elements of its monetary policy strategy:

- '[A] quantitative definition of the primary objective of price stability: a year-on-year increase in the harmonised index of consumer prices for the Euro area of below two per cent' (the explanatory statement stressed 'the Euro area as a whole').
- '[A] prominent role for money with a reference value for the growth of a monetary aggregate ... consistent with price stability. Deviations of monetary growth from the reference value would, under normal circumstances, signal risks to price stability.'
- '[A] broadly based assessment of the outlook for future price developments ... while the monetary aggregates contain important and relevant information for monetary policy making ... there is also a clear need to look at other indicators ... this assessment will be made using a wide range of economic and financial variables as indicators for future price development' (ECB president's statement).

Instruments of monetary policy

The broad aim of monetary management is to influence the rate of monetary expansion by controlling the cost or supply of credit. An increase in interest rates reduces the demand for credit by raising its cost, without the central bank having to control the volume of credit directly. Alternatively the central bank may directly alter the amount of liquidity it makes available to the banking system. In principle, various techniques and instruments of monetary management are available to central banks. The Bundesbank and the Banque de

France have operated an interest rate 'corridor', with a 'floor' interest rate payable on overnight liquidity deposited by the banking system and a 'ceiling' interest rate at which the central bank makes overnight liquidity available to banks needing it, called the Lombard rate in Germany. The EMI made various recommendations as to the monetary instruments the ECB should adopt, including standing facilities to provide or absorb liquidity on a day-to-day basis (ECB documentation, 1998). The ESCB will have:

- A marginal lending facility to allow counterparties (for example banks) to obtain overnight liquidity at a prespecified interest rate against eligible assets. This provides the ceiling for the overnight market rate.
- A deposit facility whereby counterparties may make overnight deposits at a prespecified interest rate, the floor for overnight rates.

Other important monetary policy instruments will also allow the ESCB to steer interest rates, manage liquidity and signal its monetary policy stance to the markets. These include open market operations known as reverse transactions or repurchase operations by which the ESCB will buy or sell eligible assets to decrease or increase liquidity. These operations cover a span from *ad hoc* fine-tuning operations conducted with very little advance notice, to longer-term operations conducted monthly on the basis of contracts with three-month maturity, to *ad-hoc* structural operations. The main operations will, however, be conducted weekly with contracts maturing after two weeks. These are expected to be the vehicle by which the ESCB will send key policy signals to the market and manage liquidity.

As well as market operations of this kind, a number of central banks have an administrative device for influencing bank liquidity known as reserve requirements. Under this system commercial banks have to place an amount equivalent to a certain percentage of their total deposits (as defined in some manner) at the central bank, on which they may or may not be paid interest at commercial rates. During stage two there were wide variations across Europe as to whether reserve requirements were imposed at all, and as to the interest rates that were payable, if any.

A crude and long discredited view of reserve requirements is that by adjusting the reserve ratio imposed on banks, upwards or downwards, the total money supply can be varied in a precise and mechanistic manner. A more recent and subtle justification is that if the requirement has to be met *on average* over a period such as a month, it provides a cushion to the banks by which transitory liquidity shocks can be smoothed out, for example those arising from large tax payments by corporate customers of banks to therevenue authorities. Without reserve requirements to achieve such averaging, the central bank would have to intervene very frequently in the money market in order to smooth out such disturbances, perhaps on a day-to-day basis. For example in the UK, reserve requirements do not exist as a policy instrument and the Bank of England has to intervene very frequently in the money markets.

On the other hand, reserve requirements can distort competition between banks in different countries and between banks and non-banks, such as the financial subsidiaries of giant (often American) corporations which accept deposits from, for example, corporate treasurers or even bank treasurers. The competitive distortion arises from the tax-like effect of a reserve requirement which increases in proportion to the required cash reserve ratio or to the shortfall between any interest paid and that available in the market. To the extent that cash reserve requirements distort competition without serving a useful monetary policy purpose, it is argued that they should not be used by the ESCB. This argument found most favour in the UK. It is also argued that a zero requirement would avoid distorting competition while imposing a more rigorous regime than a positive reserve requirement. Whereas the second may only need to be met over a period of several weeks, the first requires commercial banks to end each trading day in balance or credit with the central bank, or face penal borrowing rates.

Any reserve requirement imposed by the ESCB has to be at a uniform rate throughout the monetary union. Any move towards uniformity, therefore, would significantly change the relative competitive positions of banks in different member states. The German banks faced the most onerous reserve requirements before EMU (positive, unremunerated reserves), the Dutch were remunerated while the Belgians, Danes and the British had no reserve ratio at all. The adoption of the German system would have imposed heavy burdens on the banks in other member states, while the adoption of the Dutch or the Belgian approach would have provided a windfall gain to the Germans; either way the German banks stood to gain competitive advantage. The ECB governing council finalised its recommendation for an EU Council regulation on minimum reserves in July 1998. This confirmed the view of several continental central bankers that minimum reserves create a demand for central bank money that allows it to stabilise short-term interest rates through the terms on which it makes liquidity available. (It is argued that, with a minimum reserve requirement, the banking system needs central bank money in proportion to total deposits, almost irrespective of the interest rate it has to pay; and that it is therefore in its interests to reduce its total deposits when interest rates are increased, so that it can reduce the minimum reserves it is required to hold.) The ECB (General Documentation, 1998) stressed that unless banks had to meet some positive minimum reserve requirement averaged out over a period, the ESCB would be faced with volatile money markets, and it would have to make frequent use of open market operations to stabilise interest rates. It was concerned that such frequent intervention could blur market perceptions of its interest rate intentions by making it difficult to distinguish fundamental policy signals from frequent technical adjustments.

The governing council acknowledged that minimum reserves imposed a potential burden on the banking system. It decided that the reserve ratio would be between 1.5 per cent and 2.5 per cent of the relevant liability base (especially deposits and a variety of financial instruments) but it would remunerate reserve holdings at a market rate (the rate on its main refinancing operations). This meant that the impact of the reserve requirement on the profitability of banks would, on average, be neutral across the EMU zone but in some countries, such as Germany, banks would be better off since, as noted above, they had received no remuneration prior to stage three.

TARGET

A further controversy centred on the introduction of the TARGET mechanism for linking the real time gross payment systems (RTGS) of all 15 member states. These are systems for the transfer of euros from one institution to another; being real time they are instantaneous; being gross payment systems, euros can only be transferred if the remitting institution has the funds at the moment of transmission. In contrast 'net' payment systems are those where institutions transfer funds to one another, keep a tally of debits and credits and settle the net amount at the end of the day. A gross payment system is, by its very nature, less exposed to the risk that one institution may not be able to meet its obligations.

TARGET links the national RTGS system and contributes to the reduction of risk in payment systems across Europe. It also facilitates the operation of monetary policy by offering facilities for the transfer of liquidity throughout the monetary union. Because funds can only be transferred over RTGS systems if the remitter has them in the first place it is essential, to avoid gridlock, that the central bank should be able to offer intraday credit (that is, credit during the hours of the operation of the system). Otherwise the timing and size of the outgoing and incoming payments of the participants may not necessarily match in the course of the day.

It had been suggested that banks, or rather the national central banks, of EU member states not in EMU should not be able to borrow euro liquidity from the ESCB, as this would conflict with monetary management by raising the money supply. While acknowledging the importance of monetary management, it is essential to distinguish between intraday and overnight spillovers of credit. Intraday extension of liquidity to facilitate payments in the RTGS systems, by its very nature is distinguished by the end of the TARGET day and does not threaten monetary stability so there are no fundamental monetary policy grounds for distinguishing between the 'ins' and 'outs' in this respect. The proposal to exclude the 'outs', especially the City of London, no doubt had a genuine monetary policy rationale, but this was not the only issue. The competitive position of the City in regard to financial centres within the monetary union was also an important factor, especially if the ESCB were to impose a non-remunerated reserve requirement. To some extent the effectiveness of such a restriction on the 'outs' would have been undermined insofar as their banks had branches within the monetary union and collateral (for example government bonds) against which they could borrow euros from the host NCB.

Some continental bankers, concerned about the competitive threat from the City of London suggested that the use of even eligible collateral by non-EMU-based banks should be limited or even prohibited. But any such restriction would have had to apply to all non-EMU banks, including especially those from the United States. Those favouring a restriction shelved the idea for fear of US retaliation against their own branches operating in the world's largest financial market, New York.

'Out' NCBs took the view that any risk of overnight spillover from intraday credit could be avoided by imposing penal interest rates on any such credit or by imposing a requirement that the 'outs' should have access to intraday euro credit from the ESCB up to some point prior to the closing of the TARGET day, such as an hour, after which they would only retain full access to the TARGET payment system if they were in credit. They also emphasised that access to payment systems throughout the EU was a core feature of the single market for financial services embodied in the Second Banking Co-ordination Directive, that TARGET was an important means for reducing risk in European payment systems and that the monetary union as a whole would benefit from the enormous liquidity and payments traffic generated by Europe's largest financial centre, the City of London.

In the event the general council of the ESCB decided that it could meet both the needs of the payment system and its own monetary policy concerns through limits on intraday credit and safeguards against spillovers into overnight credit. Non-euro NCBs are not allowed overdrafts from the ESCB but they may place a deposit with the ESCB – up to three billion euros for the Bank of England and one billion euros for other non-euro NCBs – against which they can obtain euro liquidity to cover intraday settlements with the other RTGS systems involved in TARGET. The deposit will be remunerated. Commercial banks in non-euro countries are able to obtain intraday credit from their national NCB (until 5 pm, after which they need to be in credit), but they face a penalty interest rate of 5 per cent over the marginal lending rate for spillovers. Positive balances with their NCB may be remunerated and they can use bonds issued by their government as collateral to borrow euros. This solution satisfied the concerns of both 'ins' to 'outs' and removed what had threatened to become an acrimonious source of contention between them. It may be interpreted as a gesture of goodwill towards those not participating in the first wave of EMU. But it was also facilitated by the decision of the governing council to remunerate required cash reserves. This meant that 'in' banks would not be placed at a competitive disadvantage by giving 'outs' – who had no obligation to make unremunerated reserve requirements – access to liquidity.

Prudential supervision

Article 105.6 states that the Council may 'confer upon the ECB specific tasks concerning ... the prudential supervision of credit institutions and other financial institutions with the exception of insurance undertakings', provided that the Council decision is unanimous on the basis of a proposal from the Commission and after consulting the ECB itself (Levitt, 1995). In practice the role of central banks in the prudential supervision of banks and other financial institutions differs from country to country in Europe. In some, banking supervision is the responsibility of a separate body; in others the NCB has principal responsibility; in others the NCB and another body share supervisory responsibilities. It is sometimes argued that supervision of the banking system creates a conflict with an NCB's primary responsibility for price stability, since it may have to pump more liquidity into the banking system than is compatible with the control of inflation. The principal counterargument is that central banks are better at determining and implementing monetary policy where supervisory responsibility gives them 'hands-on' experience of the banking system.

With regard to EMU, two questions arise. Is supranational supervision at the level of the EMU zone needed? If so, should the responsibility lie with the ECB or some other body? Concern about the supervision of banking and financial markets across the EMU zone, or indeed across the EU itself, has arisen because of the prospect that EMU will combine with the developing single market for financial services to encourage the formation of larger financial institutions such as banks, futures and stock exchanges with greater cross-border presence. One concern involves the responsibility for crises of liquidity when the entire banking system of a particular country comes under stress, for example following a run on a particular bank which cannot meet its immediate obligations to counterparties. Under previous arrangements, national central banks preserved systemic stability by injecting liquidity into the system. Under EMU, however, it is the ESCB which is responsible for managing the liquidity of the euro area as a whole. By its very nature the threat of a systemic liquidity crisis requires immediate response from the authorities. But there is no explicit or formal mechanism under the statute of the ESCB for handling such an eventuality. This carries the risk of a rushed, ineffective response without adequate contingency planning. On the other hand any explicit assurance that the ESCB will approve bank bail-outs involves a risk of moral hazard, whereby banks may be inclined to engage in imprudent behaviour in the secure knowledge that if they mismanage their affairs they will not have to face the consequences. The very uncertainty about the arrangements for dealing with a liquidity crisis may be defended as a deterrent to moral hazard. On the other hand the problem should not be exaggerated: central bankers talk to one another regularly on the telephone and in the event of any crisis in a particular country they appear to be confident of being able to handle it within the ESCB framework at very short notice.

A liquidity crisis arises when an institution does not have central bank money or currency readily to hand, even though its assets are greater than its liabilities. It can be distinguished from an insolvency crisis, where liabilities are greater than assets and the institutional faces total collapse (Lannoo, 1998). In practice, however, the distinction between liquidity and insolvency crises may be impossible to determine. But the key point is that the authorities in monetary union countries differ in the following ways: in the manner in which they perceive risks of contagion (where a crisis facing an individual bank poses a threat to the banking system); in their preparedness to bail out an individual institution under threat; and in the degree to which they are prepared to use taxpayers' funds for bail-outs. Recent European banking collapses which illustrate these differences include Banesto in Spain, Barings in the UK and Credit Lyonnais in France.

A further concern is whether home-country prudential control will be sufficient as individual banks extend the scale of their activities, assets and liabilities across the single currency zone and as major cross-border banking mergers develop. As detailed supervision is a matter for the authorities on the ground and as individual institutions are licensed in their country of origin, it is difficult to see how a supranational supervisor, remote from day-to-day supervision at the national level, could represent an improvement. As responsibility for liquidity monitoring and supervision rests with the *host* country where the banks operate, and as ultimate responsibility for prudential supervision rests with the authority which licensed them in their *home* country, the answer for the foreseeable future appears to be effective and regular cooperation between the home and host country supervisors of every bank with cross-border interests and activities. At present, numerous informal contacts are maintained in practice and formal fora exist, such as the Banking Advisory Committee and the Groupe de Contact. However a particular concern does arise in the case of institutions which are created by 50:50 mergers between banks based in different countries with the deliberate intention of avoiding home-country supervision. The collapse of BCCI pointed to the need for transparent, single supervisory arrangements. This principle was embodied in the so called Post-BCCI Directive, so the creation of 50:50 groups does not so much argue for pan-European supervision, as raise the question of why national supervisors are allowing such organisations to be created in the first place.

A further concern is the creation of cross-sectoral financial conglomerates with cross-border activities. Here the immediate need is for more effective cooperation between banking and insurance supervisors, and at present this does not exist in Europe to a satisfactory degree. Again, it does not necessarily point to the need for a new supranational supervisory body but it certainly demonstrates the need for effective cross-sectoral supervision at the *national* level, without which infrastructure cross-frontier cooperation is impossible.

Perhaps the most pressing need is for effective cross-border cooperation between securities supervisors, given the immediate and major impact of EMU on wholesale financial market trading and structures. European securities supervisors meet in the forum of European Securities Commission (FESCO), although national authorities operate different rule books and policies. A broad contrast may be drawn between those supervisors, such as in the UK, who have traditionally favoured market innovation and devised supervisory arrangements around it, and those for whom supervisory led market arrangements have traditionally been the norm. As for the potential supervisory role of the ECB, there appears to be no strong momentum in this direction at the time of writing, neither within the ECB itself nor from national authorities. It is probably impossible to adjudicate between the following contentions: that there would be a conflict of interest were the ECB to be given a broad supervisory role; that involvement in financial markets and supervision complement one another.

Conclusions

The European Central Bank is intended, as a matter of policy and law, to be politically independent and devoted to the attainment of price stability within the monetary union. These desiderata were essential to win German support for monetary union. Moreover it is intended that the ECB should build on the credibility of the Bundesbank. At the same time it is expected to replace the Bundesbank by focusing on the development of a monetary policy for the euro area as a whole. As long as national inflation rates differ there may be tension between the expectation that it should be as single minded and independent as the Bundesbank and the requirement that it should take the needs of all into account. This problem is not helped by the minority position of the ECB executive on the governing council in relation to the NCB governors. On the other hand the legitimacy of this new central bank probably requires the representation of all NCBs for the foreseeable future. With time, the precise division of labour between the ECB and the NCBs with regard to the operational implementation of policy will also need to be resolved.

Nonetheless it is safe to assume that the ECB/ESCB will be devoted to achieving low inflation across the euro area as a whole, although differences in inflation rates and differences in the responses of economic agents – employees, households and firms – across countries to changes in interest rates may make this a difficult task for some years to come. One may expect increasing attention to be devoted to supervisory arrangements, given that EMU may encourage the development of large financial institutions that cross both frontiers and sectors. But at the time of writing there appears to be no strong appetite for giving the ECB a major role in this area.

Chapter 9

Fiscal Policy

While responsibility for the formulation of monetary policy is centralised in the ECB, fiscal policy remains in the hands of national governments. As a result of the abolition of each country's ability to control its own exchange rate and the centralisation of monetary policy, it is the only instrument of economic management under national control. However the Maastricht Treaty set criteria of fiscal discipline that countries would have to meet to join the monetary union. A question also arises as to what constraints will be needed now that monetary union is under way.

Whereas the objective of monetary policy is price stability, fiscal policy serves several economic and social objectives. From the viewpoint of EMU, its main role is as a tool of macroeconomic management, influencing the level of economic activity. It is therefore necessary to consider the scope for fiscal policy within the framework of disciplines set by the treaty, as subsequently amplified by the Stability and Growth Pact (Buti and Sapir, 1998; Allsopp and Vines, 1996; Fatas, 1998; Gros, 1995; Melitz, 1997; Mortensen, 1990). The role of the EU budget – tiny in comparison with national budgets – also needs to be reviewed in the context of monetary union, especially its inability to act as an instrument for cyclical stability. Finally, special attention needs to be given to effective coordination between monetary and fiscal policy.

Fiscal discipline

The treaty requires that 'member states shall regard their economic policies as a matter of common concern and shall co-ordinate them' (Article 103) and that 'member states shall avoid excessive government deficits' (Article 104c). It sets out a framework for the multilateral surveillance of national economic and fiscal positions. It also specifies detailed procedures for the examination and correction of excessive deficits, including the possibility of fines. These procedures have subsequently been amplified by the Stability and Growth Pact. The tone and underlying concern of the treaty emphasises the maintenance of fiscal discipline and reflects rejection of the Keynesian approach to fiscal policy, by which the budget balance was used to 'fine tune' the overall level of economic activity, for example by budgeting for a deficit to boost demand, output and employment during periods of recession.

The intellectual case for this rejection rests on the argument that the Keynesian fiscal policy is ineffective: a budget deficit might stimulate demand in the short run but it raises interest rates. This reduces private sector investment, and in the long run depresses household consumption by increasing the taxation needed to pay interest on the increased national debt. Increased public spending together with higher interest rates 'crowd out' more productive private sector investment, thereby depressing the future growth prospects of the economy. All these points are theoretically and empirically contestable, most notably on account of Keynes' argument that interest rates may be ineffective in times of severe recession and uncertainty. Not only may fiscal policy be the only means of stimulating demand under such conditions, the subsequent growth of aggregate output, income and consumption may generate additional fiscal revenue while reducing unemployment-related expenditure. However it was the case for fiscal discipline that dominated the shaping of both the treaty and the Stability and Growth Pact (Buti and Sapir, 1998; Gros and Thygesen, 1998).

The rejection of Keynesian fiscal policy was reinforced by anxiety that an increase in the government deficit in one member state could have spillover effects elsewhere. By raising interest rates in other countries it would depress investment, growth and employment throughout the monetary union. However it is unclear how far a fiscal expansion in one country has a net deflationary effect on others, since the country initiating the fiscal stimulus also draws in imports from other member states. The size of these positive and negative spillover effects is likely to be the greater the larger the country initiating the fiscal expansion. The example of increased deficits in Germany following reunification (to fund the Eastern *Länder*) is often quoted. But the overall net effect is difficult to estimate. Moreover the conventional economic models used to quantify these effects are, of course, based on pre-EMU structural relationships both within the economies concerned (for example the response of wages and prices to changes in the level of activity) and with regard to trade flows and cross-border interest rate effects.

A concern of the Dutch and German governments in particular, was that many of the countries that aspired to join the first wave of EMU had a relatively short history of fiscal prudence. Although it was a condition for entry that countries should attain a 'sustainable' fiscal position, as assessed by reference to an annual budget deficit of no more than 3 per cent of GDP and outstanding government debt of no more than 60 per cent of GDP, there was an underlying worry that the achievement of those targets might not be sustained over the longer term. Indeed the assessment of 'sustainable' fiscal positions on the basis of those deficit and debt ratios was based on achievements in one year only – 1997. In a number of countries one-off fiscal devices were used to achieve the 3 per cent deficit target for 1997. There was concern, therefore, that once countries had passed through the fiscal gateway into EMU they might return to their bad old ways. This concern was reflected in the convergence reports of the Dutch and German central banks, issued in spring 1998.

Fiscal indiscipline, reflected in very high debt to GDP ratios in a number of countries, had been caused by governments yielding to pressure groups or making fiscal inducements in the run-up to general elections (Buti and Sapir, 1998). A return to fiscal indiscipline would increase interest rates throughout the monetary union or put pressure on the ECB to avoid interest rate rises that it judged necessary. Countries with high government debt would be especially exposed to interest rate increases, whose impact on debt servicing costs might push them over the 3 per cent annual deficit target. In these circumstances it was feared that there could be a conflict of interest between economic and finance ministers – anxious to hold down debt servicing charges – and the ECB. The more prudent course embodied in the treaty was to introduce binding rules on debts and deficits.

Before examining the rules in the TEU and the Stability and Growth Pact, it is necessary to consider their intellectual basis. Although the arithmetical definition of sustainability is clear – it is achieved when the rate of interest does not exceed the rate of growth of GDP – it is harder to arrive at a policy rule that guarantees delivery. One approach might be to argue that the debt to GDP ratio thought to be sustainable at the time a country is judged eligible for membership should not increase further. But this implies that the debt to GDP ratios of all participants was optimal or at least acceptable at the point of entry to monetary union. In contrast, several of the countries deemed eligible in May 1998 had debt to GDP ratios that were well above the 60 per cent target. These will be most vulnerable to fiscal deterioration should the ECB raise interest rates. The rule also implies that, with a common rate of interest across the monetary union, the faster growing members could expand their deficits faster than the rest. The trouble is that interest rates tend to vary unpredictably over time. There can therefore be no guarantee that the faster growing economies will indeed maintain a stable debt to GDP ratio into the future. In short it is difficult to devise *a priori* rules for fiscal prudence.

In practice the treaty established a more or less arbitrary but unambiguous reference target for debt, that is, it should not exceed 60 per cent of GDP. It also set out a procedure for multilateral surveillance, backed if necessary by sanctions, including fines, to avoid excessive government deficits (Article 104c). These procedures were then given legal form under the Stability and Growth Pact. They are to be initiated by the Council of Economic and Finance Ministers (Ecofin) on the basis of reports from the Commission, and any action is to be based on qualified majority voting. In short, enforcement procedures lack formal automaticity and the timescale is extended. Moreover, because many member states are entering EMU with deficits close to 3 per cent of GDP, doubts have been expressed as to the credibility of sanctions and fines should there be a downturn in economic activity, which will of itself increase deficits further. Another concern is whether the rules allow enough flexibility for fiscal policy to be used to cushion economic downturns, given that member states will no longer be able to devalue their currencies or cut their interest rates.

The Stability and Growth Pact

The concern of the German minister of finance, Theo Waigel, that fiscal discipline should be maintained once EMU had started was voiced with increasing vigour throughout the Madrid, Florence and Dublin (December 1996) European Councils, where a formal stability pact was proposed. A resolution of the June Amsterdam

European Council eventually established the Stability and Growth Pact. This stressed that:

> In stage three of EMU member states shall avoid excessive general government deficits ... the European Council underlines the importance of safe-guarding sound government finances as a means to strengthening the conditions for price stability and for strong sustainable growth conducive to employment creation. It is also necessary to ensure that national budgetary policies support stability oriented monetary policies. Adherence to the objective of sound budgetary conditions that are in balance or in surplus will allow all member states to deal with normal cyclical fluctuations while keeping the government deficit within the reference value of three per cent of GDP (Resolution 97/C 236/01, para. 1).

The Maastricht Treaty had already specified procedures for avoiding and sanctioning excessive government deficits (European Commission, 1992, Article 104c):

> Member states shall avoid excessive government deficits. The Commission shall monitor the development of the budgetary situation and of the stock of government debt in the member states ... it shall examine compliance with budget discipline on the basis of the following two criteria:
>
> - (a) whether the ratio of planned or actual government deficit to gross domestic product exceeds a reference value, unless either the ratio has declined substantially and continuously and reached a level that comes close to the reference value; or alternatively, excess over the reference value is only exceptional and temporary and the ratio remains close to the reference value;
> - (b) whether the ratio of government to gross domestic product exceeds the reference value, unless the ratio is sufficiently diminishing and approaching the reference value at a satisfactory pace.

If the member state does not fulfil the requirements under one or both of these criteria, the Commission shall prepare reports. The Commission may also prepare a report if ... it is of the opinion that there is a risk of an excessive deficit in a member state. The [Economic and Financial Committee] shall formulate an Opinion on the report of the Commission. The Council shall, acting by a qualified majority on a recommendation from the Commission and having considered any other observations which the member state concerned may wish to make, decide after an overall assessment whether an excessive deficit exists. Where the existence of an excessive deficit is decided ... the Council shall make recommendations to the member state concerned, with a view to bringing the situation to an end within a given period. Where it establishes that there has been no effective action within the period, the Council may make its recommendations public. If a member state persists in failing to put into practice the recommendations, the Council may decide to give notice to the member state to take, within a specified time limit, measures for deficit reduction ... as long as a member state fails to comply with the decision, Council may decide to apply, or as the case may be, intensify one or more of the following measures:

- to require the member state concerned to publish additional information, to be specified by the Council, before issuing bonds and securities
- to invite the European Investment Bank to reconsider its lending policy towards the member state concerned
- to require the member state concerned to make a non-interest-bearing deposit of an appropriate size with the Community until the excessive deficit has been corrected
- to impose fines of an appropriate size.

The trouble, in the view of the German Ministry of Finance, was that the procedure in the treaty lacked automaticity and a clear timetable, hence the pressure to introduce more rigorous procedures in the form of the Stability and Growth Pact. Following the adoption of the resolution on the Stability and Growth Pact, the Council adopted two key regulations on 7 July 1997, one on strengthening the surveillance of budgetary positions and the surveillance and coordination of economic policies, the other on speeding up and clarifying the implementation of the excess deficit procedure.

The first regulation (1466/97) defined the content of the submissions member states would have to make under mutual surveillance, as well as the procedures for their examination and for the monitoring of subsequent undertakings 'so as to prevent, at an early stage, the occurrence of excessive general government deficits and to promote surveillance and co-ordination of economic policies' (Article 1).The following must be included in stability programmes:

- Information on the medium-term prospects for budgetary positions with a view to achieving a positive fiscal balance.
- The key underlying economic assumptions behind national budgets.
- Descriptions of the budgetary measures being taken or proposed to achieve the objective of the programme; quantitative assessment of the effects of the budget.
- Information on the government surplus and the deficits for the current and preceding years and for at least the following three years.

Stability programmes had to be submitted annually from March 1999. Later entrants to EMU will have to submit stability programmes within six months of any Council decision on their participation. The Council will take account of assessments by the Commission and the Economic and Finance Committee. It will examine medium-term budget objectives and the realism of the measures and assumptions, and it may make recommendations to member states. Article 7 of the regulation requires non-members of stage three to supply the same information in their 'convergence programmes' as full participants provide in their 'stability pro-grammes'. It should be pointed out that under Article 109e (4) the 'endeavour to avoid excessive deficits will continue to apply to the United Kingdom'.

The regulation (1467/97) on speeding up and clarifying the implementation of the excessive deficit procedure is intended to give greater precision and rigour to Article 104c, described above. Member states are 'urged to meet the deadlines for the excessive deficit procedure'; they are 'invited always to impose sanctions if a participating member state fails to take the necessary steps'; they are 'urged always to require a non-interest bearing deposit whenever the Council decides to impose sanctions'; and they are 'urged always to convert a deposit into a fine after two years unless the excessive deficit has been corrected'. Although these exhortations lack auto-maticity, they are intended to reassure those who doubt the commitment of those member states which only recently converted to fiscal rectitude. The resolution on the excessive deficit procedure limits circumstances when a government deficit in excess of three per cent of GDP 'shall be considered exceptional and temporary' to those

> resulting from an unusual event outside the control of the member state or when resulting from a severe economic down-turn ... A severe economic down-turn [is] exceptional only if there is an annual fall of real GDP of at least two per cent. The Council ... shall in its overall assessment take into account any observations made by the member states showing that an annual fall of real GDP of less than two per cent is nevertheless exceptional in the light of further supporting evidence.

The regulation specifies the following timetable for the excessive deficit procedure:

- Within two weeks of a Commission report in accordance with Article 104c, the Economic and Financial Committee has to formulate an opinion.
- After taking that opinion into account the Commission shall 'if it considers that an excessive deficit exists address an Opinion and a Recommendation to the Council which must decide on the existence of an excessive deficit within three months'.
- If the Council also considers that a deficit exists, it must make a recommendation to the member state concerned, simultaneously setting a deadline of four months for taking action, which must be completed in the year following the identification of the excessive deficit 'unless there are special circumstances'.
- Where the Council believes no effective action has been taken, the Council 'shall impose sanctions in accordance with Article 104c' within two months of a Council decision to give notice to the country concerned.
- If the Council believes that a member state has deliberately planned an excessive deficit, the whole procedure may be expedited.
- The sanctions take the form of 'a fixed component equal to 0.2 per cent of GDP and a variable component equal to one tenth of the difference between the deficit as a percentage of GDP in the preceding year and the reference value of three per cent of GDP'.

- In following years the Council will assess whether or not the member state has taken effective action and it may intensify the sanction by additional deposit requirements; any single deposit 'shall not exceed the upper limit at 0.5 per cent of GDP'.
- After two years the sanctions may be converted into a fine if the excessive deficit has not been corrected. Interest on the deposits and any fine will be distributed among the participating member states without a deficit.

The excessive deficit procedure in Article 104c will not apply to the UK while it remains outside EMU, although it still has an obligation to avoid an excessive deficit. In the event of UK participation, the timetable for the excessive deficit procedure will be somewhat different from those of the other member states, because the UK financial year does not correspond to the calendar year as in other countries.

Contracyclical fiscal policy

As noted above, the assumptions behind the treaty and the Stability and Growth Pact are dismissive of fiscal fine tuning as a tool of cyclical stabilisation. Yet they express concern about the following potentially adverse effects of fiscal expansion: negative spillover effects to other countries and the possibility that high levels of debt will induce governments to oppose ECB decisions to raise interest rates.

Critics of this position have emphasised that a combination of monetary rectitude by the ECB and the fiscal constraints of the Stability and Growth Pact could exacerbate or prolong recessions. A deterioration in the fiscal position during a recession (as revenues fall and expenditure on unemployment rises) may even require fiscal tightening under the pact. This will further depress economic activity. In short the risk is that policy could be pro- rather than anticyclical in recessionary circumstances. Given that discretionary fiscal fine tuning has rarely been practised for some time, the debate tends to focus on the role of automatic fiscal stabilisers. As the level of output falls or its rate of growth slows, tax revenues will fall or decelerate faster than the slowdown in overall economic activity, whereas social security and other public expenditures will tend to rise. The net effect is to cushion the slowdown in the economy.

The treaty and the Stability and Growth Pact accept that a deterioration in the fiscal position may arise from time to time. As seen, Article 104c of the TEU concedes that the ratio of the annual deficit to GDP might exceed 3 per cent provided that 'the excess over the reference value is only exceptional and temporary', and that the ratio of debt to GDP may exceed 60 per cent provided that 'the ratio is sufficiently diminishing and approaching the reference value at a satisfactory pace'. These statements do not necessarily imply that governments *should* proactively expand the deficit in recession (the Keynesian approach). But they do reflect acceptance that recessions tend to cause a deterioration in the fiscal position, because of built-in flexibility in tax and expenditure structures (especially unemployment benefit).

But the Stability and Growth Pact and the treaty also provide for sanctions or even fines unless the fall in the level of GDP exceeds 2 per cent per year. Such a drop in GDP only happened three times in the EU between 1980 and 1995: twice in France and once in Sweden. In other words the concession allowing an increase in the deficit over 3 per cent provided that GDP has fallen by more than 2 per cent seems likely to apply only in exceptional circumstances. In more common slowdowns, the operation of the pact may require discretionary tax increases or expenditure cuts to offset the effect of automatic stabilisers. The likelihood of this happening in practice, however, is difficult to establish.

Research among OECD countries suggests that, on average, approximately 50 per cent of a decline in the level of aggregate output is likely to be offset by a relaxation of the fiscal position as a result of automatic stabilisers; a 1 per cent fall in GDP is accompanied by fiscal loosening (lower taxes, higher spending) equal to about 0.5 per cent of GDP. The percentage is probably somewhat higher in the EU because of the higher levels of taxation and public spending in relation to GDP than in other OECD countries, especially the largest, the United States. Some numerical examples illustrate the implications of the Stability and Growth Pact using such assumptions of how fiscal balances deteriorate with GDP. If the average EU member state tends to grow at 2.25 per cent per annum in real terms but in one year the absolute level of GDP falls by 2 per cent (the limit up to which sanctions/fines may apply under the Stability and Growth Pact), and if the built-in flexibility of the automatic stabilisers is indeed 50 per cent, then the fiscal deterioration would amount to 2.125 per cent of GDP (that is, half of the 4.25 per cent GDP swing). This is well within the 3 per cent ceiling on permissible fiscal deficits. But this relaxed view *requires that the country starts from a position of fiscal balance.* Clearly a fiscal deterioration of 2.125 per cent of GDP would be beyond the limits set by the Stability and Growth Pact if the deficit was 3 per cent in the first place. If GDP fell by 1 per cent the deterioration in the fiscal balance would be 1.6 per cent of GDP (assuming previous GDP growth of 2.25 per cent and that the automatic fiscal stabilisers were equivalent to half the downturn in GDP). If the country started with a 3 per cent budget deficit, the resulting deficit would be 4.6 per cent of GDP. But a 1 per cent fall in GDP would be too low to avoid sanctions if a majority of other member states chose to impose them. Even if a country's initial deficit were 2 per cent of GDP it would rise to 3.6 per cent of GDP, again too high to avoid sanctions.

The implication is clear: unless member states achieve rough fiscal balance before the next recession the Stability and Growth Pact, if strictly interpreted and enforced, could require taxes to be raised or expenditure to be cut in conditions of declining economic activity, thereby exacerbating the recessionary tendency of the economy. To avoid this they will have to maintain and reinforce fiscal discipline once they enter stage three, so that in non-recessionary years their budgets are in balance or even surplus, thereby allowing some leeway for a deterioration in the fiscal position when the next recession strikes. Some suggest that monetary union will itself help in this endeavour: a sustained reduction in the debt to GDP ratio should permit a sustained reduction in interest rates (and the tax required to service the national debt), thereby reducing the cost of capital and stimulating investment in the long term (although a reduction in the cost of investment by itself will not stimulate additional investment unless demand for the output is also in prospect). Those who argue that there is sufficient flexibility within the constraints of the Stability and Growth Pact include Buti and Sapir (1998), whereas concern about excessive fiscal tightness, especially in the early years of EMU, is expressed by Eichengreen and Wyplosz (1998).

The EU budget

Modern federal states that form single currency zones typically have federal budgets amounting to at least 40 per cent of GDP. Not only do these redistribute resources from richer to poorer regions, they also have a contracyclical effect because of the automatic, built-in stabilisers provided by federal income taxes and social security systems. The distinction between redistribution and contracyclical policy is important. Redistribution from rich to poor regions may take place at any level of aggregate GDP and irrespective of whether it is rising or falling. In contrast contracyclical fiscal policy involves the transfer of resources from faster growing regions to those where economic activity is slowing or falling, irrespective of the level of GDP from which it falls – even prosperous regions experience economic downturns.

Such contracyclical transfers via the budget mechanism tend to come about through the normal operation of the tax and social security system: rising activity is associated with an increase in the tax take and falling expenditure on unemployment benefit, the opposite being the case with declining activity. So, within a given fiscal area, faster growing regions will pay more to the common budget while those facing a downturn take more from the common fiscal pool. The larger the overall budget and the more it is composed of taxes and expenditures which automatically vary with the rate of growth of GDP, the greater the 'built-in' fiscal flexibility. Research shows that although the individual states of the United States demonstrate asymmetric reactions to economic developments, the federal budget dampens this effect because of its built-in, automatic stabilisers, especially the reduction in federal tax revenue when states go into recession. But estimates of this automatic stabilising effect vary from as little as a 17 cent reduction to as much as a 40 cent reduction in the federal tax take for a dollar fall in regional income.

The EU budget, however, represents no more than 1.27 per cent of EU GDP, about half of it devoted to the Common Agricultural Policy. Most of the rest goes to the 'structural funds' to fund long-term programmes of economic regeneration and development. The budget is funded by member governments and it involves neither direct taxation on firms and individuals nor social security benefits/ contributions. All of this means that it is not only ill-structured to serve a contracyclical role, it is also too small for this purpose.

In 1974 the MacDougall committee of advisers examined the Community budget, paying particular attention to the potential need for a contracyclical function in the event of economic and monetary union in Europe. It noted that the main contracyclical contribution of federal budgets came not from special redistributional funds but from the normal operation of federal tax and social security arrangements. When it reported to the Commission in 1977 it recommended an expansion of the budget, partly for contracyclical purposes (the Commission never commented). At the time of writing, however, the net contributors oppose any expansion, which, even if agreed, is likely to be modest. This means that it will fall to member states to provide automatic stabilisers or discretionary contracyclical policies.

The opposition to a significant expansion of the EU budget partly reflects the self-interest of the main net contributors and the low levels of social and political cohesion across the EU as a whole: unlike interpersonal transfers within individual nation states, major intercountry fiscal transfers lack legitimacy. But a further problem is lack of confidence in the quality of the financial management of the EU budget. Reports from the Court of Auditors since 1975 have demonstrated significant fraud, waste and mismanagement. This is partly the result of weak *ex ante* appraisal of proposed expenditures, inadequate monitoring of expenditure and weak *ex post* evaluation to see what lessons might be learned. But mismanagement also results from faults within the member states themselves, where the funds are spent via local and regional agencies of government. For whatever reason, lack of confidence in the efficiency and effectiveness of the budget means that, irrespective of the member states' reluctance to dig deeper into their pockets, any significant expansion is unlikely until there is clear evidence of significant improvement, for example from reports of the Court of Auditors. However even within the Commission itself, concern about the quality of financial control probably explains its reluctance to take any public position on the MacDougall Report. Indeed there is no evidence that the Commission has ever debated the report.

The coordination of monetary and fiscal policy

Article 109c provided for the creation of a Monetary Committee in stage one to promote policy coordination, with representation from the central banks and Ministries of Finance of each member state. With the arrival of stage three this was replaced by an Economic and Financial Committee. Its role is to provide opinions and support the Council. However there is no single body to ensure the coordination of monetary and fiscal policy in stage three. As noted earlier the ECB will face eleven separate Ministries of Finance, and although the treaty requires member states to regard their economic policies as a matter of common concern and the Council to draft broad guidelines for the economic policies of the member states, supported by peer group multilateral surveillance, it is not absolutely clear what this might mean in practice. A number of risks have been identified: a tight monetary policy operated independently by the ECB might coincide with tight fiscal policy under the constraints of the Stability and Growth Pact to depress growth; or the ECB might react to what it regards as an over-loose fiscal policy by raising interest rates in circumstances where finance ministers believe that fiscal expansion is needed to stimulate growth and employment. While governments might argue that the ECB should refrain from raising interest rates unless there is a risk of inflation, there is nothing they can do if the ECB disagrees (Arrowsmith and Taylor, 1996; Dornbusch, 1990; Eichengreen and Von Hagen, 1995; Melitz, 1997).

In short there is no single body to determine the optimal mix of monetary and fiscal policy. This largely follows from two themes central to the treaty: that the ECB should focus on price stability above all else; and the insistence on fiscal rectitude, rather than an active contracyclical fiscal policy. In practice, informal discussions between central bankers and Finance Ministries are inevitable and they will meet formally in the Economic and Financial Committee. It was partly to promote monetary–fiscal policy coordination that France proposed the creation of the Euro-'X' Council. It was intended that this should, on the one hand, help coordinate fiscal and economic policy between the EMU governments, and on the other provide for a more structured monetary–fiscal dialogue between the Council and the ECB, including a mechanism for conflict resolution. Any idea that such a body could give orders or even propose policy guidelines to the ECB was anathema to countries such as Germany and the Netherlands. Instead, and perhaps to the chagrin of some of its advocates, the first discussions of the Euro-X Council were characterised by insistence by the European Commission (which provides technical/secretariat support) and Ministry of Finance officials from Germany and the Netherlands that countries with high debt to GDP ratios should do much more to reduce their structural deficits, while other countries should use the fiscal dividends from economic recovery to repay debt and reduce deficits rather than increase public spending. These are policy priorities very much in line with those of the central bankers.

In short, if monetary–fiscal policy coordination is seen as a means of bringing pressure to bear on the ECB it is likely to fail. If it is seen as a means by which the ECB can warn that fiscal looseness will be met by monetary tightening, it is difficult to see what has been added to the provisions of the treaty. If, on the other hand, coordination mechanisms such as the Economic and Financial Committee or even the Euro-X Council provide a setting in which the economic and monetary outlook can be debated by central bankers and finance ministries with a view to reconciling differences in their forecasts or policy responses, the risk of suboptimal monetary–fiscal policy mixes might be reduced. Even so, agreement on basic facts and technical forecasts may not come easily, not to mention the difficulty of reaching consensus on an appropriate policy stance.

Conclusions

Various factors condition the size of the risk assumed by any one member state in accepting the fiscal constraints created by the Stability and Growth Pact in order to participate in monetary union: the extent of economic asymmetries between it and other members; the degree to which it forfeits a useful instrument of economic policy in relinquishing the freedom to devalue its currency; and the extent to which lower interstate labour mobility puts Europe at a disadvantage to the United States. Optimists believe that the risks posed to the eleven founding states are minimal. Pessimists believe that there are still significant risks, particularly in respect of those countries which were unable to maintain consistently stable exchange rates against the Deutschmark prior to monetary union, usually the more geographically peripheral countries. Likewise opinion is divided on the other three themes covered in this chapter: the issue of whether the Stability and Growth Pact inhibits contracyclical policy; the need for a larger EU budget; and appropriate methods of delivering monetary–fiscal policy coordination.

Much analysis can be little more than speculation at this stage, and the regime will only be truly tested in an economic downturn, or as a result of severe cyclical differences between member states. A downturn might come from an external economic shock, such as a political and economic crisis in Russia or a further and severe deterioration of the major Far Eastern economies. Such external shocks would have asymmetric impacts on the different economies forming the monetary union and could exacerbate policy tensions. Leaving such external risk aside, the development of an effective fiscal policy and the achievement of balance between monetary and fiscal policy require a learning process in which trial and error are likely to be less dangerous so long as economic conditions are favourable in all member states.

Chapter 10

The Euro as a Global Currency

The euro will be the currency of an economic bloc whose economic importance potentially rivals that of the United States. For example the combined GDP of all 15 EU member states is marginally greater than that of the United States but half as large again as that of Japan; while the combined GDP of the initial 11 EMU members is marginally below that of the United States but larger than that of Japan. The share of global trade of the 15 EU countries (excluding intra-EU trade) is likewise marginally greater than that of the United States but double that of Japan, while the share of global trade of the initial 11 is marginally below the US's global trade share and larger than that of Japan. This chapter reviews the potential role of the euro in global trade as a reserve currency and in private portfolios. It then considers the role of the euro in global currency stability, both among EU members and non-members of EMU and in the world at large. It includes a brief discussion of the potential external value and stability of the euro against other currencies.

Visions of the euro

Until late 1997 there was remarkably little debate in the rest of the world about the global implications of EMU, apart from the contribution of a number of American economists. On the whole governments, officials and the private sector adopted a policy of 'benign neglect' if not downright indifference to what was happening in Europe, many of them feeling that the European countries would never complete EMU.

From the start a major goal of some proponents of EMU has been the creation of a European currency bloc that is independent from the vagaries of the global currency markets, especially the volatility of the US dollar. They have aimed for a currency which will symbolically represent Europe and further its global political power, notably by giving it a greater voice in international monetary management. A further consideration – exemplified by the United States – is that a major economic power with a currency that is used in the rest of the world is able to finance trade deficits and raise capital more easily and cheaply than if it has to borrow money from other countries. This also means that its exporters are in a stronger position to invoice their sales to the rest of the world in their own currency, thereby shifting the exposure to currency risk onto the importer.

There is, however, a contradiction at the heart of the geo-economic and political vision for the euro. While some want to see it established as a strong, credible currency that is attractive to investors and issuers throughout the world, others – sometimes even the same people – have been motivated by a perception that Europe has been at a disadvantage to the United States, whose authorities, they believe, have been able to gain competitive advantage for American producers by practising a 'benign neglect' of the dollar. The problem is that a like strategy would imply a soft single currency for Europe.

There is no mechanistic relationship that determines the value of one currency against another, their exchange rate being the product of supply and demand in global markets. There are three broad ways of looking at the matter which are relevant to the external value of the euro. According to 'the purchasing power parity approach', long-term movements in exchange rates between currencies tend to reflect inflation differentials: if one country experiences a higher rate of inflation than another (implying loss of competitiveness in trade) its exchange rate will tend to depreciate in value. Even the expectation of higher inflation, and hence currency depreciation, may make investors less willing to hold the currency in the first place. Consequently the expected success of the ECB in containing inflation will be crucial to the external value of the euro. For example attacks on the ECB's prudence shortly after the launch of the single currency in January 1999 led to a weakening of the external value of the euro.

Looked at from another, complementary, point of view, the external value of a currency tends to change in line with the size of its external current account surplus or deficit – a growing surplus means rising demand for the currency on the part of the rest of the world, putting upward pressure on the exchange rate. Over time the trend in the surplus/deficit position of an economy reflects its competitiveness. The external competitiveness of the EMU zone will depend not only on the success of the ECB in containing inflation, but also on underlying fundamentals, including the relative productivity/efficiency of European industry and Europe's ability to reallocate capital and labour to industries where demand is rising and comparative advantage can be sustained. In this regard the flexibility of labour markets in terms of mobility between occupations and regions, and the responsiveness of wage costs to changes in the pattern of demand, are crucial.

A third way of looking at exchange rates is to examine the balance between the demand and supply of financial assets denominated in a currency. To the extent that the ESCB establishes credibility in the sense of sustaining a stable and low rate of inflation, global demand for financial assets denominated in euro will be strengthened. At the same time the creation of a single currency zone embracing an economic area broadly comparable in scale to the United States potentially allows the development of large, liquid financial markets denominated in euro which could be attractive to issuers and investors in a wide variety of financial assets. The *supply* of government and corporate bonds, together with corporate stock and other financial assets denominated in euro, is potentially huge, as is the potential *demand* for those assets. It is, however, impossible to predict how the interaction of these forces will move yields in euro financial assets or the resultant euro exchange rate (Bergsten, 1998; Portes and Rey, 1998).

Europe as an economic bloc

What is absolutely crucial to the emergence of the euro as a major global currency is the development of its credibility as a currency demonstrating strong internal stability, that is, low inflation. This in turn means that the ECB must establish credibility in the pursuit of its objective of price stability, but it also requires that the ECB should not be frustrated in achieving its goal by profligate government fiscal policies. Assuming that the desiderata are met, what then determines the global role of currencies?

Clearly the economic size and stability of the country issuing the currency is crucial. Sterling became the world's leading currency in the days of the British Empire. It was then superseded by the US dollar as the United States emerged as the dominant global economic power, but this switch did not happen quickly and sterling continued to play a major role in the British Commonwealth and Empire for several years after the relative decline of the UK as a dominant economic force in the world.

In purely arithmetical terms, the fact that the EMU zone, or the potential euro zone represented by the EU as a whole, has a GDP broadly comparable to that of the United States meets a necessary condition for the emergence of the euro as a major international currency. Moreover the EU's share of global trade (20 per cent) is broadly similar to that of the United States (18 per cent). However there is a difference: around half of global exports are currently denominated in dollars but only just over a third of exports are denominated in the principal European currencies (and around one twentieth in Japanese yen). This means the US dollar is used to denominate many exports from countries other than the United States, and the United States is able to minimise its exposure to global currency movements because a significant share of its own imports are priced in its own currency, especially petroleum and other primary commodities.

Clearly the EMU countries will denominate their own exports in euro. Other European countries, and especially EU countries not inside stage three, will be under pressure to do likewise, particularly when exporting to the EMU zone. Over time, other countries with exposure to the euro may be tempted to follow suit, notably those strongly dependent on imports from Europe. But even if they adopt the euro for imports or exports to the EMU area, it does not follow that countries in the rest of the world will use the euro in trade relations with one another, or that the euro will displace the dollar as a 'vehicle currency': that is to say, a currency used as an intermediary between the users of two others because of its superior liquidity and lower transaction costs (it can be readily bought and sold throughout the world with a lower spread than alternatives between bid and offer prices). Whether or how quickly the euro could acquire this role in trade and currency transactions between third countries cannot be forecast with any degree of confidence. But certainly the potential is there for the euro to become a dominant currency in trade relations between the EMU zone and the rest of the world, including the displacement, at least in part, of the dollar in Europe–US trade.

Trade

The fact that Europe has a current account surplus with the rest of the world (over US $100 billion in 1997 whereas the United States had a deficit of around $200 billion) means that the rest of the world will *need* euros anyway. But it also means that the EMU zone as a whole can act with more independence in determining its monetary and economic policies than if it faced the constraint of an external deficit while simultaneously trying to create credibility for its currency. Moreover, both the EU as a whole and the EMU zone are more self-sufficient than any of the individual member states, that is, the EU/EMU economy is less open than that of any of its national parts.

The degree of openness of an economy may be measured by comparing its exports or imports with its GDP. In the EMU zone at the end of the 1990s, this measure of openness varies from approximately 18 per cent in the case of Spain to around 50 per cent for Belgium, whereas for the entire EMU area it is 11 per cent and for the EU it is 9 per cent. In general, the more open an economy the greater the cause for concern about the impact of domestic monetary policy on external competitiveness, and hence on the overall level of activity. If a national central bank raises interest rates for domestic counterinflation purposes the exchange rate will tend to appreciate, thereby worsening the competitiveness of the economy, resulting in a reduction in the levels of activity and employment and a worsening of its external trade position. The more open the economy the greater the adverse effects are likely to be. Given that the EMU zone will be less open than any of the individual member states, it follows that the operation of monetary policy by the ECB will be less inhibited by any adverse impact on the external position than would be the case for any single member country. Likewise it will be less concerned than any individual member state about the impact on internal inflation induced by higher import prices in the event of any depreciation of the external value of the euro. These considerations point to the likelihood that the ECB may well adopt a policy of 'benign neglect' towards the impact of its monetary stance on the euro exchange rate.

However it should be recognised that movements in the external value of the euro will have a differential impact across industries and across countries. Some industries will be more exposed to changes in the euro–dollar exchange rate than others, and some countries (especially the Republic of Ireland and the UK) are more dependent on exports to the United States than others, though membership of EMU may itself induce greater concentration on intrazonal trade.

Reserves

Another dimension of the global role of the euro is its possible use as a reserve currency by national central banks around the world. Prior to the start of stage three the US dollar constituted around 60 per cent of global reserve holdings (totalling around $1.5 trillion) with EU currencies representing about 20 per cent and the yen a little under 10 per cent. In purely mechanistic terms it can be argued that the relative shares of the euro and the dollar should be equivalent, given their similar shares of global GDP and trade. But reserve holdings are not driven by simple arithmetic of this kind. They also depend upon confidence in the stability and liquidity of the currency. By removing currency volatility among member states, the creation of EMU reduced the need for currency reserves in the EU itself. These reserves include not only European currencies (principally the Deutschmark) but also the US dollar. Yet a reduction in dollar holdings may not happen immediately as the European authorities will not wish to destabilise markets or damage the competitiveness of the euro-zone against the US economy by unloading dollars precipitously. More interesting is the extent to which reserve holdings in third countries will be switched, at any total level of reserves, into euro. EU members not in the monetary union will need to hold the euro, as will and Eastern and Central European countries. At the start of stage three in 1999, the United States held an estimated $20 billion in Deutschmarks. Although these will be automatically switched to euro, it should be noted that such a move will represent neither an intentional decision to hold the new currency nor any increase in the share of European currencies in global reserve holdings at the expense of the US dollar.

Beyond a substitution of the euro for pre-existing European currencies, it is plausible that the euro could reduce the share of the dollar in official reserve holdings if developing countries, Japan, the United States itself and the 'pre-ins' were to increase their holdings of the euro in the expectation that it will indeed be a major global currency in trade, exchange markets, private portfolios and capital markets. In arithmetical terms, equal shares in official holdings for the euro and the dollar (assuming a rough split of 40:40:20 between dollar-euro-other currencies) implies a switch from the dollar to the euro approaching $800 billion, thereby putting downward pressure on the external value of the dollar relative to the euro, and making the external US deficit more difficult to finance without higher interest rates. This is a possible long-term development but the scale and pace of any switch from dollars to the euro remains conjectural Moreover any downward pressure on the dollar would imply that the demand for euros exceeded supply, whereas it is quite conceivable that they may balance at a broadly stable price (exchange rate).

There is a great deal of inertia in the pattern of reserve holdings and, indeed, private portfolios. As seen, the global role of sterling continued for several decades after the displacement of the British Empire by the United States as a global economic power. Conversely it took some years for the French franc to be recognised as a stable currency in global foreign exchange markets, even though France successfully implemented the domestic policies needed to maintain stability in the link of the franc to the Deutschmark. With high and persistent unemployment in Europe and the possibility of political attacks on the ECB, such as that launched by the German Finance Ministry in early 1999, the ECB will have to prove its ability to emulate the Bundesbank (or the performance of the US Federal Reserve during the Volcker/Greenspan period), and demonstrate its independence during both economic downturns and upturns.

Private portfolios

The advent of the euro, together with a single market for banking and securities, creates the potential for the emergence of a European financial market comparable in scale to that of the United States, able to attract investors and issuers from the rest of the world, as well as within the EMU zone itself. But at present the European capital market is fragmented by currency, regulatory and fiscal differences. These factors reduce the liquidity of the market and inhibit pan-European trading, issuance and investment. EMU by itself will not remove the regulatory and fiscal impediments but it will intensify the pressure from market operators for their removal. Issuers have the potential to tap into the savings from the EMU zone as a whole once their issues are denominated in the single currency, while competition between banks for the mandates to manage those issues will drive down issuance costs. Once the enlargement of the euro-denominated capital market within Europe takes off, and provided the ECB wins international credibility for itself and the single currency, the euro will be a currency in which governments and companies around the world will be interested in denominating their own issues. Under the same conditions, investors will wish to take up euro-denominated investments. The process of interest-rate convergence, especially the associated reduction in yields, means that investors – whether investment funds or private individuals – are looking for superior yields. It is likely that corporations, offering a variety of risk to yield combinations, will respond by launching more bond issues in Europe. Life and pension funds will wish to match their euro-denominated liabilities with euro-denominated assets; indeed in most member states they are required by law to do so. The processes of issuance and investment will therefore help to drive the emergence of a euro-denominated capital market with the potential to rival that of the dollar over time. Some commentators anticipate that this will take several years. Others believe that the development could be rapid, particularly because the new and outstanding debt of participating states have been euro-denominated since January 1999, and major institutional issuers such as the European Investment Bank are already issuing in euro, as are a number of large corporations.

Private holdings of international financial assets at the end of the 1990s (bank deposits, bonds and corporate stock) have been estimated at somewhere in the region of $3 trillion, with about half held in dollar-denominated assets, about a third in EU currency denominations, about 10 per cent in yen and the remaining 20 per cent in other currencies. Again, an arithmetical rebalancing of private portfolios away from the US dollar towards the euro clearly implies a shift equivalent to several hundred billion dollars, but its scale and pace is conjectural. However the potential scale of euro-denominated assets within Europe alone should not be underestimated. The sovereign bond issue of the 11 EMU countries denominated in euro currently amounts to more than the US dollar sovereign bonds market, or 35 per cent of outstanding global sovereign bonds as opposed to 31 per cent in the US case. This represents, from the very start of EMU, a huge, liquid market which will grow in size as other European countries participate in EMU.

The size of the US corporate bond market is about double that of the EU, where companies have traditionally relied more on bank borrowing than issuing their own debt directly to the capital market. This partly reflects the reluctance of many companies to incur the cost of bond issuance, but it is also a reflection of the illiquidity of the European corporate bond market in comparison with that of the United States, where the scale and growth of the corporate bond market has been a self-reinforcing process. The advent of the euro creates the potential for a large pan-European bond market denominated in the single currency. Competition between banks for mandates to issue corporate bonds will drive down issuance costs, while the decline and convergence of government bond yields in line with the Maastricht criteria can be expected to give investors an appetite for the superior yields offered by corporate bonds. Traditionally, corporate bond issues in Europe have been made by the largest firms with the highest possible credit ratings, unlike in the United States, where low or even non-rated firms have been able to tap the savings markets by offering superior yields. A comparable bond market is expected to develop within the monetary union.

A further, marked contrast with the United States and the UK is the relatively low reliance upon equity issues by European corporations as a source of funding. European stock market capitalisation across the EU as a whole is only around $3 billion, as opposed to over $5 billion in the United States. There is the potential within EMU itself for the creation of a stock market comparable in size to that of the United States, given the broad similarities in the scale of the European and US economies. This may be reinforced by a number of factors: the process of privatisation; the opportunity to tap the investment potential of the entire monetary union; lower costs of issuing equity in just one currency; and the likely consolidation of stock exchanges into fewer, larger (or at any rate linked) centres.

As the process unfolds it is likely that investors in the rest of the world will be attracted to investing in euro-denominated financial assets (whether issued by European or non-European entities), while governments and corporations in the rest of the world will want to reinforce supply by tapping into this large liquid market.

To the extent that this happens, it will intensify the holding of euro currency reserves in the rest of the world. As before, the scale and pace of change is uncertain and dependent on the credibility of the euro, and it is essential that the creation of a deep and liquid pan-EMU equity market is not impeded by regulatory or fiscal restrictions on the development and distribution of financial assets (Chapter 7).

The euro and global currency stability

EMU will create a zone of currency stability among the participants and, to a degree, between them and the members of ERM2. The latter is an arrangement by which EU countries not in EMU may use fluctuation bands of plus or minus 15 per cent to link their currencies to the euro, though they can choose narrower bands, as Denmark has done in negotiating fluctuation limits of just plus or minus 2.25 per cent. The central parity is determined by mutual agreement. The linked currency may be able to call on support from the ESCB if it comes under attack, provided that this does not threaten stability within the EMU zone itself. In short, unlimited intervention is not on offer.

Prior to joining EMU, countries have to satisfy the Maastricht requirement of stability 'within the normal ERM bands' between their currency and the euro, although – as the UK authorities have stressed – it is not certain whether this means formal membership of the ERM, as distinct from *de facto* stability. In its convergence report of 25 March 1998 the European Commission noted that although the Italian lira had only rejoined the ERM in November 1996 it had not been subject to severe tensions, nor had it been consciously devalued between March and November 1996. Accordingly the Commission concluded that Italy fulfilled the convergence criteria. A similar conclusion was reached for Finland, which had only entered the ERM in October 1996. Turning to Sweden, the Commission concluded that it did not meet the exchange rate criterion as its currency had fluctuated against the rest, in part because of the absence of any formal commitment. As for the UK, no assessment was made, since none was called for. In short the importance of ERM membership for entry into EMU remains opaque (presumably deliberately) and one assumes that if and when Sweden and the UK want to join EMU the question of formal ERM membership and its duration will be a matter for negotiation. But what is beyond doubt is that a period of *de facto* exchange rate stability will be required. Amongst other things that would require the British and Swedish authorities to match movements in the ECB interest rates, with significant implications for the real behaviour of their economies at the time, depending on how their economic cycles match that of the EMU zone.

Turning to the relationship between the euro and the currencies of the rest of the world, the treaty and the transitional arrangements adopted by the Madrid Council of December 1995 required that the euro's opening exchange rate should equal the ECU's closing rate on 31 December 1998. After that it would be a market rate shaped by three separate considerations: the fundamental equilibrium rate between the euro and other currencies, the long-term trend in that rate, and its volatility. The equilibrium rate of exchange between the currencies of two countries depends on the assumption of free capital movements and, in the absence of restraints on trade, on their relative prices and hence their relative cost structures. Europe is on the verge of fundamental changes to product and labour markets, the structure of industry, and the role of the state (including the ownership of industry and participation in the provision of a wide range of services), so the structure of Europe's costs and their relationship to cost structures in the rest of the world is impossible to forecast. The major unknown is whether labour markets will become more flexible now that this is the only assured means of delivering economic adjustments in a monetary union governed by fiscal constraints, or whether the EMU countries will hold fast to established economic and social protections.

It follows that any future trend in the euro–dollar rate will be determined by the pace, scale and political sustainability of economic adjustment within Europe, together with trends in capital markets. As noted, the euro creates the potential for the development of a capital market to rival that of the United States, drawing investors and issuers from within and beyond the EMU zone. To the extent that there is a switch from dollar to euro assets, there may be an upward trend in the euro–dollar exchange rate, although this will be moderated if increased demand for euro assets is matched by an increased supply. So, in sum, there are three related uncertainties: the medium-term trend in the euro–dollar rate, the pace of economic restructuring, and the balance of supply and demand in financial markets.

Irrespective of equilibrium values and long-term trends, the volatility of euro exchange rates will be an important concern. As seen, the high degree of self-reliance of the EMU economy points to the likelihood of a policy of 'benign neglect' towards the external currency similar to that of the US authorities over many years. If both the European and the US monetary authorities were simultaneously to follow such an approach, and if the two economies displayed asymmetric cyclical behaviour, especially in their interest rates, the scene would be set for potentially marked volatility in the euro–dollar exchange rate. This might be a matter of indifference to the euro-zone and to the US, but not to others, such as the UK, which can expect to be heavily exposed to the consequences of currency fluctuation in both continental Europe and the United States. Indeed, the UK economic cycle has historically been more closely correlated with that of the United States than that of Germany. It would appear to follow that euro–dollar volatility could result in a buffeting of sterling due to factors largely out of UK control. In the long run any significant rise in the global role of the euro, together with any euro–dollar volatility, would have implications for other countries, such as primary producers who import from Europe but export commodities denominated in the dollar. Such countries may be tempted to consider redenominating their exports into euros. A decision by Gulf oil producers, seemingly expected by some in the European Commission, to price petroleum in the euro instead of the dollar would give a major fillip to the euro, and a move with major implications for the US economy, given that the United States is a net petroleum importer.

To date, institutions such as the IMF and G-7 have not focused on preserving global currency stability, or have been ineffective in achieving that goal. It has sometimes been suggested that although a fixed rate euro–dollar–yen relationship is unnecessary and unrealistic, some kind of target zone or band width for global currency fluctuations might be appropriate (more or less along the lines of the

ERM parity grid, with its fluctuation margins for European currencies). The proposal has merit but the indeterminacy of the equilibrium rate between the euro and the dollar (let alone one between
the euro and the yen or the yen and the dollar) would make its
implementation difficult, even if the authorities concerned favoured
it, which neither the ECB nor the US Federal Reserve do at the time
of writing, in part because of the constraint this would put on the
ability to determine interest rates according to domestic inflationary
circumstances, and the possibility that they could be caught between
internal and external obligations requiring them to move their rates
in opposite directions.

Consequently the scene appears to be set for periodic euro–dollar
volatility, with no rigorous mechanism to dampen that instability.
This may have adverse implications for other currencies and
economies. On the other hand this risk need not materialise if there
are stable and similar cyclical and monetary developments within
both the United States and the EMU zone. In practice the monetary
authorities concerned have frequent informal contact in addition to
institutionalised meetings via the IMF and the G-7. The threat of
serious volatility would almost certainly be raised by one or more of
the interested parties. If, on the other hand, the interest rate needed
for exchange rate stability did not coincide with the domestic
objectives of at least one of the parties, it might be difficult to
resolve matters without a crisis.

Finally, it is worth noting the scope for tension and competition
between the members of Ecofin with regard to the future conduct of
external monetary policy. Operational management of the euro
exchange rate is for the ECB. It was agreed at the Mondorf-les-
Bains Ecofin that ministers should refrain from giving the ECB
'guidance' on the euro exchange rate in the initial stages of stage
three and only subsequently if there is a fundamental currency
misalignment, and then only on a temporary basis. How this will
work in practice remains to be seen.

Conclusions

The size of the EMU zone economy and its share in global trade,
together with the potential for the emergence of a large, common,
liquid, euro-denominated capital market, raise the possibility that

the euro could rival the US dollar in terms of official foreign exchange reserve holdings, as the currency for trade denomination, and as a capital market attractive to both investors and issuers throughout the world. Such a development will require the ECB to establish the euro's credibility as a currency with a stable internal value, that is, low and stable inflation. But early efforts by the ECB to establish credibility will not be viewed in isolation by financial markets: high and persistent unemployment in Europe may be perceived by international investors as casting a long-term shadow over the ability of the ECB to maintain a vigorous monetary stance. Likewise evidence that national governments are not undertaking sustained reductions in their structural fiscal deficits or that they disagree with ECB policy will raise doubts about the long-term ability of the ECB to counteract fiscal looseness by monetary tightness if high unemployment persists. On the other hand the combination of a politically independent ECB, reductions in unemployment and fiscal discipline will contribute to the rise of the euro as a major global currency.

Any switch in official and private holdings around the world from dollar-denominated financial assets to the euro could induce an upward movement in the value of the euro against the dollar, except insofar as this is matched by a parallel increase in the supply of euro-denominated assets. Moreover the level and trend in the euro–dollar exchange rate will be influenced by the presence or absence of fundamental reform of the structure of the European economy, especially its labour market.

To the extent that the ECB follows a policy of 'benign neglect' towards the external value of the euro and the EMU zone is economically self-reliant, the scene may be set for increasing euro–dollar volatility, with potentially adverse effects on other European currencies. However the treaty (Article 109) states that the Council may only conclude formal exchange rate agreements if the decision is unanimous, if the Council has consulted the ECB and if such agreements do not threaten internal price stability. At present such arrangements are not planned, but pressure could grow for external agreements in the event of currency volatility.

Chapter 11

EMU and the Single Market for Financial Services

A single currency, when combined with a single market in financial services, creates the regulatory environment for the emergence of pan-European asset management companies and securities markets, together with a more efficient and competitive banking industry. This reduces the cost of capital, improves the opportunities for portfolio management and increases the range of financial assets, while reducing prices to the personal and business customers of banks. There is widespread belief that EMU will encourage the growth of liquid and deep securities markets across Europe and that it will induce the restructuring of the banking sector on more efficient lines. However national restrictions on cross-border competition and the diversity of national regulations mean that the single currency will not automatically lead to these developments. Various impediments to competition in financial markets and the banking sector may inhibit exploitation of the full potential of the single currency.

The impediments

Impediments to the creation of a single financial services market make it difficult and sometimes impossible to:

- Develop standard, pan-European products.
- Market or sell certain products from a branch in some countries but not others.
- Provide some services on a cross-border basis into other member states.
- Process data or products on a pan-EU basis.
- Manage institutional fund assets on a pan-EU basis.

This situation results from:

- Failure to implement or fully implement key directives, especially the Investment Services Directive (ISD).
- Ambiguities in certain directives which allow host states to introduce regulations which restrict innovation or foreign competition on the basis of general good or monetary policy clauses (Second Banking Co-ordination Directive, 2BCD, ISD).
- Gaps in the scope of single market legislation, including passporting for fund management (for example life and pension funds).
- In some cases national measures appear to breach the spirit if not the letter of single market legislation. With the exception of fund management the problem is not one of insufficient legislation but of its effective implementation and enforcement.
- Sometimes impediments to competition result from structural factors within certain countries, such as state aid of various kinds to national banks and extensive state ownership of retail banking. These questions require the attention of the competition authorities.
- Numerous fiscal impediments that reflect differences in national tax structures and tax rates. These may only be soluble in the very long term and any resolution in the form of harmonising measures which damage the competitiveness of the European financial sector or drive business offshore without any revenue gain should be avoided.

Principles underlying the single market for financial services

EU directives have established the concept of 'single licence': financial institutions licensed in one member state should be able to deal with customers in any other member state from their home country base without having a local presence, or they should be able to establish branches in the other member state without local authorisation. They are subject to the prudential supervision of the home authorities. In principle this means that the services an institution is authorised to provide in its home country could be provided throughout the EU – provided they are listed in the annexes to the relevant directives. The basis for the single licence or passport is mutual recognition by the national regulatory authorities, as developed in a series of directives on licensing, capital adequacy, solvency, accounting and other common prudential rules, together with the passporting clauses in certain directives. Some of these issues are considered in the European Commission's Framework for Financial Services (1998).

Investment services directive

Provisions

The ISD has yet to be implemented fully in several member states, so uncertainty about its impact remains. It provides considerable power to host member state authorities with regard to the regulation and supervision of the branches of and cross-border services offered by firms licensed in a different member state.

First, 15 different sets of national rules on primary dealership have been left in place.

Second, Article 1.13 describes the concept of a 'regulated market' but it leaves considerable discretion to member states on how the concept is interpreted. This is relevant to cross-border access to markets.

Third, Article 2.4 excludes institutions based in another member state from right of access to services offered by the local central bank that are associated with 'monetary, exchange rate, public debt and reserve management policies'. This is a wide range of exclusions, used by virtually all member states to restrict sovereign bond dealing to nationals. But the improper use of such restrictions may be open to challenge in the European Court of Justice (ECJ). Nor is it clear how they will be affected by the advent of euro-denominated government debt.

Fourth, as with the Second Co-ordination Banking Directive (2BCD), the host member state has the power to draw up 'general good' restrictions on the conditions under which the branch of an investment firm based in another member state may conduct its business (Article17.4) (again, this is open to challenge in the ECJ). The Commission has not yet clarified what will be permissible here, although it has published communications clarifying the general good clauses in the banking and insurance directives.

Fifth, Article 14.3/4 provides host country authorities with the power to insist that trade in instruments listed on regulated markets should be carried out 'on market' (the 'concentration' concept) when the trade involves an investor who is a resident in that member state. The effect could be to ban off-exchange or over-the-counter transactions.

Sixth, Article 15.5 enables member states to refuse authorisation for access to 'new markets'. This may not only restrict the opportunities to exploit technological innovations, it may also be used to prevent remote access for existing markets that do not yet have trading screens in member states which want to keep them out – especially where the remote market trades in securities listed in that member state.

Finally, under the licence, an investment firm may be subject to dual reporting requirements – imposed by both the home member state authorities and the host country, the latter having discretion to determine the frequency and content of the required 'particulars' (Articles 19.1, 19.2).

The effect of these ambiguities and loopholes in the ISD is to restrict the opportunities for cross-border competition in investment services. As in the case of 2BCD, the assurance that the ECJ may be relied upon to stamp out possible abuses ignores the punishment which might face those who complain and the great delays involved in litigation.

Non-implementation

At the time of writing, several states have not fully implemented the ISD and their national laws are impeding the provision of cross-border services to their residents. Even where the ISD has been implemented, problems arise: several countries impose restrictions on the solicitation of customers and counterparties, even though they may be financial institutions or professional investors themselves; the business conduct rules applied by several countries fail to distinguish between professionals and others, who may need greater protection; although the ISD places responsibility for prudential supervision on the home country, several member states impose burdensome prudential reporting on branches of investment firms from other EU countries; and a number of member states restrict the ability of investment firms in other countries to provide lead management and other investment services on a cross-border basis.

Anti-competitive behaviour

In several of the instances noted above, the effect of national practices is to impede competition, whether between domestic and foreign establishments within a country or competition from cross-border services. It is far from apparent that competition authorities – whether at EU level or within the member states concerned – have been involved in scrutinising the relevant regulations prior to their implementation.

Collective investment funds

In an ideal situation a European collective investment fund (CIF) would be subject to appropriate regulatory approval in the state in which it is domiciled, and it would then be free to market the fund to retail and institutional investors throughout the EU. Where clients hold shares or units in a fund domiciled in another member state, they should receive the same tax treatment as if the fund were domiciled in their own country. But current practice is far from this single market ideal:

- National regulations hinder or prohibit the marketing of such funds outside their home state.
- There are restrictions on the allocation of assets by funds (especially insurance and pension funds) with regard to (1) currency matching, for example 80 per cent of assets often have to be in the domestic currency (within EMU this constraint will apply to the euro zone as a whole, although some member states appear tempted to offset the relaxation of the national currency constraint by offering tax privileges for investment in purely domestic assets); and (2) the mix of assets (bonds/equity/property/money/other funds).
- There are various other regulatory barriers to the development of cross-border products and services in particular countries.

The potential for the creation of deep and liquid securities markets across the EU will not be fully exploited if the restrictions and impediments remain in place, quite apart from the persistence of suboptimal returns to investors which the fragmentation of asset management across Europe implies.

Securitisation

The advent of the single currency raises the possibility of asset-backed securities across the EU. But in some instances, notably mortgage-backed securities, differences in national rules on the assignment of title and the rights of lenders in the case of default, as well as differences in prepayment practices and charges, mean that this kind of market will not develop automatically now that the single currency has been introduced. However other forms of debt securitisation seem likely to develop on a cross-border basis.

Listing

Differences in listings requirements for equities and in the cost of regulatory compliance inhibit pan-EU issuance of equities and, especially, the willingness and ability of small and medium enterprises (SMEs) to enter the market. Another source of diversity in national practice with regard to listings concerns commercial paper (CP), where, again, differences in the information required by regulators and compliance costs inhibit the development of a market that otherwise has the potential to rival the United States following the advent of the EMU. In some countries the CP market is inhibited because issuance is prohibited for firms involved in banking activities, and this can include corporations because of intercompany loans, even though they are not licensed credit institutions.

The Second Banking Directive

General good clauses

Under the Second Banking Directive (2BCD), any intention to provide new services (listed in the Annex for the first time) or to establish new branches in other member states must first be notified to the competent authority of the home state. Prudential supervision is a matter for the home authorities, but the host state 'shall retain complete responsibility for the measures resulting from the implementation of their monetary policy. Such measures may not provide for discrimination or restricted treatment based on the fact that a credit institution is authorised in another member state' (Article 19.2). The host country is responsible for stipulating 'the conditions under which, in the interest of the general good, those activities may be carried out in the host member state' (Article. 19.4). The possibility of introducing regulations on grounds of the general good or monetary policy provides host countries with considerable discretion.

Non-discrimination

Member states do not have *carte blanche* to impose restrictions on monetary policy/general good grounds; in particular they must not discriminate between domestic institutions and those based in another member state. But what does this mean? If a foreign institution wished to introduce a new product or technological delivery system, and domestic institutions without the will or ability to provide the product were to lobby for a ban, would that be truly non-discriminatory in a legal sense? The only real loser from a ban that apparently applies to all would be the foreign institution with the initiative and ability to innovate.

Structural impediments to competition

In a number of countries economic structures and cultural traditions mean that it is difficult to develop standard, pan-EU products, or for others to penetrate the domestic market. The following are the most important examples:

- Large-scale public sector involvement in financial markets, including privileged issuance of personal savings/investment products.
- State guarantees for regional/municipal banks, which therefore need less regulatory capital and are able to raise capital more cheaply.

- Restrictions on the access of foreign banks to cash-dispenser card networks maintained by local cartels.
- Major cross-shareholdings between banks and large corporations.

Such impediments to competition and the evolution of a genuine single market for financial services are not amenable to resolution by legislation alone. However they do raise questions of competition policy under the treaty (especially Articles 59 and 92), but progress in addressing them has been glacially slow.

Consumer protection

Differences in consumer protection laws and practices mean that the marketing of standard pan-EU products is difficult if not impossible. Research into the differences in marketing/sales regulations across Europe is beyond the scope of this book but contributions from a number of the institutions have demonstrated marked differences between national practice with regard to advertising, off-the-page selling, the ability to quote prices in advertising and marketing material, and the extent to which customers or target customers have to provide positive affirmation that they wish to hear about new products and services, even if they are free.

In the case of retail financial services, national regulations are often justified by considerations of consumer protection, especially as consumers cannot be expected to understand the conduct of business rules in the foreign countries from which the financial services are provided. There is, however, a risk of this legitimate concern being abused to protect local service providers from foreign competition. There are at least three possible solutions to the dilemma:

- All retail service provision should be subject to host country control, provided that the relevant regulations have been scrutinised and approved by the Commission's competition authority.
- Home country regulations should apply but national consumer protection agencies (for example ombudsmen, although these do not exist in every member state at present) should act as agents for domestic purchasers of financial services provided by institutions based in other member states where the consumer

has a grievance. In other words the agency in country A should address the complaints of consumers in country A to the agency in country B where the service provider is located.

- Complete harmonisation of all consumer protection rules throughout the EU. This would be an excessively bureaucratic process – probably impossible to establish and involving the risk of inhibiting financial innovation and competition.

The first solution is the least bureaucratic and cheaper than the others. At present none of these solutions are available, and all too often the effect of national 'consumer protection' regulations is to protect inefficient local service providers and deny consumers wider choice and the opportunity to obtain cheaper services.

Conclusions

A single market in financial services together with a single currency provide the opportunity for the creation of a pan-European securities markets and a more efficient and competitive banking industry. This would reduce the cost of capital, increase the range of choice, reduce prices to personal and business customers, and improve opportunities for optimal asset management.

In practice numerous regulatory and other impediments to the creation of a genuine single financial services market make it difficult and sometimes impossible to develop standard, pan-European products, to market or sell certain products from a branch within some countries but not others, to provide some services in other member states, to process data or products on a pan-EU basis and to manage institutional fund assets on a pan-EU basis. This situation is the result of ambiguities in EU directives, gaps in their scope, differing interpretations and failure to implement and enforce key directives, especially the Investment Services Directive (ISD).

The 'general good' provisions in the ISD have been the basis of restrictions on cross-border solicitation of business, interprofessional dealings, access to new markets and dealing by local residents in locally listed securities in regulated markets, as well as dual reporting requirements. However, different national wholesale financial market regulators and supervisors have different traditions, and some are more open to financial innovation than others.

Restrictions on the marketing and provision of retail financial products and services in some member states are justified on consumer protection grounds, though they may deny consumers access to a wider range of choice and cheaper services. At the same time there are genuine consumer concerns, especially those that relate to the possibility of gaining redress against foreign suppliers without a local presence. Proper cross-border mechanisms are needed here.

Overall the impediments to competition and the creation of a genuine single market for financial services detailed above demonstrate the need for better and faster implementation and enforcement of the existing single market legislation. The problems are not attributable to insufficient legislation, except in the case of fund management. The issues were recognised in the Commission document 'A Framework for Financial Services', published in October 1998, which was attacked by some as being too 'Anglo-Saxon' in approach. A Financial Services Policy Group, composed of ministers and senior officials and chaired by Commissioner Monti, was established to address the matter and to report to the Council in June 1999. Considerable consensus was reached on wholesale markets and the basis for further liberalisation of pension fund management was established, although effective follow-up actions remain to be seen, and significant differences remain on the issue of personal (retail) financial services.

Chapter 12

Executive Power under Monetary Union 1: the European Central Bank

Monetary union and the EU political system

Now that the origins of monetary union have been explained and its economics analysed, it is possible to turn to its implications for the European Union's overall political system. The management of any currency requires its own political subsystem: its own distinctive cluster of interinstitutional relationships within a more general system of government. This must include at least the following: a body to issue and control official money; an executive power capable of coordinating public budgets in line with monetary policy; and some mechanism of public representation and accountability.

The character of monetary union is likely to be profoundly affected by its location within the highly distinctive institutional structures of the EU, where it will create one new EU institution (the European Central Bank) and draw on several existing ones (the Commission, the Council of Ministers, the European Council and the European Parliament). Conversely the wider EU is likely to be substantially changed by the addition of monetary union, so creating a complex feedback loop, the full effects of which may take many years to resolve. Not only is the power to issue money a highly visible stage in the acquisition of political authority (Dyson, 1994), it may also catalyse the development of flanking policies, alter the balance between existing institutional players, encourage the direction of new demands and expectations into the political system and fashion new relationships between institutions and their publics.

In concluding the book with three chapters on the interaction between monetary union and the EU institutions, there is no intention of pursuing a narrowly procedural analysis. For while institutions matter to the point at which just small changes in structural design can produce major differences in policy outcomes (Arrow, 1963; Riker, 1982; Shepsle, 1989) they also have a chameleon-like tendency to take on the colours of their surrounding political and social terrain: to reflect *in*formal rules, power distributions, the preferences of principal actors, the historical experiences and standard operating assumptions of bureaucracies, patterns of social consensus and division, and philosophical views as to what makes political and administrative power legitimate (March and Olsen, 1984). It follows that it is important to be cautious about the 'transferability of models'. A particular 'monetary constitution' is likely to operate in different ways when transposed from a single country to a political system that is transnational, fundamentally contested, and an umbrella for a still wide variety of state–market relationships.

A useful starting point is the observation that political systems can either integrate or separate powers over the different dimensions of economic governance. In integrated systems the political authority is not only responsible for taxing, spending and borrowing, it also looks after monetary policy by issuing instructions to the central bank. In those based on a separation of powers, central banks set monetary policy independently of governments. Apart from West Germany, and since the 1970s the Netherlands, a firm attachment to the integrated model of economic governance was a key aspect of the postwar settlement in most West European societies. The political determination of monetary policy was considered indispensable to effective economic management, democratic accountability and social compromise.

As seen in earlier chapters, economic thinking changed during the 1970s and 1980s. A 'new orthodoxy' suggested that governments could only make choices between inflation, growth and employment for short periods. This analysis was as much a challenge to the political systems of Western Europe as to their economic ones: if governments could achieve short-run illusions without long-run improvements they could be opportunistic in their management of the economy, fooling voters with artificially benign economic conditions at election time, after which the public would, in reality, be worse off than if policy had never been changed at all (Nordhaus, 1975). Price and wage fixers would soon identify those political systems that allowed governments to act in such a way, and anticipate a drift towards inflation in their own behaviour. The implication was plain: the achievement of price stability was a challenge of institutional, even constitutional design. Even governments that were firmly wedded to anti-inflationary rigour could only achieve it within political systems capable of convincing the publics and markets that decision makers had absolutely no incentive to create inflation. All of this made it more attractive to adopt systems based on the separation of economic powers. Even before monetary union, national governments were moving towards a sharper separation between economic and monetary policy in the domestic arena by granting more operational independence to their national central banks (Goodman, 1992). As well as creating a single currency, monetary union takes the separation of powers between monetary and fiscal authorities to new lengths, and arguably puts a more secure lock on central bank independence by embedding it in a supranational framework.

All of this suggests an agenda for the next three chapters. Within the new separation of powers the ECB will have responsibility for monetary policy. The Council and Commission will undertake any fiscal coordination that will be conducted at the EU level. The Council and European Parliament will play various roles of representation and accountability. The next two chapters will accordingly focus on executive power under monetary union, showing how the ECB and the Commission–Council tandem exemplify two contrasting ways in which executive authority may be institutionalised in any supranational political system. The subsequent chapter will examine the means by which these executive bodies can be held politically responsible. As several of these institutional arrangements were introduced in foregoing chapters, the focus will be less on their mechanics than on how they fit together, on their implications for the wider EU political system, and, conversely, on what their construction as a subsystem of the idiosyncratic EU institutional order means for monetary union.

Ways of comparing central banks

Chapter 8 introduced the basic structures of the ECB and discussed its approach to monetary policy. This chapter considers the implications of adding the ECB to the EU political system.

FIGURE 12.1   Composition and decision rules of the European Central Bank

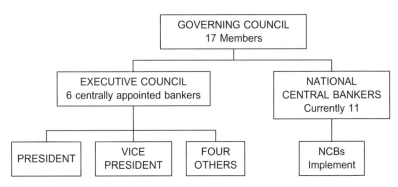

Both the executive council and the governing council take decisions by simple majority, with the president of the ECB exercising a casting vote in the event of a tie. On the governing council, each national central bank governor has one vote regardless of country size.

To avoid repetition from the earlier chapter, the composition and decision rules of the ECB are set out in Figure 12.1. There are four characteristics of central banks that both distinguish them from one another and have important implications for the wider political systems in which they are situated: the extent of their independence from the political authority; the 'terms of their agency' – the tasks and powers delegated to them; their federal or unitary character; and the nature and degree of their accountability. This chapter will deal with the first three of these themes. The last will be covered in Chapter 14.

A political system will be affected not only by the question of whether or not its central bank is independent, but also by the degree of that independence and the precise manner in which it is constructed. As the chair of the European Parliament's Economic and Monetary Affairs Committee (EMAC) has put it: 'The Statute of the ECB and the Maastricht Treaty take to new lengths the principle that a central bank should be independent. No other central bank – in any other political system – has been as independent (European Parliament, 1998b).

Before examining the contention that the independence of the ECB is likely to be more thorough-going and securely based than any previous central bank, including the Bundesbank, it is necessary to make an essential, if slightly pedantic observation. Independence should only be considered to be at threat if a central bank is purposefully *constrained* from pursuing the monetary policy of its choice by a political institution. It is not compromised by any attempt to influence the central bank, where this consists of the non-coercive communication of information on economic conditions or policy preferences. On the contrary, central banks may only be effective when they interact with a wide variety of private and public actors.

Box 12.1 summarises the provisions that give a legal basis to the ECB's independence. But it has to be emphasised that its independence cannot be reduced to a list of treaty provisions. The fact that independence is contained in the treaty at all is as significant as the specific clauses that seek to give it effect. In addition, it is important to the character of the ECB's independence that it is nested in a supranational political system with some federal features. The following paragraphs expand these points.

First, *central bank independence based on a treaty between members of a multinational political system is more secure than any based on ordinary law in a single national arena*. Independent central banks can only be established through the legal delegation of decision-making powers from a legitimate political authority. But this means that central bankers can always be threatened with the withdrawal or redefinition of their powers if they do not comply with the wishes of elected politicians. Hans Tietmeyer claims that the Bundesbank had to ride out five such threats between its foundation in 1957 and the end of the Adenauer period in 1963. Only then could it be confident of its independence (*Le Monde*, 9 May 1998). The EU political arena may, however, have one decisive advantage over national systems in its ability to entrench institutional powers beyond challenge or amendment by normal political processes. Whilst, for example, the Bundesbank's powers and independence are based on ordinary statute law, reversible by a simple majority of both houses of the German parliament, the ECB was established by an EU treaty. This is only amendable if all fifteen member governments can reach agreement and persuade their publics and parliaments to ratify changes. Politicians will therefore find it difficult to make credible threats to change the ECB's statute.

Second, *the ECB is subject to a sweeping prohibition on the purchase of any kind of public debt* (TEU, Article 104). This is

Box 12.1 Treaty provisions giving legal effect to the ECB's independence

- There is a sweeping prohibition on the 'seeking or taking' of 'instructions' and on attempts to 'influence the members of the decision-making bodies of the ECB or of the national central banks in the performance of their tasks' (TEU, Article 107).
- The appointment of members of the ECB executive board is for a single term of eight years. The non-renewable character of the appointment is thought to protect the executive from attempts by the governments to reward or sanction their careers (TEU, Article 109.2)
- The ECB objectives are defined to give priority to the control of inflation. In the absence of any indication to the contrary in the treaty, it is also to be assumed that the ECB will be judge and jury on whether price stability has in fact been attained. These provisions are designed to defend it against pressures to pursue other goals.
- All national central banks whose governors are represented on the ECB governing council must themselves be independent. Before a country can be admitted to stage three, the Commission is required to assess the adequacy of any arrangements to make its central bank independent (TEU, Article 109.j).
- Permanent members of the ECB cannot be dismissed by governments. They can only be removed by other members of the executive board or by the governing council. An application has to be made to the European Court of Justice and it has to show that the individual 'no longer fulfills the conditions required for the performance of his duties' or that he has been guilty of 'serious misconduct' (ECB statute, Article 11).
- To avoid 'placemen' being appointed to the executive board, the treaty specifies that only persons of 'recognised standing and

$\longrightarrow$

intended to insulate it from pressure to support loose fiscal policies or bail out indebted public authorities, either of which could force it to accept a different rate of monetary expansion from that it judges compatible with price stability. Like the last point, this safeguard is related to the multinational character of EU federalism: in federal systems, central banks can only offer a helping hand to struggling authorities if there is a high level of political support for the

$\longrightarrow$

professional experience in monetary or banking matters' can be selected. As the European Council has to reach a unanimous decision on each of the six appointments, it will be sufficient for just one government to seek to uphold the spirit of the treaty (TEU, Article 109).

- Because national central bank governors will also be members of the general council of the ECB, the treaty even constrains their appointment and dismissal. All governors will have to be appointed for a term of at least five years, and they will only be dismissable for the same reasons as the permanent members of the ECB: inability to perform their functions or serious misconduct. In the event of removal by a member government, any national central bank governor can appeal to the ECJ to determine whether the conditions for dismissal were justified under the terms of the treaty (ECB statute, Article 14).

- Arrangements for the salaries, pensions and working conditions of members of the ECB executive board will be set by an independent process, to avoid their being used as a source of political leverage. Recommendations will be made by a committee with equal representatives of the ECB governing council and the Council of Ministers. But the final decision will be taken by the governing council alone (ECB statute, Article 11).

- The ECB will effectively finance itself (from the returns on capital transferred from central banks).

- The treaty protects the confidentiality of the meetings of the governing council, and binds both national central bank governors and ECB staff to obligations of professional secrecy. These arrangements are designed to protect members of the governing council from attempts to monitor the way they vote (ESCB/ECB statute, Articles 10.4, 14.2).

interstate redistribution of public resources. Low levels of such acceptance may well have the paradoxical effect of making it easier to develop independent central banking in multistate federations than in single-state ones.

Third, *the ECB is less likely than the Bundesbank to have to support external currency commitments*. Obligation to support an external currency regime may also inhibit a central bank from pursuing the monetary policy of its choice. At first sight the ECB is in much the same position as the Bundesbank used to be: the political authority is responsible for the external management of the currency and the central bank for internal monetary creation. However the Council of Ministers can only 'conclude formal exchange rate agreements' with 'non-Community countries' if it succeeds in negotiating what may well prove to be a tougher obstacle course than any which would have had to be crossed by a national government before monetary union: the Council has to consult the ECB; it can only act if it has received a recommendation from the Commission; it has to secure a unanimous vote of all its members; and it has to show that the external currency regime is 'consistent with the objective of price stability' (which would presumably be difficult in the absence of ECB support) (TEU, Article 109). Once again, it is the EU's character as a multistate political system that ensures that the political authority has to follow complex and demanding decision rules if it is to impose a currency obligation on the central bank.

Differences of economic context also make it less likely that the ECB will have to sacrifice internal independence to honour external obligations. Because the Bundesbank operated in a multicurrency single market, most of whose governments had a preference for some element of exchange rate stability, it found itself having to manage a currency tied by tight fluctuation bands (plus or minus 2.25 per cent from 1979 to 1993) to countries covering more than half of Germany's trade. As the bank responsible for the anchor currency in the ERM zone, it was often exposed to political pressures from other governments as well as its own. It frequently had to weather accusations that it was putting the entire European construction – and thus the whole framework of Germany's external relations – at risk. Although it broadly held its own, economic studies suggest that it did not follow the exact policies of its choice during the more rigid phases of the ERM (Frattiani and Von Hagen,1993).

In contrast to all of this, monetary union will internalise most of the currencies of the EU single market. The only external currency regime that is likely is an ERM-2 with countries that are preparing either for full membership of the monetary union or for entry to the EU. But even this will employ the current loose bands of plus or minus 15 per cent.

Finally, *the ECB will enjoy both 'goal independence' and 'instrument independence'*. Some independent central banks choose their own targets. Others are given targets by the elected government and only have independence in selecting the means to achieve goals that are not of their own making. The first are said to have 'goal independence' while the second only have 'instrument independence' (Rogoff, 1985). The ECB clearly enjoys the first and more comprehensive form of independence. In Chapter 14 it will be seen how hard it would be for things to be otherwise in a federal system of central banking.

In one crucial respect, however, the independence and effectiveness of the ECB may be less well founded than that of the Bundesbank. It is important to be aware of this problem because it is one that could be averted by appropriate political strategies and institutional construction. It is often observed that the ultimate guarantee of Bundesbank independence is not legal in nature. Rather it is the depth and evenness across most social and political groups of the consensus that supports the right of the central bank to pursue price stability independently of the policy preferences of elected political authorities. So, for example, the Bundesbank often wins showdowns with the political authority because it has the majority of public opinion on its side (Berger and De Haan, 1997). It will be difficult to know whether a like social consensus in support of the ECB's role can be replicated at the EU level until such moment as the central bank is confronted by the need to make difficult and unpopular decisions.

The nature of the ECB mandate

In political systems where democratic authorisation and supervision are taken to be indispensable for the legitimate exercise of public power, only elected bodies can claim the right to wide-ranging discretion in policy making. In contrast unelected and independent bodies can only claim the right to make public policy when explicitly delegated to do so by a legitimate political process, and when their mandate corresponds to those rare circumstances in which a role for an independent technocracy is justifiable even in a democracy. The objectives set out in the founding statutes of independent central banks, accordingly, go a long way to define them as institutions, providing benchmarks beneath which they dare not fall and beyond which they dare not stray. To underperform would be to undercut the argument that there are some socially desirable objectives that can only be achieved by independent bodies. To attempt other objectives would be to provoke challenges to the initial policy delegation on the ground that it is open to abuse.

When asked to account for the success of the Bundesbank, its current president felt that the 'first reason' was that it had 'a clear mandate to defend the stability of money and that it was only obliged to support other objectives insofar as they put that stability at risk' (*Le Monde*, 9 May 1998). The preference of many central bankers for a simple mandate confined to the delivery of price stability has both an economic and a political logic. It reflects the economic theory of no long trade-offs between inflation and growth on which the case for independent central banking is founded. But it also captures the political sensitivity of the position in which independent and unelected central bankers find themselves. As will be seen, such arrangements are easier to justify when they are pareto improving (that is, they have the potential to make everyone better off) than when they are redistributive or non-neutral in allocating political values. So long as central bankers are only expected to deliver price stability in contexts of no long-run trade-offs with other values, the pareto condition holds. A simple statement of responsibility for price stability may also help to protect central bank independence, as well as the integrity of any separation of economic powers. It makes it clear that the bank is responsible for inflation and the political authority for long-run growth and employment. This in turn reduces the scope for political authorities to blame central banks for any economic underperformance that is properly their own responsibility. Without such safeguards the main consequence of independent central banking may be the evasion of accountability (Lohmann, 1997), rather than improvements in public welfare.

Table 12.1 shows how the objectives assigned by the TEU to the ECB compare with those of other central banks. None would seem to attain the central bankers' ideal of a single objective limited to price stability. The ECB does, however, have a hierarchy of goals in which the control of inflation is the most important, and other objectives only come into play if they do not endanger price stability.

Table 12.1 *Comparing the objectives of independent central banks*

Bank	Objectives
Deutsche Bundesbank	To regulate the amount of money in circulation and the credit supplied to the economy with the aim of safeguarding the value of the currency.
European Central Bank	The primary objective of the ESCB is to maintain price stability: 'without prejudice to price stability, the ESCB shall support the general economic policies of the Community'. The general economic policy of the EU is defined by cross reference to Articles 2 and 3 of the treaties. The latest version agreed at Amsterdam is as follows: 'The Community shall have as its task, by establishing a common market and an economic and monetary union..., to promote throughout the Community a harmonious, balanced and sustainable development of economic activities, a high level of employment and of social protection, equality between men and women, sustainable and non-inflationary growth, a high degree of competitiveness and convergence of economic performance, a high level of protection and improvement of the quality of the environment, the raising of the standard and quality of life, and economic and social cohesion and solidarity among Member States' (European Commission, 1997).
US Federal Reserve	To promote conditions of maximum employment, stable prices and moderate long-term interest rates.

Given that the ECB itself will be the judge of this matter, the TEU can be considered to leave it with considerable discretion to concentrate on the control of inflation. It is, however, worth noting that the goal of price stability could require the ECB to act against 'deflationary pressures' as well as inflationary ones (European Parliament, 1998b).

The federal character of the ECB

The ECB resembles the Federal Reserve of the United States and the German Bundesbank in its federal structure. As seen, national central banks continue to have two crucial roles under full monetary union: they are the implementing arm of the ECB and they hold a majority (presently 11:6) on its highest decision-making body, the governing council. Systems such as these raise two problems of institutional design. The first is ensuring that decision makers drawn from different parts of the currency area are capable of making policy judgements appropriate to the area as a whole; the second is guaranteeing the consistency and completeness of a decentralised pattern of implementation. Both these problems were raised in Chapter 8. However it is now possible to consider institutional solutions. It will be suggested that these will most plausibly involve the application of distinctive forms of federalism that are widely employed in other EU institutions, so providing an interesting cross-pollination between the practices of European integration and federal central banking.

As seen, national central bank governors have a clear legal responsibility to form policy judgements appropriate to the EU as a whole (ECB statute, Article 12). If they were to represent national interests it would be impossible to justify decision rules which left the votes of national central bank governors unweighted to country size, so that the governor of the Luxembourg central bank would have the same voting power as the president of the Bundesbank. It is likewise clear that the ECB would systematically underperform if board members were to base their decisions on national circumstances. Since policies would be no more than the chance aggregation of different judgements about what was best for particular member states, overall price stability would only be achieved occasionally and accidentally.

Drawing on the German experience, Hans Tietmeyer stresses that the successful operation of federal central banks can only be assured by making the 'intellectual leap' to collegiality:

> The decisions of the Bundesbank are collegial. Its members come from different political and professional backgrounds. But once nominated they are independent. It is like a little parliament, which takes its decision after deliberation. This gives it authority

in the eyes of the public and makes it less influenceable by the political powers ... the representative of Bavaria, Hamburg or Berlin is not considered as the advocate of a region of origin but as the guardian of the stability of the whole area. The same will have to happen at the European level. I must not look at Germany but at the whole of Euroland (*Le Monde*, 9 May 1998).

The difficulty, according to some commentators, is that the ECB is more likely than single-state central banks to be dominated by a fragmented pattern of preference formation, because it is anchored in a supranational federation rather than a national one. Members of the ECB board will apparently find it psychologically more difficult than their counterparts in Germany or the United States to decouple their decisions from the circumstances of their state of origin. To the extent that the convergence criteria are not rigorously applied, there could, as seen in Chapter 7, also be some conflicts of interests: between those from countries where price stability has already been achieved and those where the transitional costs of eliminating inflation have yet to be suffered; and between those with a preference for fiscal prudence and those whose borrowing or debt can best be handled by creating 'surprise inflation'.

One response to all of this is to accept that national preference formation may well occur, to calculate its probable policy implications under the ECB decision rules, and to ask whether those rules are sufficient to protect monetary union from some of the more harmful outcomes of domestically biased decision making. Under the present membership, nine votes will be needed for a majority on the governing council (if there are no absentees or abstentions). If all six members of the executive board were to vote the same way and stick to policy judgements appropriate to the overall euro economy, their views would probably dominate: to form a majority they would only need the support of three out of eleven national central bankers, and the chances are that there would always be that number of countries whose ' ideal national positions' were relatively close to what the executive board judged appropriate to the EU as a whole.

In addition to operating coherently on the general council, the executive board will also be able to counter particularist pressures by making forceful use of its powers of recommendation and policy leadership. If the executive board uses its responsibility for preparing the meetings of the governing council to present the latter with concrete recommendations for monetary policy (ESCB/ECB statute, Article 12), an EU-level perspective will always be the starting point for discussions. This will increase the pressure on national central bank governors to justify any departure from the executive's proposals by reference to alternative interpretations of general economic conditions, rather than those prevailing in their own countries only. Socialisation, and a decoupling of perspectives from national particularities, may also be promoted by arrangements that are currently being made for the general council to meet every second week, or more than twice as often as formally required by the treaty. National central bank governors will normally have to be present in person if they are to cast a vote. The only exceptions are provisions for teleconferencing and for governors to appoint an alternate if prevented from voting for a long period (ECB/ESCB statute, Article 10). In any case, things have been so arranged that national central bank governors may neither be found out nor have anything to lose if they base their decisions on what is appropriate for the euro zone as a whole. To insulate national central bank governors – and even permanent board members – from particular-ist pressures, the treaty provides for the general council to keep their proceedings confidential (ECB statute, Article 10). This important theme will be returned to in Chapter 14 on accountability.

Things would, however, be less clear-cut in one of three circum-stances: if the executive board failed to act as a cohesive body; if members of the executive board were influenced by patterns of national preference formation; or if national central bankers at-tempted to reduce the executive board to the status of a technical secretariat. The latter is one alternative prediction of what might follow from frequent meetings of the national central bank gover-nors in Frankfurt, or from the still dramatic imbalance in staffing resources between the ECB and national central banks.

Turning from voting behaviour to implementation, it was seen in Chapter 8 that the treaty requires the governing council to lay down the 'general guidelines for implementation'. But it will be for the executive board to turn these guidelines into practice by issuing instructions to nation central banks (ESCB statute, Article 12.1). If the governing council feels that a particular national central bank has not carried out the instructions of the executive board, it can take action in the ECJ. The ECB will be expected to draw up a 'reasoned opinion' of why it thinks that a national central bank is in default of its obligations. The national central bank will then be able to reply and the ECJ will adjudicate between the two points of view (ESCB/ECB statute, Article 35). The obvious question is whether this procedure is likely to be sufficient to avoid all types of implementation gap. One danger is that national central banks that have lost a vote on the general council may attempt to move outcomes closer to their preference by failing to implement the agreed policy in full. Another concern is that the governing council – on which the national central banks have a majority – is the key body in any decision to take proceedings against a national central bank. A final difficulty is the absence of any sanction on the part of the ECJ beyond the mere delivery of a negative judgement against the national central bank in question.

However the following factors can be expected to prevent significant problems of implementation from arising. The nature of the task and of the chosen instruments will either make it costly for a single national central bank to depart from the agreed policy, or make it administratively simple to detect and correct any deviation. One national central bank would be unable to sustain an interest rate that was different from the rest of the euro zone for a long period without having to assume the burden of financing the entire area. If it were to provide more credit than allocated by the ECB, this would be rapidly picked up in the accounts and corrected in the next period (author's interview at the ECB). The internal structure of the ECB can also be used to anticipate problems of implementation. A present plan is to establish some ten or eleven working groups in addition to the executive board and general council. The working groups will bring together senior officials of the national central banks at one level below the top decision makers. When the general council needs to make a decision about a detailed policy framework, it will ask the working groups to study the problem and come up with proposals that all the national central banks will feel able to implement (author's interview at the ECB).

In a federal system the institutional solution to both problems discussed in this section – nationalistic voting and implementation gaps – is usually considered to lie in the balance of votes between centrally appointed bankers and state bank governors: the more decentralised a federal central banking system in its arrangements for implementation, the more important it may be to shore up the

TABLE 12.2   The balance between central appointees and state representatives in federal systems of central banking

	Number central appointees	Representatives of state banks
Deutsche Bundesbank	8	9
European Central Bank	6	11
US Federal Reserve	7	5

capacity of the centre to police the consitutent parts by giving permanent appointees a substantial presence in the central decision-making body (Gros and Thygessen, 1992, pp. 397–8); the stronger the incentives for state central bankers to vote along particularist lines, the more important it may be to create a sizeable bloc of centrally cast votes. As discussed in Chapter 7 and summarised in Table 12.2, central decision makers are weaker in the case of the ECB than in other systems of federal central banking, even though its decentralised implementation structures would suggest that things ought to be the other way round.

Solutions that focus exclusively on the mechanistic consequences of voting weights may, however, underestimate the power of institutions over the shaping of preferences: they assume that national central bankers are likely to have a fixed propensity (probably governed by domestic circumstances) for nationalistic voting or incomplete implementation, and that the only thing to do is to create enough centrally cast votes to eliminate the effects of the first and police the second. But the need for a response of this kind would be lessened if it could be reliably assumed that other institutional features of the ECB were likely to reconfigure the interests of the national central banks in a collegial direction. The ECB looks set to develop two features that could have just such an effect. Both are evidence of the ECB borrowing policy-making styles from the wider EU political system in which it is located, either as a straightforward piece of institutional learning or because the two structures face a similar challenge of rendering a multilevel structure of governance viable.

The first federal characteristic common to both the ECB and the wider EU is what is known as *Politikverflechtung*, or administration fusion. National and EU institutions do not practise a form of

TABLE 12.3 *'Politikverflechtung'* under monetary union: ways in which the ECB and national central banks will have to mix their policy instruments

Function	Mix of responsibilities between national central banks and the ECB
Control of monetary policy	Governing council of the ECB formulates monetary policy, including intermediate monetary objectives, key interest rates and the supply of reserves in the ESCB. To implement policy, the ECB gives the necessary instructions to national central banks (ESCB statute, Article 12)
Issue of bank notes	The governing council of the ECB has the exclusive right to authorise the issue of bank notes. Their physical issue can be undertaken either by the ECB or by national central banks (Article 16)
Open market operations	Either the ECB or national banks will be able to carry out open market operations, but both cases will be covered by general principles established by the ECB (Article 18)
Minimum reserves	The minimum reserves which credit institutions will be required to hold with either the ECB or the national central banks will be determined by the general council (Article 19)
Clearing and payments systems	Since the drafting of the ESCB statute, it has been agreed that national financial systems will be locked into an integrated clearing and payments system – TARGET – which will be administered by the ECB.
Prudential supervision	Either member states or EU authorities may undertake prudential supervision (Article 25). Member states will have the comparative advantage of knowing their own financial systems, the ECB of knowing what is compatible with monetary targets for the euro zone (Gros and Thygessen, 1992, p. 404)
Foreign reserves	The ECB may manage up to 50 billion euros of foreign reserves credited to it by national central banks (Article 30)

federalism in which each level of governance functions separately of the other, each fully in command of their own list of tasks. Rather they have joint responsibility for each problem or issue, and they merge or fuse their policy instruments in order to get things done. In short they are tied together like two runners in a three-legged race, constrained to coordinate their activities if they are to achieve anything at all (Peters, 1997; Scharpf, 1988; Wessels, 1991). Monetary union will mesh the effectiveness and credibility of each national central bank with that of the ECB, a factor that cannot be ignored by institutions that stand or fall by performance alone. Table 12.3 builds on the analysis of Chapter 8 to show how national central banks and the ECB will merge their instruments across a whole range of functions.

National central bankers may also behave collegially because they form a strong 'policy community': a tightly knit group of experts with a shared professional commitment to a common view of what counts as high performance in policy making, and a more or less uniform view of the likely consequences of any action (Haas, 1992; Rhodes, 1997; Richardson, 1996; Peterson, 1995). It may even be more important for central bankers to impress one another than it is for them to be unduly influenced by national idiosyncrasies, which they are liable to dismiss as either temporary (if monetary phenomena) or structural problems that the politicians should sort out for themselves. Given that national interest is a 'plastic concept' that will be differently interpreted according to analytical frameworks and time horizons, central bankers may well be inclined to believe that the best way to serve domestic interests is to follow the shared commitment of their professional community. Again, the prevalence of policy communities is a pervasive feature of EU-style federalism, with an obvious link to *Politikverflechtung*: the continuous need for professional policy makers at the EU and national levels to merge their powers if they are to get anything done puts them under pressure to adopt a dense network of communications and convergent understandings of how policies work.

Chapter 13

Executive Power under Monetary Union 2: the European Council, Council of Ministers and Commission

The ECB corresponds to a model of supranational executive power that is both a throwback to some of the earliest experiments in European integration and, in the view of some, a challenge to the dominant method of EU governance: the Commission–Council tandem. Like the European Coal and Steel Community of 1952, but unlike the institutions set up under the Treaty of Rome of 1957, policy is delegated in a precisely defined area to a strictly independent technocracy that only needs to *report* to the Council of Ministers, rather than seek its approval for decisions (Haas, 1964, pp. 52, 459). It is this model – more than the conventional Commission–Council tandem – which best fits Giandomenico Majone's notion that European institutions can emerge as an independent fourth branch of government: policy specific, rather than discretionary or general in their scope; legitimised by the need to provide essential public goods that are beyond the reach of conventional politics, rather than through links to elected govern-ments or a directly elected European Parliament (Majone, 1996a, p. 287).

But by breaking with the principle that all executive power should accumulate in the one place, monetary union can also be seen as challenging the Commission–Council tandem. After all, one author has urged the creation of just such fragmented and issue-specific executive authorities as a means of meeting needs for supranational institution building while averting the emergence of a single govern-ance structure at the European level (Vaubel, 1994). However it would be a mistake to push such an analysis too far. This chapter is committed to the theme that monetary union has not just added a new form of executive authority in the form of the ECB. It is also likely to catalyse and transform existing ones, with important feedback effects into the management of the single currency. After a brief section reviewing the role of the European Council in appointing the ECB and revising the constitutional basis of its operations, the main body of the chapter considers the day-to-day activities of the Council of Ministers and the Commission under monetary union.

The European Council and the power of appointment

It is easy to see why the six permanent members of the ECB executive board should be considered so central to monetary union as to require their appointment by the unanimous consent of the European Council: the executive will set the agenda for meetings of the governing council, hold a third of the votes on the initial governing board, and supervise the implementation of EU monetary policy by national central banks. Chapter 7 considered whether appointment by the European Council could affect the credibility and independence of the ECB. This chapter asks a further question: do the politics of the European Council expose the ECB executive to recurrent risks of adverse selection? Support for rival candidates can turn into contests in which particular heads of government are unable to back down without loss of national or personal prestige. This can lead to suboptimal choices. Examples might be the appointment of compromise or lowest common denominator candidates, or attempts to split mandates. Even when agreement is more easily reached, the European Council has a tendency to appoint according to a 'consociational pattern', in which the spread and rotation of nationalities is considered more important than technical competence.

Consider the evidence of what happened on the first occasion when the European Council was called upon to exercise its power to appoint the executive board. During 1997 an assumption developed in central banking circles that Wim Duisenberg would be the first president of the ECB. He was a well-known 'inflation hawk'; his management of the Dutch central bank had been both lengthy and successful; and as he was the sitting president of the EMI, continuity between the bodies responsible for stages two and three of monetary union would be assured, so minimising any need for the ECB to earn reputation and credibility. But in November 1997 Chirac counter-proposed the president of the French central bank, Jean-Claude Trichet. Two justifications were made for this move. One was the claim by several leading French politicians that it was a 'convention' in the politics of international organisations that if the seat of an institution was in one country, its presidency should go to an appointee from another, and that since the ECB was in Frankfurt, and France was the next largest member state after Germany, it should have the first opportunity to appoint the president of the ECB (Milesi, 1998, p. 290). The other defence of Chirac's position was that the policy community of central bankers was getting too big for its boots. Duisenberg's appointment as president of the EMI upon the unexpectedly early retirement of Alexandre Lamfalussy looked like an attempt to pre-empt the choice of ECB president. According to this point of view, Chirac was merely asserting the constitutionally correct position that it was for the heads of government to appoint the executive board: the latter might have very considerable independence but its appointment by heads of government was an important reminder that central bankers were delegates of the political authority and were selected to perform a specific purpose, rather than people who could effectively 'annoint' themselves by encouraging the markets to believe that certain individuals were 'natural' candidates for particular positions.

However Chirac had little success in convincing other heads of government, not least the Dutch prime minister, who was in no position to compromise since a general election was due to be held within a week of the European Council called to select the ECB at the beginning of May 1998. Given that the decision rules required unanimity, there was a severe risk that the French and Dutch governments would simply veto each other's candidate, so removing the two figures who were widely considered as most suited to the job. The European Council moved towards a compromise in which Duisenberg was appointed as the first president. But the conclusions of the meeting took note of the likelihood that he would retire before the completion of his eight-year term and recorded an agreement that his successor should be French.

Table 13.1   *Appointment structure of first Executive Board of the
European Central Bank*

	Position and Responsibility	Nationality	Experience
Wim Duisenberg	President	Dutch	National finance minister 1973–77; president of national central bank 1982–97; president of European Monetary Institute, 1997–98.
Christian Noyer	Vice president: administration and personnel	French	Finance Ministry official since 1976; member of the Monetary Committee of the EU 1990–92 and 1993–95.
Otmar Issing	Board member: chief economist	German	Member of the board of the Bundesbank, 1990–98
Sirkka Hämäläinen	Board member: market operations	Finnish	Governor of the Bank of Finland, 1992–98
Tomasso Padoa-Schioppa	Board member: international relations	Italian	Deputy director general of the Bank of Italy, 1984–98 ; secretary of the Delors Committee on monetary union, 1988–89
Domingo Solans	Board member: statistics and banknote issue	Spanish	Member of executive board of the Spanish central bank, 1994–98

Although subject to much less political grand-standing, the appointment of the rest of the board clearly followed a consociational pattern. Not only were the seats distributed between the member states as shown in Table 13.1, there even seem to have been some political undertakings as to the future rotation of positions. A feature of the first board is that the members have been appointed to terms of varying duration, rather than for the full eight years. This will allow future executives to be appointed on a rolling basis, rather than in one fell swoop. However it has also opened the way for informal promises to be made to the 'outs' that countries joining at a later date will have a good claim on the next seat to fall vacant.

It is unclear why the heads of government were prepared to invest so many political resources in a tussle for the presidency and a consociatonal carve-up of the rest of the board unless there was some expectation that the national origin of appointees would have an impact on the formation of monetary policy. A further worry has already been reviewed in Chapter 7: the compromise on Duisenberg's appointment raises the spectre of informal understandings being used to override treaty rules that were painstakingly constructed to ensure the independence of the ECB, in that instance the provision that the members of the executive board should serve an eight-year term.

The European Council and the power of Treaty Change

A second role for the European Council will be to consider any changes to the treaties that are relevant to the functioning of monetary union. The agenda of the Amsterdam IGC was carefully controlled to prevent any proposals for treaty change being tabled during the introduction of monetary union. Nonetheless at least one change affecting monetary union crept into the treaty: the economic objectives that the ECB would be expected to pursue once it had secured price stability were amended. Amongst other issues that particular governments or EU institutions could well seek to raise at future IGCs are the following.

First, *the composition of the governing council of the ECB*, notably the balance between the executive board and the national central bank governors. As shown in Table 12.2, this already gives less weight to central decision makers than might be expected in a system dependent on decentralised implementation, and the imbalance will only get worse with enlargement of the currency zone or the EU as a whole. Assuming that expansion of the executive in proportion to the number of national central banks will eventually produce an unwieldy decision-making body, it may be necessary to break with the principle that each national central bank can expect permanent membership of the governing council. Germany, for example, has 'state-overlapping banks', while the United States has regional clusters of central banks, and even these only enjoy full membership of the Federal Open Markets Committee on a rotating basis. However arrangements such as these may only be politically acceptable in single-state monetary unions, characterised by a well developed sense of political identity. In multinational monetary unions, each national segment may need full representation if decisions are to enjoy full and even acceptance.

Second, *national central bank structures*. The possibility that the institutional characteristics of national central banks might be reshaped by EU treaty is a matter of some sensitivity given the principle that member states should be free to define their own constitutional arrangements. However it has already been conceded that this principle may need to be qualified to ensure the proper functioning of the overall monetary union: the TEU requires national central banks to be independent, and it puts limits on the appointment and dismissal of their governors. The convergence reports of both the EMI and the Commission before the start of stage three concluded that the founding members of monetary union had met their obligations under the TEU. But they also suggested that those obligations could usefully be tightened to ensure further safeguards on NCB independence (European Commission, 1998b; European Monetary Institute, 1998).

Third, *arrangements for central bank accountability*. As will be seen in the next chapter, the European Parliament is already seeking to expand its role beyond the strict letter of the treaty. It has sought to hear and even confirm the executive board, but it only has a formal right to be consulted on its appointment. It has attempted to use its powers to box the central bank into preannounced targets, in order to overcome concerns that the ECB would otherwise have too much power to manipulate the criteria by which it is itself judged. Should such evolving practices prove successful, the European Parliament could well seek to constitutionalise them in a future IGC.

Finally, *arrangements for coordination and economic governance in non-monetary matters*. It is in this area that the full institutional implications of monetary union have yet to be decided. Whereas the TEU provides a precise institutional blueprint for the central bank, evolving practices of economic coordination may require treaty changes. For example, recent discussion of fiscal harmonisation has raised the issue of whether majority voting may have to be introduced to the determination of some areas of taxation policy.

Fiscal coordination and the politics of institutional choice

Monetary union has not created a neat division between executive, representative and judicial powers. Rather it has divided executive power within itself: it has assigned monetary policy to the ECB, while leaving fiscal or budgetary powers with the member states, as organised in the European Council and Council of Ministers. Some commentators argue that this should not concern us too much. In their view governments can pursue autonomous policies without getting in each other's way, because the externalities are small and markets soon identify and punish the irresponsible (Buiter *et al.*, 1993, p. 82).

To others, however, questions of coordination between monetary and fiscal policy raise some of the largest and most politically contentious issues of institutional choice associated with monetary union. By intensifying economic integration, monetary union will increase the 'strategic interdependence' between all institutions responsible for economic policy: the capacity of any to achieve its goals will depend on the behaviour of the others. As seen, insufficient coordination of national budgetary policies could create particular problems for the institution most immediately concerned with the management of the single currency: the ECB (Artis and Winkler, 1998, p. 87). In addition to causing economic underperformance, the credibility and legitimacy of the ECB could also be adversely affected. The more inappropriate the aggregate of national fiscal policies, the more the burden of economic stabilisation will be thrown onto the ECB, and the more the ECB will have to eschew small and smooth changes of monetary policy for large movements of interest rates. Concentrating short-term sacrifice on particular occupational groups, generational cohorts and geographical regions could strain the political cohesion of the EU and raise questions about the right of an unelected body to distribute pain. Large and volatile movements of interest rates might also tempt governments to 'transfer blame' to the ECB. During the early stages of monetary union the following dilemma will be especially acute: while the ECB may only be able to perform at its best once its policy regimes are fully established, widely understood and in a stable relationship with investor and consumer behaviour, its right to take painful decisions may not be fully accepted until it has a sufficient track record of effective policy making to neutralise criticism that it is an unelected institution or a supranational interference in national economies. The remainder of this chapter accordingly considers the institutional capacity of the Council of Ministers, European Council, Commission and ECB to rise to the challenge of policy coordination.

Mutual surveillance, the Stability Pact and the politics of the Council of Ministers

It has already been decided that the Council of Ministers will be home to two new fiscal coordination procedures: mutual surveillance and the Stability Pact. In addition, there will be a series of contact points between Council, Commission and ECB. Chapter 8 provided an economic analysis of these mechanisms. This section considers the manner in which they are likely to interact with the politics of the Council.

The politics of the Council under mutual surveillance

As seen, the Council is supposed to reach a judgement for the macroeconomic policy of the EU as a whole, and show how any policy changes might be apportioned between member states. Cynics might suggest that commitments such as these are as old as the Community itself, and that they have never achieved very much. Mutual surveillance procedures are commonly accused of giving a false veneer of international coordination to policies that continue to be exclusively determined within the domestic arena. Another suggestion is that common fiscal guidelines established at the EU level will always contain the seeds of their own destruction: any indication that some governments will behave well will only increase the incentive for others to behave badly, and rational governments will anticipate this by not behaving too well in the first place. Others suggest that things are likely to be different under monetary union. The following is the appraisal of the commissioner responsible for the procedure since 1994:

> At the beginning of the 1990's, Finance Ministers did not say very much when they presented their convergence reports to one another. In a succession of monologues, each would claim to be on top of the situation. Rare was the Minister who dared pose

questions or raise objections to a programme presented by a colleague. The challenge of stage Two of monetary union has significantly changed things: debates in the Council have become more substantial and sometimes much longer. The role of Ecofin has been greatly reinforced, proof of a need to co-operate (De Silguy, 1998, p. 227).

Such scant evidence as we have of the use of the mutual surveillance procedure in stage two would seem to add some support to this conclusion. The Council does seem to have been prepared to divide its own members into 'sheep' and 'goats', with, for example, only two countries escaping criticism for excessive deficits in 1996 and the rest receiving recommendations to put things right (Milesi, 1998, p. 195).

What grounds might there be for arguing that the Council will be able to use mutual surveillance to make a useful contribution to policy coordination? One answer is that even if governments continue to play a non-cooperative game, the mutual surveillance procedure could well improve outcomes for the EU as a whole by providing all players with more reliable information about the intentions and behaviour of others. Another is that the arrangements for mutual surveillance may not be as sanction-free as they appear. They amount to a system of 'naming and shaming' in a context in which national central banks will no longer be allowed to prop up their governments by buying their debt, and liberalised capital markets will combine with a single currency to remove nationally captive pools of savings. Each drop of confidence will increase the cost of debt, and thus make it harder for governments to win elections by improving public services or cutting taxes.

Such processes of naming and shaming will, however, depend crucially on the internal politics of the Council of Ministers. Conscious of the possibility of harnessing punishment by the markets to the cause of intergovernmental coordination, the TEU allows the Council to use majority voting to decide whether it will go public with any admonition of a member state for failing to live up to its commitments under mutual surveillance. But the work of Ecofin is only part of a vast complex of business handled by the Council of Ministers at any one time. The need to obtain the willing cooperation of a member state on other matters may constrain any move to name and shame it in the area of budgetary coordination. Indeed a body that usually strives to avoid identifying governments as winners and losers, to the point of minimising recourse to formal voting even when it is available under the treaties (Hayes-Renshaw and Wallace, 1997), may be singularly reluctant to name and shame. Another difficulty is that the political cost of offending particular governments varies, with the result that the procedure may not be applied with impartiality, if it is ever used at all. A final suggestion is that the club of governments may respond with a kind of mutual disarmament pact or a no-first-use policy, in which no group of governments dares use the naming and shaming procedure for fear that it might one day be on the receiving end. One MEP has spoken of the danger of surveillance turning into a 'mutual complicity procedure' (author's notes, Institutional Affairs Committee, European Parliament, 29 October 1998).

However, it is at this point that the EU interinstitutional structures assume a crucial importance. Although the Council makes the final decisions, it does not fire the first shots in the mutual surveillance procedure. Whether laying down broad guidelines, monitoring economic developments or proposing corrective measures to the member state concerned, the Commission starts the ball rolling with a recommendation to the Council that is public knowledge. The transparency of the process is increased still further by the obligation of the presidents of the Council and the Commission to report the results of multilateral surveillance to the European Parliament (TEU, Article 104). This may at least force the Council to justify any decision not to follow a Commission recommendation. It could also mean that the procedure does not have to run the whole way to successful conclusion in the Council for it to impose a cost on an uncooperative government: market confidence in the policies of a particular government could be adversely affected at an earlier stage in the procedure.

The politics of the Council under the Stability Pact

To avoid repeating ground covered in Chapter 8, the main details of the pact are represented in Box 13.1. The procedure involves a subtle mix of flexibility and sanction. On the one hand, countries in excessive deficit have a reasonable time in which to adjust their finances: penalties only come into play two years after the excessive deficit first appears and only turn into non-refundable fines after four years. Throughout the member state has the opportunity to

---

Box 13.1 Summary of Council Procedures under the Stability Pact (see also Chapter 9)

1. Council decides whether a member state has run a deficit on its public finances of more than 3 per cent of its GDP.

2. If the deficit has been more than 3 per cent, the Council ascertains whether the member state has suffered a decline of more than 2 per cent of its GDP in the year in question. If it has, no further action is taken.

3. If in the year of assessment the member state has suffered a decline of its GDP of between 0.75 and 2 per cent, the Council must decide (by Qualified Majority vote) whether it is to accept any explanations offered for a deficit of more than 3 per cent of GDP.

4. If the member state's public deficit is not excused under 2 or 3, the Council may require it to take corrective measures.

5. If the member state does not take corrective action, and a deficit of more than 3 per cent persists, the Council will require it to make a deposit of between 0.2 and 0.5 per cent of its GDP on which it will not earn interest. The deposit will rise by 0.1 per cent for each 1 per cent of GDP by which the public deficit exceeds 3 per cent.

6. If after a further year, the member state has still not taken corrective action, the deposit is converted into a fine.

7. The member state being assessed is entitled to take part in the voting at step 3 but not at steps 5 and 6.

---

convince its peers that it is doing something about the problem. On the other hand the penalties, if exercised, could turn out to be quite severe in their effects. As with the mutual surveillance procedure, punishment by the markets – in the form of the extra interest that governments have to pay on their debt – could turn out to be worse than any fines imposed by the EU itself (Artis and Winkler, 1998).

The decision rules which the Council applies to its various stages will be a critical factor in shaping the political economy of the pact. The question of whether a country has an excessive deficit is decided by normal qualified majority voting – in other words by 71 per cent of the block votes on the Council, including the country that is being judged, and even including those which are not members of the single currency. Only when a decision has to be made on sanctions are the 'outs' – and the country under judgement – barred from voting. Some may argue that all of this makes the Stability Pact implausible: as with the mutual surveillance procedure, there is room to doubt whether a club of governments would pass adverse judgements on one another. Governments will be able to avoid sanctions by persuading just two or three others to join it in forming a blocking minority. If several go over the 3 per cent limit at the same time – and they may well do if the euro zone is governed by a single economic cycle – there may be some collusion between groups of governments to thwart the operation of the pact (Winkler, 1997). But as with the mutual surveillance procedure, the process is exercised in view of the public and the markets, with both the ECB and the Commission playing important roles. This could constrain governments from letting transgressors off too lightly. In addition the pact may well function as a 'conditional power', moderating behaviour well before it has to be invoked.

How will governments behave under the Stability Pact? As shown in Chapter 8, the pact will effectively constitutionalise balanced budgets when allowance is made for the temporary effects of the economic cycle. Some see the Stability Pact as the mainstay of both forms of policy coordination discussed in this chapter, that between the governments on the Council, and that between the Council and the ECB: to the extent that governments only have to follow the one rule, the need to rely on elaborate institutional structures of common economic governance, with high transaction costs and considerable scope for inefficient forms of decision making, is short-circuited; if on the other hand the ECB knows that governments have an incentive to aim for balanced budgets over the cycle, it will be able to set monetary policy with a far more predictable understanding of how it is likely to interact with the fiscal plans of member states. The treaties do, however, allow for more *discretionary* forms of coordination between the Council and the ECB, to which we now turn.

Interinstitutional relationships: the ECB, Council and Commission

As EU decision making is usually governed by *inter*institutional relations, outcomes are only imperfectly understood by studying one institution at a time. In anticipation of the policy coordination needs of monetary union, the TEU and subsequent agreements allow for two forms of relationship between the Council, the Commission and the ECB:

- *Reciprocal rights of attendance at meetings.* The president of the Council and a member of the Commission will be able to participate in meetings of the governing council of the ECB, and the president of the ECB will be invited to participate in meetings of the European Council that are relevant to the objectives of the central bank (European Commission, 1992, Article 109b).
- *A role for the Commission and the ECB in the preparation of Ecofin meetings.* Of great potential significance to coordination between Ecofin and the ECB is the replacement of the old Monetary Affairs Committee by a new Economics and Finance Committee (ibid., Article 109c). This consists of two representatives of each member state, two of the Commission and two of the ECB. Because it prepares the meetings of the finance ministers it effectively provides Ecofin with its own Committee of Permanent Representatives (COREPER), upon which the ECB is represented. It meets as often as once a week and allows for the appointment of one high-ranking official from each finance ministry and one from each national bank (ibid.). This pattern of representation ensures that national fiscal authorities are not only confronted with pressures from the ECB, but also from their own national central banks, eleven of which are heavily implicated in the work of the ECB through the governing council and its network of working committees.

An interesting question is how far these arrangements will involve the Commission. The Commission is often neglected in analyses of monetary union because of its slender formal powers: a reading of the treaty would suggest that its primary function is to make arrangements for the introduction of stage three, after which it will take a back seat to the ECB and the Council. But the Council's dependence on an active and effective Commission is much more than juristic in character: the Commission can save Council members the high transaction costs of having to negotiate tricky distributional questions between themselves; and the presence of an impartial referee allows governments to make more credible commitments to one another, with the result that they can be more ambitious in their coordinated policy making. The result is that the Commission is often a significant agenda setter even where its formal powers are relatively slight (Pollack, 1997; Smyrl, 1998).

But there is a further reason to expect the Commission to remain an important actor in stage three: because the Commission enjoys various rights of initiative in relationship to the fiscal coordination procedures (mutual surveillance and the Stability Pact) the ECB will have an incentive to align with the Commission to help it solve problems of policy mix. Indeed the Council and the ECB may even have reason to compete with one another to influence Commission positions on monetary union issues. After the Brussels European Council of May 1998, the Commission and the ECB made a coordinated effort to persuade member states to eliminate remaining structural deficits (*Financial Times*, 10 July 1998). On the other hand the ECB was clearly embarrassed, and the French and German governments delighted, by a proposal from Commissioner Monti that the 'golden rule' should apply to the Stability Pact: in other words it should take account of public sector capital expenditure net of depreciation (*Financial Times*, 17 November 1998).

How monetary union is changing the Council of Ministers

In showing how coordination outcomes are likely to be shaped by the distinctive politics and institutional practices of the Council, previous sections cautioned against a static analysis of the latter body. The time has now come to gather together evidence of how the Council is already undergoing change in response to monetary union.

First, *as a result of monetary union Ecofin looks set to become the most elaborately institutionalised of the sectoral councils of ministers, with the possible exception of the General Council of Foreign Ministers.* The Council of Ministers does not function as a unitary body, but as a series of sectoral councils, each related to a particular issue area. These can be said to vary in their institutionalisation depending on the degree to which they substitute collaborative public administration at the EU level for previously encapsulated patterns of national policy making. All sectoral councils preside over a substructure of working parties, supported by direct and continuous contacts between counterpart agencies in national capitals (Hayes-Renshaw and Wallace, 1997). The more elaborate and intensive of these practices make it hard to regard the Council as just a mechanism for member states to supervise the EU. On the contrary, they internationalise some of the official advice given to national ministers and they erode the unity of national public administration, as each department has to be given the autonomy to participate effectively in the work associated with its sectoral council (Dehousse, 1997). The following is an insider's assessment of how Ecofin's responsibilities under monetary union have intensified the contact between officials in national finance ministries and increased their ability to act with transnational coherence:

> Multilateral surveillance is a very heavy, time-consuming process. The intensity of communications between ministers and key civil servants has grown, not just in the Council, but on an everyday basis, through international meetings and bilaterals. These people form a club because they have shared problems and they tend to have shared beliefs about sound economic policies. They also have to fight against other ministries. The stability pact has also strengthened the hand of Finance Ministries demonstrably (author's interview at the Council of Ministers, December 1998).

Second, *Ecofin has moved up the hierarchy of sectoral councils.* As a result of monetary union, finance ministers have been admitted to full meetings of the European Council, formerly the exclusive power base of prime ministers and foreign ministers. As seen, the new Economic and Finance Committee will effectively take Ecofin out of the COREPER structure by which other sectoral councils are constrained, and, uniquely, allow it to prepare its own business. Although the work of Ecofin is largely self-contained, there are overlaps that have required it to collaborate with other sectoral councils, such as those concerned with taxation, employment and single market policy. This means that the General Affairs Council (GAC), made up of foreign ministers, has had to cede some of its coordinating role to Ecofin, so partially terminating an anomaly whereby Finance Ministries tend to be the key coordinators of domestic public administration, while Foreign Ministries are the key policy coordinators at the European level. One measure of the growing importance of Ecofin is a series of proposals to clip its wings. One is for deputy prime ministers to be appointed to a new

General Affairs Council, senior both to the foreign and finance ministers and capable of balancing the claims of all EU projects, monetary union included, so that none dominates. The exact outcome of these various power plays between sectoral councils of ministers may, however, depend crucially on the subject matter of the rest of this chapter: the more the range of institutional choice raised by monetary union is resolved in favour of an ambitious approach to policy coordination, the less easy it will be to displace the finance ministers from a prominent role in EU policy making.

Third, *because of monetary union, Ecofin has come under pressure to find innovative institutional solutions to the challenge of flexible integration.* One institutional response to the division of the EU into single currency 'ins' and 'outs' has been to vary the voting rules for Ecofin: when Ecofin deals with single currency questions – notably mutual surveillance, the imposition of fines and the external parity regime – only single currency countries will be eligible to vote. Another innovation, as discussed in previous chapters, has been to set up a Euro-11 Council specifically for those countries that have made the transition to stage three. It is still not entirely clear how the Euro-11 Council will relate to Ecofin, but the following is the outline agreement reached at the Luxembourg European Council of December 1997. Agendas for the Euro-11 Council and Ecofin will be prepared by the same body (the new Economic and Finance Committee). The two will meet on the same day and at same venue. 'Outs' will not attend meetings solely concerned with single currency questions, but they will be able to participate in other discussions, either by invitation or at their own request. Ecofin has also been confirmed as the final decision-making body, with the Euro-11 Council only functioning as a 'court of first instance'.

The importance of presidencies – of the Council, the Commission, Parliament and the ECB – in interinstitutional negotiations in the EU will, however, introduce one curiosity which may have the effect of moving the balance of influence back and forth between Ecofin and the Euro-11 Council. When the presidency of Ecofin is held by an 'out' country, interinstitutional dealings with other EU institutions will have to be handled by the presidency of the Euro-11 Council, which will be held by the next 'in' under the normal rules of rotation for the Council of Ministers. It is yet to be seen whether these arrangements will operate smoothly, or have the effect of fragmenting Ecofin at the very moment that monetary union promises to accelerate its institutional development and raise it in the hierarchy of councils.

Fourth, *there are signs that monetary union is mobilising political actors into the EU arena with the express purpose of influencing the work of Ecofin*. On the one hand the task of economic coordination has increased the incentive for national governments to structure their bilateral relations around the work of Ecofin. For example the institution of a Franco-German Finance Council from as early as 1988 produced no matching initiative from the British government until the start of full monetary union in 1998–99, when it moved quickly to establish an Anglo-German working group (*Guardian*, 21 November 1998).

But there are also signs that Ecofin's role in economic co-ordination may provoke a more novel form of political behaviour, in which non-government actors such as parties and organised interests begin to organise themselves to influence a specific sectoral council. There are some signs that finance ministers have started to coordinate positions in their transnational party federations (the Party of European Socialists, PES; the European People's Party, EPP; the European Liberal and Democratic Reform Party, ELDR; and the Federation of Greens) prior to Ecofin meetings. In 1996 the Irish finance minister proposed that the PES should discuss a common economic programme for the EU in stage three, so that it would be well prepared to set the agenda once the Council had assumed responsibility for coordination under monetary union. The results of this study were presented to a meeting of PES finance ministers immediately prior to the Ecofin meeting of November 1998. The work of Ecofin under monetary union may also influence party competition and cooperation at the national level. For example the coalition agreement between the German SPD and the Greens contains a clause 'committing the parties to drive forward economic and financial co-ordination' at the level of the Euro-11 (SPD/Grüne, Koalitionsvertrag, 20 October 1998).

Similar patterns are emerging at the level of organised interests. Finance ministers hold informal meetings every six months with the UNICE (European employers) and ETUC (European Trade Unions). The ETUC, in particular, has attempted to follow the internal dynamics of Ecofin, issuing statements of its own preferred position on agenda items. Examples include opposition to moves to tighten the Stability Pact and the adoption of an agreed position on how Ecofin should react to the prospect of a global financial crisis in the autumn of 1998.

Conclusion: the open questions of European economic governance.

The foregoing analysis suggests another key political contrast between the two main aspects of monetary union: the institutions that govern the setting of monetary policy have been tightly specified in advance and may even be subject to stasis for fear that any proposed changes to the ECB will be taken as an attack on its independence; in contrast the coordination of budgetary policies through the Council offers a wide and open-ended range of institutional choice. At one extreme the member states could adopt an almost 'institution free' solution, consisting of little more than a few simple and self-enforced rules of good neighbourliness. At the other they could attempt to construct a full-scale process of discretionary economic governance at the EU level. It may even be a healthy aspect of the project that it contains 'open questions' such as these: that it has a variable institutional component in the form of how the Council is organised to provide fiscal coordination as well as a fixed institutional component in the shape of the ECB. The first ensures that monetary union is less exposed to the charge that it is founded on the entrenched preferences of long departed governments, and that it lacks any capacity for contemporaneous 'democratic will formation': for responsiveness to the needs and values of present-day society.

The extent to which there is likely to be a winning coalition for any particular approach to fiscal coordination can be expected to change with the average left–right position of the governments that go to make up the Council. At the time of the TEU, centre-right governments held power in seven of the twelve member states. By the time stage three was launched in January 1999 the left–right balance of the Council was very different: centre-left parties were in coalition in 13 of the 15 member states. Of particular importance was the change in government in Germany in October 1998. Whereas the French government had long been in favour of using monetary union to build up the Council of Ministers as a site for coordinated demand management, the Kohl administration had steered the agenda for coordination towards the Stability Pact, with its simple rule-based mechanism whereby all members would aim for balanced budgets, and away from more discretionary approaches. In contrast the incoming German finance minister, Oskar Lafontaine, immediately aligned himself with the view that the Council should attempt coordinated policies to ensure full employment.

It would, however, be a mistake to suggest that these choices will be just down to the preferences of governments. They will also be governed by the capacity of EU institutions to develop in various directions. So far the EU has concentrated on the regulatory aspects of economic governance, rather than those directly concerned with stabilisation or redistribution (Majone, 1996b). This makes sense given its limited administrative resources and the greater legitimacy that may be needed if the institutional structure is to accept responsibility for a discretionary approach to economic management, or to make overtly redistributive decisions. Some of the forms of macroeconomic coordination that have been suggested for stage three of monetary union would certainly involve responsibility for stabilisation matters such as full employment, and quite probably involve the determination of redistributive questions, such as the incidence of taxation.

A further consideration is that simply by virtue of the number of players involved, the institutionalisation of budgetary coordination between public authorities is likely to be far more complex under monetary union than under any previous political system. So far the most complex examples of monetary–fiscal coordination have probably been provided by single-state federations such as the United States and Germany. The principal players in both these cases might be characterised as follows: one central bank; one federal authority responsible for about one half of public spending; and a whole series of state governments responsible for the other half. In contrast the European Union is an 'upside-down' and somewhat consociational federation. That is to say, the states are amongst the principal decision makers at the centre as well as in their own territorial segments, and one of the purposes of the EU is precisely to enable states to preserve many of the idiosyncrasies of their own internal governance in an overall context of prosperity and security.

This means that, in contrast to the German and US cases, any game of economic coordination in the EU would have the following, more complicated structure: a single central bank faces a Council of Ministers that can dispose of just one fortieth of public resources through a process that requires high levels of agreement between 15 states, not all of which are members of the monetary union; the remaining 39 parts of public spending, taxation and borrowing can only be sanctioned in the domestic political systems of the member states, and sometimes only at local or regional level at that. Even if it were physically possible to assemble all those responsible for spending, borrowing and taxes in the one place, a coordinated fiscal stance could not be directly authorised within the rules of a single political system common to all. Apart from the small proportion of public resources covered by the EU budget, national political systems remain the sovereign budgetary authorities. Finance ministers cannot easily be bound by undertakings given in Ecofin: they can only endeavour to persuade their cabinet colleagues to follow suit and this may not always be easy. First, public budgets are conditioned by the particular characteristics of the economic and social structures of the individual member states, and they often demonstrate an intractability to political control even by national institutions, let alone supranational ones. Second, governments may risk their very survival if they fail to adjust public budgets on an almost continuous basis to the demands of domestic reelection or those of maintaining a multiparty coalition. Because politicians compete for power in the national rather than the European arena, they are unlikely to be directly rewarded for Ecofin-based coordination, and may sometimes have an incentive to ignore it.

Chapter 14

Representation and Accountability under Monetary Union

An institutional structure is democratic to the degree that it is publicly authorised, representative and accountable. Against this background it is often argued that democratic politics can have very little to do with monetary union. One suggestion is that any meaningful form of political accountability would undermine the independence of a central bank. Another is that the representation of public preferences has little relevance if there are no long-term choices to be made between inflation, growth and unemployment. In contrast to such arguments, this chapter begins by showing that democratic politics are both necessary and possible in relation to a system of independent central banking. It then goes on to review likely channels of democratic representation and accountability under monetary union: the Council, the European Parliament, national parliaments, and direct communications between the ECB, the public and its economic and social intermediaries.

To see why democratic sanction may be the logical consequence of independence and not its opposite (Briault *et al.*, 1996, p. 1), it is necessary to set out the normative justifications for independent central banking more systematically than has been possible elsewhere in this book. By using comparative historical data to show that inflation has tended to be lower in systems run by independent central banks, several studies imply that democratic societies would be prepared to delegate important powers to unelected bodies if they were likely to make a better job of achieving an agreed objective. But even if an objective is agreed its delivery may involve denying values to one set of people in order to confer them on another. Many take the view that such decisions ought only be made by a body that is regularly accountable to the electorate: the argument that independent central banking is in the long run value neutral between inflation and unemployment may therefore be as important to its political legitimacy as to its economic justification. But even this does not get to the core of the problem. Commitment to democratic process is primarily ethical, rather than utilitarian. The prospect that everyone might be better off if a task were delegated to a technocratic body may therefore only be a necessary condition of such an arrangement, and not a sufficient one: only a convincing argument that a public good is essential and that conventional democratic politics are inherently incapable of delivering it to minimum standards is likely to defeat a normative preference for the latter.

Three such arguments are relevant to independent central banking. One is that democratic politics may not be all that good at settling those questions of individual justice where majorities can achieve electoral approval by appropriating minorities. There could therefore be an argument for putting some basic protections of property rights beyond normal democratic politics. Independent central banks might be justified as constraints on the power of governments to appropriate assets by creating surprise inflation. Another suggestion is that the democratic process itself works imperfectly when governments have the power to manipulate the economic and electoral cycles so that the two coincide (Nordhaus, 1975). As seen, this may eventually put the control of inflation beyond even the reach of governments that are committed to such a goal. When rational price and wage fixers know that a political system affords governments the power to create illusory economic expansion, they will anticipate this in their economic behaviour, however much their rulers intend otherwise. A third possibility is that independent central banking might be justified at a supranational level as binding countries into a process of collaboration and reducing the probability of aggressive forms of interstate behaviour.

So to summarise, policy delegation to a technocratic body may only be justifiable when (1) there is an agreed objective that can (2) be delivered without denying values to some and conferring them on others, and (3) that objective corresponds to some essential public good without which the wider political and social system is unlikely to perform to what the overwhelming majority would consider to be an acceptable standard. All of this makes it important to have a system of accountability to ensure that the independent authority delivers 'on the nail', neither falling below its mandate nor straying beyond it. If the good in question is so important to public well-being as to justify its removal from the normal democratic process, there has to be a means of ensuring that the independent authority delivers its objective. If, on the other hand, the act of delegation is to be strictly controlled and not expanded by stealth to cover goals that could be achieved by normal democratic processes, a system of accountability is needed to ensure that the independent authority does not exceed its mandate. As executive board member Thomasso Padoa-Schioppa told the European Parliament, 'the powers that the central bank exercises are not its own, but powers that have been delegated by the voters' (European Parliament, 1998c).

Economic arguments also suggest that democratic accountability may reinforce the credibility and performance of central banks, rather than threaten their independence. In his written answers to questions put by the European Parliament during confirmation proceedings, Duisenberg wrote that 'the ECB will implement these provisions (its reporting obligations to the EP) not only because it is required to do so by the Treaty, but also because transparency increases the effectiveness and credibility of a central bank'. His deputy, Christian Noyer, took up the same theme: 'dialogue with the political authorities of the European Union, and in particular with the European Parliament, is absolutely crucial if the single currency is to be accepted and monetary policy understood by the general public. It is a vital factor in the credibility of the European Central Bank'(European Parliament, 1998c). As one study rather grandly puts it, 'transparency is pareto improving within any institutional set-up characterised by preference uncertainty' (Briault *et al.*, 1996, p. 9). The more an independent central bank can induce the public and markets to set prices and wages in a manner that anticipates its own determination to achieve its objectives, the fewer frictional or transitional costs it is likely to incur in the realisation of its goals. In the jargon, it can minimise the 'sacrifice ratio': the short-term loss of output or employment needed to achieve any reduction in inflation (Gros and Thygessen, 1992). As unelected bodies, independent central banks will often be in search of public platforms that allow them the opportunity to explain the nature of their policy regimes. Obligations to make their policies transparent to representative institutions may therefore be more of an opportunity than a threat.

Nor is it clear that the theory of 'no long-run trade offs', upon which independent central banking is based, removes all need for a process of public representation. As Charles Goodhart has pointed out, central bankers do have a choice about the speed with which they attempt to return to long-term equilibrium if they are ever knocked off course. As this is a purely subjective choice between a short sharp shock and a long slow squeeze, it is just the kind of matter upon which it would be appropriate to use representative structures to gauge public feelings (Charles Goodhart, evidence to the EMAC of the European Parliament, January 1998).

Two models of accountability

The belief that democratic politics cannot be combined with independent central banking may, in any case, be based on a confusion; or to be more precise, on a concentration on hierarchical methods of accountability to the exclusion of those based upon a separation of powers in a political system. Under hierarchical methods, representative institutions appoint and dismiss senior executive office holders. In a world in which everyone wants to retain their jobs, the politically appointed leaderships of executive bodies issue instructions to subordinates that they can defend to the elected body, and representatives then put administrative leaderships under continuous pressure to show that their decisions serve the needs and values of the electorate (Page and Wouters, 1994).

The New Zealand model probably provides the only conceivable means of applying such hierarchical methods of accountability to an independent central bank. It is worthy of some consideration, since one critique of the TEU is that its authors were too preoccupied with generalising the Bundesbank approach to consider an alternative that comes closer to squaring the circle between independence and political responsibility. The New Zealand central bank is handed a quantified inflation target by the elected government, which it is expected to deliver subject to a precise contract of rewards and penalties, including dismissal and political override: in other words, effective loss of franchise. Not only does this confine technocratic or non-democratic decision makers to the selection of means rather than ends, it also reconciles independence with systems of account-ability based on the dismissal of office holders. The central bank can still be considered independent because (1) it has the freedom to choose the instruments it considers appropriate to the achievement of its targets, and (2) the political authority can only dismiss the central bank for not achieving the preannounced targets, and not at whim.

By the standards of hierarchical democratic accountability used in the New Zealand model, the ECB has been criticised as being well placed to elude accountability. Apart from the absence of arrangements for dismissal or override, it would appear to be able to set the standards by which it will itself be judged. It may even be able to 'move the goal posts' to avoid evidence of underperformance. Yet there are at least four reasons of time and place why the New Zealand model might be inapplicable to the European Union:

- Doubts about the rigour with which the Council of Ministers might define the inflation target, given that its primary purpose is to organise intergovernmental consensus, even at the cost of lowest-common-denominator decision making, or splitting the difference between positions.
- Whilst the electoral sanction might deter single national governments from playing fast and loose with the inflation target, the somewhat diffuse and non-transparent setting of the Council of Ministers allows greater opportunity to evade political responsibility for decisions.
- The difficulty of applying the New Zealand model to a quasi-federal structure. However forceful the policy leadership of the executive board, the majority of votes on the governing council will be held by the governors of the national banks, who could only be made dismissable from the centre by terminating the federal structure of the ECB and moving it in a unitary direction. In addition the delivery of price stability may depend on the policy mix with fiscal authorities, not just on the unilateral actions of the ECB.

The hierarchical approach may not, however, be the only means of institutionalising accountability. Other models emphasise the separation of powers, rather than their integration into a single system of democratic control. Under such models, powers are divided between institutions in such a way that they can only attain their goals if they are able to offer a sufficiently convincing account of their performance and intentions to secure the willing cooperation of other bodies (Kielmansegg, 1996; Kohler-Koch, 1996; Jachtenfuchs, 1997). To their defenders, such systems have three advantages: they adapt the practice of accountability to a world in which fewer organisations seem to be able to operate as pure hierarchies or obtain their goals unilaterally; they combine accountability with deliberation; and they are better suited to situations where account-ability requires specialist forms of knowledge (Héritier, 1997; Joerges and Neyer, 1997).

Accountability through reason-giving may be an especially cogent weapon in the case of independent central banks. Those which fail to give convincing explanations and justifications of their policies will soon find themselves unable to perform their functions at an acceptable cost. Given that they are unelected institutions that function under an act of policy delegation to carry out a narrowly defined task, performance is the only basis for their legitimacy, and without it they can expect to decline in influence. As explained, the ECB may be independent, but to achieve its goals it will need to command the credibility and active cooperation of a large range of other actors. According to the reporting process laid down in the treaties, there are no fewer than four institutions that might lay claim to a role in bringing the ECB to account through explanation of its policies: the Commission, the Council, the European Council and the European Parliament (European Commission, 1992, Article 109b). The incentive for the ECB to maintain the confidence of the Council and the European Council will arise from its need to seek adjustments to national fiscal policies if it is to achieve the desired policy mix; and from the advantage of having governments that are staunch public defenders of central bank independence when hard decisions have to be made. The incentive for the ECB to maintain the confidence of the Commission will arise from its position as the agenda setter in the two fiscal coordination procedures: mutual surveillance and the Stability Pact. The more the Commission can be persuaded to frame public recommendations that are close to the ECB's ideal preferences, the more difficult it will be for the member states to evade their responsibility for the problem of policy mix.

These formal reporting requirements will, in addition, be played out in the full gaze of two other actors whose confidence the ECB will need to maintain: the public and the markets. The ECB will also have to answer to the European Parliament, which looks set to become a significant inquisitor and mouthpiece for heterogeneous public concerns. Although the ECB could choose just to rely on press conferences to announce and explain its policy regimes to those whose cooperation it needs, a strong parliamentary committee would be able to offer the bank one distinctive advantage: the credibility and legitimacy that comes from being able to defend policies under rigorous cross-examination by the people's representatives.

The need for dual accountability to Council and Parliament

To the extent that the ECB can be seen as an 'agent' that has received a policy delegation from member states to deliver price stability, the Council might seem to be the proper body to bring it to account. In addition to reporting arrangements, the right of its presidency to attend meetings of the ECB will give the Council a unique right of accountability. However there are a series of reasons for believing that accountability to the Council cannot be enough.

First, the Council and the ECB both exercise executive powers under monetary union. To a certain extent their coresponsibility will lead to a fusion of operations, rather than a separation of powers upon which a fully detached process of accountability can be based. As seen, the Council and the ECB will be represented in each other's decision-making processes, and a new monetary committee made up of representatives of the Commission, Council and ECB will have a crucial role. As one MEP has put it, a substantial role in the management of the European economy could be about to pass to an 'ECB/Ecofin' axis (Pierre Herzog to EMAC, 27 January 1998). In an ideal world the ECB, Council and Commission should not just be accountable to one another, but politically responsible to a body that is completely independent of the complex of intra-executive relations.

Second, a related point is that the expansion of the Council's responsibilities for fiscal coordination under mutual surveillance and the Stability and Growth Pact will itself need to be covered by adequate mechanisms of accountability. Since these procedures will operate by qualified majority voting, the Council should, logically, be answerable to the European Parliament in order to protect the interests of those whose viewpoints may not have been covered by the majority position adopted by the member states.

Third, efforts to make the ECB accountable to the Council may arouse suspicions that the governments are attempting to reimpose a system of political supervision. In contrast the European Parliament is a supranational body whose members are widely assumed to have a strong interest in the institutional development and effective performance of the EU. Unlike the member governments, it probably lacks the means to threaten the independence of the ECB. Dual responsibility to the Parliament and the Council could add to the obligation of the ECB to explain itself, while providing a check on the Council in its dealings with the ECB. If this were to make the ECB less defensive and reassure markets, it could even improve ECB–Council relations.

Fourth, given that the ECB's main interest in accountability lies in the opportunity to explain its policy regimes to the public and the markets, it needs to be politically responsible to the most transparent institutional process available. Whereas the Council is an essentially secretive institution geared towards permanent intergovernmental bargaining, the Parliament is a body in search of an audience. It has been quick to recognise the political opportunity offered by the ECB's need for a political platform.

Fifth, the Council is organised for the expression of preferences along national lines. Given the earlier observation that the ECB will systematically underperform unless it makes policy judgements appropriate to the euro area as a whole, it would be better to hold it politically accountable to a democratic body organised for the aggregation and expression of needs and values at the EU level.

The European Parliament's role under monetary union

The Parliament will have four kinds of role in relation to monetary union.

First, *legislative powers*: These are set out in Table 14.1. The broad conclusion would seem to be that the Parliament's role in framing the rules of monetary union ranges widely but does not go very deep. On most matters it is limited to consultation: once the Council has received the Parliament's opinion, it is free to proceed as it wants. There are, however, exceptions: the Parliament's approval is needed under the assent procedure for most amendments to the ECB statute, and to confer powers on the ECB to undertake the supervision of financial institutions.

Table 14.1 *Legislative powers of the European Parliament in relation to monetary union*

Description of power	Already exercised?	Frequency of exercise	Decision rules
Choice of countries participating in single currency	Yes, in relation to the 11 founding members (2 May 1998)	Whenever a European country wishes to enlarge the single currency to include new countries	Consultation
Nomination of president, vice president and other members of the board	Yes, appointment of first executive board (14 May 1998)	Eventually, every 1–2 years, as the terms of the original board have been structured to create a 'rolling' pattern of appointment	Consultation
Legislation needed to prepare the introduction of the single currency	Yes		Consultation
Legislation needed for the introduction of new notes and coins	Yes		Consultation
Legislation setting out procedures for the control of excessive national deficits	Yes, when the stability pact was enacted	Every time that the governments want to revise the rules of the Stability Pact. Also need to inform European Parliament of any decisions taken/fines imposed	Consultation
Agreements on external exchange rate regimes between the euro and other currencies	No	If any G8 currency accords; if an ERM2 is established with other EU countries; every time the Council wants to change the euro central rates	Consultation
Modifications to the ECB statute or to powers delegated to the ECB in control of financial institutions	No		Assent procedure

Second, *rights in relation to the process of executive appointment.* Technically, the treaty only gives the Parliament the right to be consulted on the appointment of the president of the ECB, the vice president and other members of the executive board (European Commission, 1992, Article 109a). However the Parliament has often used the fact that it is master of its own procedures to put a maximal interpretation on the powers assigned by the treaties. True to form, it has sought to turn its right to be consulted on the appointment of the ECB executive into a power akin to that of the US Senate to 'hear' and confirm nominees for the Federal Reserve. Its documentation describes the procedure as 'European Parliament confirmation hearings'. In this it has been able to draw on its own experience in developing similar arrangements to confirm the appointment of new EU commissioners. The Parliament's own rules of procedure accordingly require that nominees to the ECB executive board should make a declaration before the relevant parliamentary committee (the Economic and Monetary Affairs Committee, EMAC) and answer its questions; that EMAC should then make a recommendation to the Parliament to accept or reject the candidate concerned; and that the Council should be asked to withdraw any candidate rejected by the Parliament and substitute a new nominee (European Parliament Rules of Procedure, Article 36). When this procedure was first used in May 1998 EMAC took the additional step of requiring each candidate to submit a curriculum vitae and respond in writing to a detailed questionnaire. Regardless of how the Parliament's power is best classified on a scale from consultation to confirmation, it is worth noting that it is comparatively unusual for parliaments to have any role at all in the appointment of central bankers.

Third, *the power to request explanations from the ECB.* The president of the ECB has to present the annual report of the bank to the European Parliament in person (European Commission, 1992, Article 109b). To obtain maximum publicity, the Parliament intends that this should be at a plenary session of the Parliament, and that there should be both a debate (as allowed by the treaty) and a vote on the ECB's performance during the year under review. In between annual reports the president of the ECB and other board members may be heard by EMAC, at the request of either the Parliament or the ECB itself. During the hearings on his appointment, Duisenberg indicated that he would like to appear before the Parliament at least once a quarter (European Parliament, 1998c).

Fourth, *powers to scrutinise the work of the Commission and the Council under the mutual surveillance procedure and the Stability Pact*. These powers include the right to be informed of all recommendations that the Commission makes under the multilateral surveillance procedure and Stability Pact, and of the subsequent steps adopted by the Council. In the event of a Council decision to make a public recommendation that a particular member state should change its economic policies, the president of the Council may be invited to appear before a parliamentary committee to explain the grounds for such a decision (European Commission, 1992, Article 103).

The obvious question is whether these obligations to the Parliament are enough to put the ECB under real pressure, such that if it does not give convincing explanations it is likely to suffer loss of credibility with the public and the markets. To answer this question it should first be noted that the Parliament has sought to link its various powers into a continuum: the confirmation hearings are to be used to clarify the criteria by which the ECB will be subsequently brought to account; the three-monthly hearings are then to be used to review the performance of the ECB against those targets; and it is anticipated that the Parliament will then use its power to request an emergency meeting if the targets are not met. In addition to using the confirmation proceedings to specify an initial definition of price stability, the Randzio-Plath report specifies that the ECB should be asked to provide each subsequent hearing with updated inflation projections and targets, and indications of the means it intends to employ to achieve those targets (European Parliament, 1998b).

As the Parliament approved all nominees to the first board by a substantial margin, the first use of the procedure in May 1998 did not test whether the Parliament had succeeded in turning its right to be consulted on appointments into a *de facto* power of confirmation. However all candidates were asked to state in writing whether they would 'wish to pursue their nominations' if rejected by the Parliament. Duisenberg's own response suggests that a vote of parliamentary disapproval would not invariably be effective, but it could become so under certain conditions. He thought that it would primarily be for the European Council to decide how to respond to a negative parliamentary vote. But he went on to say that he would 'look very carefully at the grounds on which the Parliament's decision was based and at the degree of support it had received'.

This suggests that an adverse vote could prevent a central banker from taking office if the Parliament succeeded in calling the credibility of the bank into question, either through the size of the vote against a nominee or because the reasons for rejection were pertinent to the independence of the board or its ability to deliver its objectives (European Parliament, 1998c).

If the ability of the Parliament to claim a full-scale power of confirmation remains undecided on the evidence of May 1998, it would seem to have been more successful in using the hearings to clarify benchmarks by which the ECB might be brought to account at a later date. The questionnaires that EMAC sent to the executive board nominees required them to specify their definition of price stability, and all of them indicated that they would aim to keep inflation within a range of 0–2 per cent. Duisenberg confirmed that he expected the ECB to be accountable for *pre*announced targets and that normal lags in monetary policy making would make it appropriate to judge the performance of the ECB board against decisions made some 18–24 months earlier (European Parliament,1998c). By boxing the ECB into *pre*announced targets in such a way, the Parliament can help overcome the objection that the TEU leaves the ECB with too much discretion to define the goals by which it will itself be judged.

In parenthesis, it is worth noting that confirmation hearings are an occasion for the Parliament to review the performance of the European Council in appointing the executive council as much as they are an opportunity to consider the candidates themselves. In this regard there may be a role for the Parliament as a safeguarder of ECB independence and credibility. As seen, the European Council attracted considerable criticism for concerning itself more with the nationality of the candidates than with their suitability as European central bankers. The indication that Duisenberg might be replaced at some stage of his eight-year term by another candidate, who 'would probably be French', was seen as damaging to the credibility of the ECB.It presented the danger that informal deals between heads of government might be used to by-pass the formal rules that the drafters of the TEU had judged necessary to the independence of the ECB; in this instance the requirement that central bankers should be appointed for a single eight-year term. Duisenberg was, however, able to use his hearing before EMAC to clarify that he had made no promise to step down before the eight years elapsed and that it would have been illegal for him to have done so (European Parliament, 1998c).

The first parliamentary hearing of an ECB president in office took place in September 1998. Duisenberg presented the Parliament with a written statement summarising the ECB's principal decisions over the previous three months and then took questions, which the committee chair had grouped into three themes: the democratic accountability of the ECB, the nature of monetary policy, and the ECB's views on how the euro zone should respond to crisis in the international financial system. Questioning was rigorous and lasted almost three hours. More than two hundred members of the international press corps were represented. However the process probably failed in its aim of reproducing the public impact of appearances of US Federal Reserve President Alan Greenspan before Congress, in which every question and answer is weighed and sifted, to the mutual benefit of both the bank and the representative assembly.

Yet to be demonstrated is the effectiveness of the power of the Parliament to summon the ECB to an unscheduled hearing before the Monetary Affairs Committee. Given the importance of market credibility to effective central banking, the right of the Parliament to invite the executive board to an unscheduled hearing in the event of it missing a predefined target could well be a powerful source of accountability and a considerable deterrent against poor perfor-mance. If an executive board either declined the invitation or failed to give convincing answers under cross-examination it would probably suffer severe damage to its reputation. The Parliament's internal rules of procedure indicate that the procedure for summon-ing the ECB to an extraordinary hearing of the Parliament will be initiated by EMAC and confirmed by the Conference of Presidents: that is, the president of the Parliament and the chairs of the political groups. This means that the decision will effectively be taken by weighted vote of the parties in the Parliament (European Parliament, Article 39).

But what institutional resources will the Parliament have to carry out a process of accountability that is essentially based on extracting explanations for decisions and testing their validity? There may be inherent limits to which any central bank can be held to quantified tests of its performance. One reason for this has to do with variable lags in economic policy making: the interval between the making of policy and its impact on economic behaviour may vary in a way that makes it difficult to judge which decisions – and whose – are responsible for particular outcomes. Another problem is that monetary outcomes may be subject to shock developments that the ECB can legitimately claim to be beyond its control. A possible difficulty here has already been indicated by Duisenberg. While concurring with the Parliament's drive to get the ECB to state precise and preannounced targets, he has observed that these may need time to bed down: the switch to monetary union will itself create turbulence in private economic behaviour, with the result that the ECB may need to make a series of adjustments before it is fully content with its policy targets and statistical series. To hold it into a straitjacket of precisely quantified tests during such a phase of adjustment could only diminish its performance.

The implication of the foregoing point is that the capacity of the Parliament to exercise meaningful accountability in the conduct of monetary policy by the ECB will depend a great deal on expertise. Given that quantified targets will not always be sufficient, the real test of any failure to deliver price stability will be to weigh the credibility of any explanations offered by the ECB. To achieve this goal the Parliament may be able to draw on outside advice, as when it invited academics and central bankers to EMAC in January 1998 to advise it on procedures of central bank accountability. However there will probably be no real alternative to the internal construction of a committee with both political weight and technical understanding of monetary policy. The Parliament has therefore set itself the ambitious goal of endowing EMAC 'with tasks similar to that of the US Senate Banking Committee' (European Parliament, 1998b). One obstacle to the accumulation of expertise could, however, be presented by the very high turnover of MEPs between European elections. This may require party groups to give priority to ensuring the continuity of EMAC when they make committee assignments.

Given that the politics of accountability under monetary union will also involve a whole complex of interinstitutional relationships, the Parliament has also considered requesting an interinstitutional agreement. This would embrace the ECB, the Commission and the Council, and give more formality – as well as public transparency – to its right to hold other bodies to account. Perhaps concerned that a formal interinstitutional agreement would be seen in the markets as a challenge to independence, the ECB has, however, indicated that it would prefer a relationship to emerge 'through custom and practice' (European Parliament, 1998c). The Parliament likewise seems to have pulled back from pursuing a written understanding that would give member states a say in any evolving relationship between the Parliament and the ECB.

Another problem is that of transparency. One possible view is that anything short of full publication of the minutes of general council meetings would only produce an abridged and sanitised version of discussions: the public and its representatives would be denied a full account of the conflicting considerations involved in any policy choice. The alternative view, however, is that collective responsibility is precisely what the ECB should be aiming to achieve. Anything that made it possible to identify who had taken which positions on the governing council would open central bankers to domestic pressures and deflect them from their responsibility for achieving price stability in the euro area as a whole. The following is the view of the ECB's chief economist:

> the governors of the national central banks do not sit on the ECB Governing Council as representatives of their countries but as representatives of the institution as a whole. Making individual members' voting behaviour public would encourage scrutiny of members' voting patterns. This, in turn, would encourage external pressures on the Council members arising from local interests. Independence, granted by the Treaty would be at risk (Issing, 1998; see also Issing, 1999).

Duisenberg has accordingly taken what at first sight seems the somewhat drastic line of suggesting that the ECB minutes should not be published for 16 years, that being the longest possible period that any single person could be a member of the governing council. In any case the ECB's duty of clear and coherent explanation would arguably be better expressed in a summary document than in a verbatim report of committee discussions.

In contrast it has been suggested that publication of the minutes may even be needed to protect independence. It would make it easier to detect any undue influence or nationalistic voting, and secrecy could lead to the worst possible outcome: information on voting behaviour could leak out without any explanation to the public that it is the duty of each national central bank governor to make a judgement appropriate to the euro zone as a whole (Buiter, 1999a).

In addition to these specific points, the ECB will have to deal with two general accountability dilemmas raised by monetary union. It was noted earlier that it would be unreasonable to make the executive board liable for dismissal for decisions that may have been taken by a majority constituted by national central bank governors. A similar problem could arise with accountability through explanation and justification. The executive board could find itself having to defend to the Parliament decisions that it has not itself supported in the governing council.

The second problem is that although the ECB has indicated that it will cooperate willingly in a European parliamentary process that will give it the opportunity to explain its own policy regimes, the two institutions may not always have the same concept of accountability. For a start the ECB is almost certain to insist that it should only be held politically responsible in a manner that acknowledges its narrow focus on price stability, as well as the core theoretical assumption of independent central banking that there are no long-term trade offs between inflation and the real economy. Whether the Parliament – or all sections of it – will always recognise these parameters is another matter. Another way in which the ECB and the Parliament may differ in their concept of accountability is that the ECB has shown signs of taking a Bundesbank-like position that it is answerable to the public as a whole and not to any one political institution. In the eyes of the ECB the Parliament is just one element of a wider strategy of communication and legitimation with the public. The Parliament, on the other hand, may feel that detailed scrutiny will require it to have privileged access to information on the internal policy making of the ECB. This tension has already produced one disagreement. Duisenberg has refused to disclose any documents to the Parliament that are not also made available to the public at large (author's notes of Duisenberg's appearance before EMAC, 22 September 1998). Some members of EMAC, on the other hand, have taken the view that they should enjoy certain rights to the confidential disclosure of documents, such as those produced by the working parties of the ECB, if they are to meet what they consider to be adequate standards of parliamentary review.

National parliaments

A final issue is whether national parliaments should also be included in the accountability process, as strongly urged by the French National Assembly. On the one hand, this raises the danger of a fragmented pattern of accountability clashing with the ECB's mission to make policy judgements that are appropriate for the single currency area as a whole. On the other hand, national parliaments will, to a certain extent, be involved whatever happens. First, national parliaments have established the right to pose questions to their national central bank governors, and it is national central bank governors who form the majority of the ECB governing council. As the Randzio-Plath report points out, national central banks are obliged to follow a 'monetary dialogue with national parliaments in ten out of fifteen member states' (European Parliament, 1998b). Second, national parliaments are responsible for holding their governments to account for their contribution to the intergovernmental processes of economic coordination associated with monetary union. Once the questions turn from monetary policy to fiscal coordination, national institutions outspend European ones by a ratio of 40 to 1. If some level of national parliamentary involvement is inevitable, it is important to ensure that they are informed players able to play out their own roles with an understanding of the objectives of monetary union and of how national economic policies contribute to an EMU-wide policy mix. One suggestion has therefore been that representatives of national parliaments and the European Parliament should hold joint hearings with the ECB twice a year (Pauline Green, leader of PES parliamentary group, reported in *The Economist*, 26 June 1998). The same effect could be achieved by merely inviting national parliaments to send key members of their monetary policy committees to meetings of the EP subcommittee on monetary affairs.

Chapter 15

The Place of Monetary Union in European Integration

Neofunctionalist and liberal intergovernmentalist interpretations

For a variety of reasons, early 'neofunctionalist' theories of European integration predicted that the process would begin modestly but then spill over from one policy to another until it encompassed a full system of government: technical interdependency between policies would make it hard to handle some issues at the European level but not others; pluralist politics would put pressure on parties and interest groups to compete to ensure that their own supporters shared in the benefits of integration; and, once created, European institutions would have an interest in new initiatives that expanded their own role (Haas, 1958; Lindberg, 1963; Tranholm-Mikkelsen, 1991). Although a hackneyed and crudely deterministic view of European integration, this is a useful way of framing our concluding discussion of monetary union. One reason for this is that both supporters and critics have represented monetary union as a staging post of peculiar potency in any spill-over process towards cumulative European integration. Depending on their point of view, they have bought into elements of the following scenario: a single market requires a single currency; a single currency cannot work without a single fiscal policy; a single fiscal policy, possibly including a greatly enlarged EU budget, would call for a massive centralisation of public administration and authoritative political decision making at the European level; and none of this would be acceptable without an elected European government accountable to a powerful and majoritarian European parliament.

Another reason for mentioning neofunctionalist theory is that it is often thought to explain the political behaviour of those who initiated the present bid for monetary union. Thus the Delors Commission is thought to have employed a 'Russian doll strategy':

beginning with the single market, governments would find that each new initiative in European integration contained another inside (Ross, 1995). Meanwhile the non-government interests who had organised themselves to promote the single market featured strongly in the monetary union initiative. Almost all those companies that had been members of the European Round Table joined the Association for Monetary Union in Europe. Likewise the Padoa–Schioppa theorem seemed to be an almost perfect example of governments caught in a process of technical spill-over: they could only have their single market with free movement of capital if they either relinquished what many considered to be the gain of a relatively fixed exchange rate regime or accepted that monetary policy would have to be even more closely determined by the policy leadership of just one national central bank. For most governments 'spill-over' in the direction of a single central bank was preferable to the predicted 'spill-back' to unmanaged currencies, or any 'spill-around' that would have been involved intensifying the current Bundesbank-led policy regime. To achieve their goal of a European central bank, however, they had to accept a political process in which they did not call all the shots. Since the 1970s the central bankers of the European Community had organised themselves into an increasingly coherent policy community, convergent in their professional understanding of the problems of monetary policy, and organised in the European arena by their experience of managing the EMS. Through the Delors Committee of 1988–89, the Commission effectively aligned with the central bankers to box the governments into a model of monetary union based on a single currency and a highly independent central bank.

On the other hand we have had reason at several points in this book to question the strength of the spillover effects associated with monetary union. Although it is true that a single market will always be imperfect without a single currency, there is no *a priori* reason to believe that gains from further market integration will outweigh the costs of eliminating national currencies. On the negative side of the balance sheet will be the costs of the transition, the loss of the exchange rate instrument as a means of easing economic adjustments, and the problems of a 'one size fits all' interest rate policy. The further argument that a single currency is needed to stabilise the single market rests on contested assumptions about the nature of foreign exchange markets and the likely performance of national and EU institutions under stress. Specifically, that the former are subject to imperfections that cause overshooting and prolonged misalignment, and that the latter will buckle to protectionist pressures in response to exchange rate volatility. In earlier chapters we likewise saw that monetary union may not require extensive centralisation of political authority over fiscal policy. A handful of constraints on irresponsible borrowing may be sufficient to meet the problem of unneighbourly behaviour or of a poor policy mix between monetary and fiscal policy. The majority of economic shocks are likely to affect sectors within states rather than whole states at a time, with the implication that national budgets will usually be adequate to soften the problems of adjustment (so long as they stay comfortably within the 3 per cent borrowing limit). This lessens the need for monetary union to be accompanied by an enlarged EU budget.

At first sight neofunctionalist approaches would seem to be more helpful when we turn from issues of policy assignment (the level of governance at which policies are made) to those of institutional structure. The reason for this is that monetary union does seem to be provoking some institutional changes in which 'form' is 'following function'. The most obvious example is the way in which the member governments have been forced down the road of creating a European Central Bank that is even more independent than the Bundesbank. Although this may well have been the outcome of the processes of intergovernmental bargaining in which Germany held the key veto over the formation of a monetary union, it also reflects the growing need for governments to respond to the power of markets to act as 'gendarmes de l'économie' (De Silguy, 1998, p. 91) by finding functional solutions that maximise credibility. Another example of form following function might be the way in which the rise of Ecofin – and its knock-on effects across all the other specialised councils – seems to be reshaping the European Council from an institution which has traditionally been dominated by Foreign Ministries and their policy-making styles to one in which national Financial Ministries have had to be accorded a far more significant role in the principal institution for intergovernmental decision making in the EU. A third is the manner in which the Commission has had to be assigned significant agenda-setting roles beyond any formal allocation of powers in the initial intergovernmental deal on monetary union.

However it is one thing to argue that the EU political system will have to undergo significant change if it is to meet the functional challenge of running a monetary union. It is another to accept that the cumulative effect of such changes must amount to a process of state or even nation formation at the European level. The euro may well provide the citizen with a daily reminder of the European Union as a unit of belonging and a system of rule, but it is being introduced at a time when it seems increasingly difficult for any identity to make exhaustive and exclusive loyalty claims. The provision for different countries to put their own national symbols on coins is itself symbolic of an era of cacophonous identities.

Although the final determination of this question must await the actual practice of full monetary union, there are good reasons to believe that the institutional ramifications of the project can be handled within the trend of recent decades towards the development of the EU as a *non*-state political system (Hix, 1999, pp. 2–5). In its pure form the state is a hierarchical political system for the final arbitration of all other economic and social relationships, backed by a monopoly of violence and capable of enforcing a universal and uniform application of its rules.

The reasons for believing that the EU can, in contrast, continue as a non-state political system under a single currency are as follows. First is the scepticism we have already shown towards the view that it should develop into a comprehensive economic governance structure, rather than one which just imposes selective discipline on tightly defined policy areas. Evidence of this is to be found in the view backed by the ECB itself that the central bank should operate according to a tightly defined political responsibility for price stability, with other kinds of macroeconomic and microeconomic policy remaining with governments, either acting unilaterally or in coordination with one another. Second is the evidence that monetary union will form a non-hierarchical, negotiated order. The nearest that it will come to a system of sanctions will be fines that the governments can levy on one another for persistent breach of rules on excessive deficit procedures. Otherwise a great deal of implementation will have to be negotiated on an almost continuous basis between the makers of policy and its addressees: between, for example, the executive board of the ECB and the individual national central banks which will be responsible for carrying out all market operations in the control of monetary policy; between the ECB, the

Commission, Ecofin and individual member states in the further example of using multilateral surveillance to achieve a desired policy mix. Third, and closely related to monetary union as a negotiated order, is its differential application: at the time of writing all 15 EU countries are part of the ESCB and Ecofin; 11 are full members of the single currency; two are part of the new ERM-2; and yet the single currency may be important for economic actors domiciled in 'out' countries and even in non-member states. We shall return to this theme in a moment.

Some may even go further: not only is it perfectly possible to institutionalise monetary union in a non-state political system that presents little threat to existing states; the project may also constitute one more European rescue of those older state structures. According to this view, a handful of key governments embraced monetary union because it would improve their capacity to realise *their* preferences; others went along with the initiative because it would be hard for them to pursue their goals outside a single currency formed by the larger states; and a third category adopted a 'wait and see' approach because it was still unclear whether their preferences would be served by such a project or whether they would have the power to get by on their own. In other words all political behaviour in relation to monetary union can be explained by the distribution of power and preferences between national governments (Moravcsik, 1993a), and it only happened where and when it suited those governments. This requires us to rethink any notion that monetary union is primarily driven by the goal of political system building at the European level.

But how exactly might monetary union be regarded as a 'state-supporting' strategy, rather than a 'state-replacing' one? One answer is that governments were unable to achieve the ideal of full employment with price stability so long as doubts about the credibility of national policies created 'inflationary drift'. Although they could respond to the problem by making their national central banks independent, none could be expected to enjoy as much credibility as the Bundesbank, and therefore all would have to follow the policy leadership of the latter so long as governments sought a modicum of currency stability short of full monetary union. A single currency substituted a monetary policy rule based on the average of conditions in all euro zone states for one based on the domestic circumstances of just one country. A second way in which monetary union can be regarded as a state-supporting strategy has to do with the role it played in the rebalancing of the European state system in the face of massive change in the wider international political system. By contributing to a dual multilateralisation of German power – through monetary union and political union – it allowed German reunification to proceed without creating excessive inequalities in state power in Western Europe and without upsetting Franco-German relations in particular.

Monetary union, multilevel governance and state–society relations

Between the two arguments so far reviewed there stands a third position: European policy regimes are shaped neither by a deterministic dynamic of integration nor by a static bargain between state interests, but as a series of compromises that intertwine the realisation of national preferences with an enlarged role for supranational actors, while substantially changing the domestic character of participating states and societies. Although initiatives such as monetary union would be unthinkable if they did not start life as attempts to serve the purposes of a winning coalition of governments, they go on to have two further effects: they put states under pressure to adjust the economic and social models supported by their policies; and they bring even the most unitary of constitutions within a multilevel pattern of governance in which individual government departments, and local and regional governments, are directly mobilised into the European arena, where they enjoy an unmediated relationship with supranational actors and institutions (Marks *et al.*, 1996). Let us now consider the evidence for these two effects in relation to monetary union.

The countries that make up the EU are thought to operate three rather different models of capitalism and four types of welfare state (Esping-Anderson, 1990; Rhodes, 1997, pp. 171–9). One view is that monetary union will sharpen the processes of policy competition between these models, as it will be easier for capital and companies to 'regime shop': governments will have to adjust their taxation systems, social security structures and public goods until they have achieved combinations that retain market confidence. Now this may not lead to a withering away of public services as some more apocalyptic commentators predict. Well-provided public goods and services may enhance competitiveness and become a source of attraction to international capital and countries. Nor need the intensification of regime competition lead to convergence on a kind of identikit European state. Governments could base their policy competition on differentiation, with each attempting to appeal to different kinds of capital and corporate actor. Likewise, differences in productivity will allow governments a margin of choice, with more ambitious public goods and social security systems being financed by the rewards of superior economic efficiency and performance (Tsoukalis, 1993). The intensification of economic integration associated with monetary union could even improve the capacity of the state to provide public services. The integration of capital markets – and the lowering of the risk premia that governments have to pay on borrowing and debt – could make it easier for governments to finance their activities. Meanwhile the process of regime competition would be a benign one if it did more to align public services with consumer tastes or remove the dead-weight costs of provision.

But there are two outstanding concerns. The first is that monetary union will increase the mobility of capital but not that of labour. The result is that the process of regime competition will work to align public services with the tastes of capital more than those of labour. As Phil Cerny points out, there may be a great many ways in which states can compete for international capital, stay in business and carry on doing a lot of things for their publics. But a 'competition state' will be of a very different character to a 'welfare state', whose relationship with society is grounded precisely in the claim to be able to enforce notions of social protection and social justice that may be unwelcome to markets (Cerny, 1997). A possible counterargument to all of this is that governments will continue to have two masters: the markets and the voters. The greater mobility of capital under monetary union will not stop governments from wanting to fund public services in a way that allows them to win elections.

A second concern is that the removal of the exchange rate instrument, the introduction of a 'one size fits all' interest policy and constraint of national fiscal policy by the Stability Pact will remove any role for governments in facilitating macroeconomic adjustment. The only way of adjusting to economic change will be for the capital and labour markets themselves to develop new powers of flexibility: people will have to accept greater variability in prices and wages, a 'hire and fire' culture and a greater probability of having to relocate or retrain during a career. Fixed entitlements under various European social and economic models may need to be reappraised.

But once again it is unclear how far monetary union will upset the existing patterns of social entitlement and economic adjustment. Even if governments remain within the constraints of the Stability Pact there is no reason why national fiscal policy should cease to have a role in the stabilisation of economic cycles. Given the internal diversity of most national economies, shocks under monetary union are more likely to hit different sectors and regions of individual countries rather than whole countries, thus preserving the relevance of states as political mechanisms that can aid adjustment by taxing those who are working at full capacity and aiding those who are not. The need for labour markets to speed their adjustment to change may lead to a polarisation of models – movement towards atomisation in some cases and improved consensus and communication in others – rather than universal convergence on the former solution (De Grauwe, 1995). In any case the main determinant of market flexibility in West European economies may not be labour market flexibility at all but the depth and sophistication of capital markets, which will be increased by monetary union.

Turning to the question of multilevel governance, monetary union has clearly allowed one important branch of the national governance structures – central banks – to come together at the European level in way that has given them greater autonomy within their respective national arenas. It may also be integrating national Finance Ministries into a more closely knit policy community and strengthening their position in the main intergovernmental institutions of the EU. There is also some evidence of it affecting relationships between national and subnational governments. In Germany the state governments of Bavaria and Baden Würtemberg have pointed out that the fiscal solidarity rule that requires rich German Länder to subsidise poorer ones may put the former at a disadvantage once monetary union sharpens the competition for inward investment.

The exercise of qualifying for monetary union has already had some impact on the domestic character of the West European state. Across the EU as a whole, reductions in government debt and borrowing have been equally split between taxation increases and spending cuts, and the overall impact on the 'size of the state' has been limited to a decline of 1–2 per cent in the share of GNP taken by government expenditure.

Yet even these relatively small changes may have occurred without monetary union. Public finances in the EU member states had undergone a broadly similar evolution since the mid 1970s. The proportion of government expenditure in the total GNP of the 15 member states rose from 38.7 per cent at the beginnnig of the 1970s to 52.4 per cent twenty years later, with half of this rise being accounted for by increased social security payments. This raised serious questions about the sustainability of member state finances. Total government debt increased over the same period from 35.3 per cent to 73.5 per cent of GNP, and more than 10 per cent of all official expenditure was now absorbed by interest payments on old debt rather than the provision of public services. Such a 'deadweight loss' presented a challenge to the long-term competitiveness of the European economy, not least because the 'quality' of government expenditure was being steadily eroded as debt charges and transfer payments to individuals came to crowd out spending on infrastructure and other components of productive potential. As the governments of the EU approached the limits of sustainability in their public finances, there were also doubts about their capacity to cushion their economies from future recessions by means of counter-cyclical expenditure. The challenge of meeting the convergence criteria – and then staying within the rule on excessive deficits – therefore provided member governments with a useful incentive and discipline to begin an overhaul of their public finances. As they also faced the demographic time bomb of an ageing population in the early decades of the new millennium, a sensible strategy for most governments was to aim at balanced budgets over the economic cycle. This would put government debt on a gentle downward trend with economic growth.

Monetary union, democracy and legitimacy

One reason for dissatisfaction with the debate between those who believe that European integration is shaped by the preferences of national governments and those who claim that it is sustained by its own structure of supranational and subnational interests, is that neither perspective addresses the normative issue of the right of EU institutions to make unpopular decisions that create winners and losers. For example the ECB may need to take decisions that affect the short-term balance of interests between savers approaching retirement and young people seeking their first employment. How might it defend its right to act in such a way, either against the objection that it is an unelected body, or that it is an interference in the right of countries to govern themselves?

The transfer of important economic powers to an independent central bank may be seen as increasing the democratic and legitimacy deficits of the EU just at a time when these have become salient in the politics of European integration. An alternative view is that the creation of independent authorities is a time-honoured practice even in democratic political systems, and one that finds justification in liberal democratic theory. Three such justifications are relevant to monetary union and the institution of an independent central bank. First, it may be legitimate to put selected powers beyond the democratic process where they might otherwise be used to interfere with the operation of that process. By preventing governments from manipulating the economic cycle to coincide with the political cycle, central bank independence might improve the quality of democratic choice. Second, there is always a need to balance the liberal and democratic components of liberal democracy: democratic processes may not be able to ensure various forms of individual rights protection if there is a danger of majorities abusing minorities. Such a danger may arise in relation to property rights, and the political control of money offers an example: the power to create 'surprise inflation' that effectively takes resources away from savers and gives them to debtors. Third, the delegation of powers to independent central banks might be justified if it could be shown that it is pareto improving: that it really does leave everyone in a better position to achieve their preferences. The assumption that there is no long-term trade off between unemployment and inflation is not only the economic theory upon which independent central banking is based, it is also important to its political legitimacy. For it implies that there is nothing to be gained in the long run from the political manipulation of money, and something to be lost by leaving it in the hands of those who are known to have an incentive to create inflation.

Independence for the ECB in its own specific domain of monetary management, need not preclude the need for it to mix its policy instruments with those of other actors if it is to achieve its objectives. This will in turn put it under pressure to explain itself and sustain public consent for its activities. A familiar argument is that the superior performance of the Bundesbank does not rest on the institutional apparatus of independence alone: it depends crucially on a high level of social support for its role. When a public believes that its central bank is competent – and that its role is justified even when its decisions are unwelcome – it can bring about changes in private market behaviour at far lower cost. These reassuring thoughts about ways in which policy delegation can be made publicly acceptable should not, however, blind us to the fact that the methods of legitimating EU-level decision making are fundamentally contested: what is a solution to one person is an aggravation of the problem to another. The right of an unelected authority to decide monetary policy is likely to remain a controversial issue in the monetary union, particularly when difficult decisions have to be made.

Monetary union and the EU as an international actor

Another major criticism of neofunctionalism is that it suggests integration can be explained as an *internally* generated process of spill-over. It offers no account of how it might be shaped by the *external* environment of the European Union, or conversely, of how European integration might contribute to the international system. We have seen that the present bid for monetary union was powerfully catalysed by the reunification of Germany in 1990–91 and the consequent need to find some new basis for Franco-German relations in particular. But can the initiative also be expected to change the EU's external relationships? The most relevant external issues are whether the euro will emerge as an international currency, and if so, what the effects of such a development will be. Another is whether adjustments will have to be made to the political management structures of the international economy, such as the G8 and the IMF. Beyond these specifically monetary questions, a single currency may have more general effects on the EU's development as a foreign policy actor, as well as its presence in the international system.

Predictions of the euro's emergence as an international currency often begin by pointing out that the EU national currencies are underused in global transactions and reserves relative to the EU GNP and its weight in world trade. They then go on to consider the factors that make a currency attractive to international holders, and to ask whether these are more likely to apply to the euro as a single currency than to the sum total of its component national currencies. One factor is a simple consideration of portfolio diversification. As risk averse actors will want to put their eggs in more than one basket, we might expect that there will always be a demand for more than one international currency. But money is a peculiar asset: the utility of a particular money rises with the number of people who choose to use it. Hence the dollar has held almost undivided sway as the leading international currency for most of the postwar period, and historically it has been comparatively rare for more than one currency to be widely used as an international money.

On the other hand the euro will clearly start off from a higher level of 'usability' than any of its component national moneys: it will be a single currency that can be used in 11 of the 15 countries of the EU single market. Moreover financial markets in euros are likely to be deeper than those in national currencies: they are likely to increase the number and variety of assets available to those wanting to park their money and improve liquidity for those wanting to retrieve their funds. A third consideration is that the euro will be attractive as an international currency in proportion to the probability that it will be as well managed as any conceivable alternative. People can be expected to prefer to hold a currency that will retain its value. A fourth is that the decision will partly be one for the EU countries to make themselves. A currency can only become an international currency if its issuer is prepared to allow others in the international system to accumulate substantial stocks. This means that it has to be prepared to run balance of payments deficits.

The balance of advantage in being the issuer of an international currency is, however, by no means clear cut. On the positive side are benefits of seigniorage: to some extent the issuer may be able to live beyond its means, running up liabilities that do not need to be met so long as they languish in the foreign currency reserves of other countries. Then there is a question of political power. If this is measured by the ability to make others do what they would prefer not to do, its essence in international economic management consists in being able to shift the burden of unwanted economic adjustments onto others, or at least in being able to shield one's own policies from such effects. International currency status will bring an improved position in this power equation. On the negative side, a currency may be demanded in a way that pushes up its value and reduces its international competitiveness. Large international holdings of a currency may also complicate its domestic economic management. As we shall see in a moment, they can also bring unwelcome political responsibilities.

The question of whether the euro will become an international currency will, in short, be an intensely political one. It may be contentious within the EU as well as outside it. While the euro has often been sold to the French public as a means of giving the EU equality with the dollar in the international economy, the German public may be more cautious of an ambition that may not always be consistent with price stability. There may also be a conflict of interests between sectors – such as financial markets – that could benefit from international currency status and those – such as manufacturing – with more to fear from an overvalued parity. On the other hand an aspiration to international status could provide a further political incentive for respecting the independence of the ECB. In a world in which financial assets have to compete for credibility, the euro will be at a competitive disadvantage to the dollar if there is reason to believe that the ECB will not be at least as well placed as the US Federal Reserve to protect the value of its currency. An aspiration to global status would also make the issue of membership of the euro more important: the more countries that are included in the euro, the wider will be its usage within Europe, and the more attractive it will therefore be to outsiders. In particular the presence of the London financial markets within the euro area could well be decisive to the rapid development of its tradability.

The arrival of the euro has raised difficult issues about the structure of global economic organisations. The responsibility of the IMF for the stability of the international financial system will clearly require the active cooperation of those responsible for European monetary union. This means that a highly anomalous situation could develop: the statute of the IMF only allows states to be members; but in the event of the euro developing as an international currency the IMF may need to work closely with non-state institutions of the euro zone (the ECB and the Commission). Even before the introduction of the single currency the EU countries contributed 30 per cent of the IMF's financial quota, and thus held a corresponding share of voting rights. Some provision has been made for this institutionally awkward situation: the government which holds the presidency of the Council of Ministers will have responsibility for representing the EU' position in IMF committees; and the Commission will collaborate with the IMF secretariat and have observer rights in committees. These arrangements may well have knock-on effects on the internal organisation of monetary union, as they will almost certainly require a high level of collaboration between the Council, the Commission and the ECB, notably to meet obligations under the IMF's mutual surveillance procedure (De Silguy, 1998, pp. 376–80).

In the case of G8 meetings things may be trickier still. Just four member countries – France, Germany, Italy and the UK – have permanent seats. The Luxembourg European Council of December 1997 passed a resolution committing members to take 'full account of the interests of the Union in international economic bodies' and the Commission president does have observer rights at the G8. But it is unlikely that the small members will be fully confident of their representation by the larger ones.

A final theme is the impact of monetary union on the wider evolution of the EU as a foreign policy actor. No political body has exclusive control over the definition of its role in the international system: this is conditioned by the expectations of others as much as its own preferences. An unintended consequence of previous efforts at economic integration has been to ratchet up the responsibilities that outsiders have expected the EU to assume for international problems. Thus the unexpected success of the single market programme at the end of the 1980s conditioned the assumption of the Bush administration that the EC was in a position to take the lead responsibility for stabilising Eastern Europe and bringing it within the new world order. But this creates a problem: foreign policy expectations that are conditioned by economic successes do not reflect the EU's political capacity to undertake international tasks (Hill, 1993). There is a clear risk that monetary union will lead to a repeat of this mistake.

On the other hand an important source of such foreign policy influence as the EU does enjoy lies in its power to grant or withhold access to its 'prosperity sphere'. Monetary union may sharpen this as an incentive for cultivating relationships with the EU and provide new sources of leverage by which access to the economic fruits of European integration can be extended to outsiders. It is possible, for example, to see the internationalisation of the euro as playing a role in the development of the EU's relationship with Eastern Europe. As emerging economies, countries of the latter region have often found it difficult to establish a floor for fluctuations in their currencies and thus insulate their development – and integration into the international economy – against destabilising crises of confidence. The euro could provide them with a useful currency peg and a more plentiful supply of foreign exchange reserves. Access to support of this kind could likewise be used as a foreign policy instrument in the EU's efforts to stabilise the transition in the East, and to prepare for the enlargement process. However one further external issue will be the attitude of the US administration to the development of the euro as an international currency: in order to prevent any sudden dislocation of US interests or disruption of the wider international financial system, it may be necessary for the US and European authorities to coordinate their responses to any switch of market demand from dollar to euro holdings.

Monetary union and flexible integration

It is a mistake to regard monetary union as an unambiguous step towards further European integration: it has always had the potential to divide the EU as well as unite it. The point is well made by the economist and MEP Paul De Grauwe:

> Politically, it would maximise conflicts over membership: those countries left out would not readily agree to a union from which they were barred. Economically, it would also create a divide: those left outside EMU would face greater volatility in their exchange rates than those inside. This would make trade more difficult in the single market, and might even reverse the process of European economic integration (De Grauwe, 1995).

Monetary integration has probably done more than anything else to shatter the convention of the uniform *acquis communautaire* and it is likely to continue to do so for the foreseeable future. On the one hand the founding membership of 11 countries has produced a far wider monetary union than the average estimates of just two years earlier that only eight or nine countries would qualify. This has averted the possibility of the EU membership being divided evenly into 'ins' and 'outs'. On the other hand the isolation of the 'outs' has been increased by the large founding membership. In addition, institutional solutions to the problem of insider–outsider relations are likely to be complicated by the way in which the 'outs' fall into three categories: those committed to joining once they are judged to have met the criteria (Greece and Sweden); those that have 'opt-outs', with the result that immensely difficult domestic choices still have to be made before participation is possible (Denmark and the UK); and those that are inside the ERM (Denmark and Greece) and those that are not (Sweden and the UK).

In addition, monetary union can be expected to complicate the process of enlargement. Although, as we have seen, some applicant countries may find the euro to be a useful source of currency stabilisation, there is no avoiding the fact that monetary union dramatically increases the 'integration threshold' that any country will have to cross to secure membership of the EU. The 1995 enlargements established the principle that derogations from automatic and obligatory transition to stage three (on satisfaction of the criteria) would not be granted to new entrants. There will be no more opt-outs after Denmark and the UK. This means that countries entering the EU – most at a far lower level of economic and political development – will have just a few years to adopt a complex set of policy regimes that existing members have been able to absorb at a more leisurely pace. Another likely implication of enlargement is reduction of the probability that the mismatch between membership of the EU and of the single currency will be a temporary one. Any decision by the present 'outs' to join stage three may well be counterbalanced by the admission of new member states at the beginning of a long transition to full membership of the monetary union. One issue is that of timing: how to dovetail the monetary union and enlargement processes to preserve the numerical preponderance of single currency 'ins' over 'outs'. However by far the most important problem will be this: enlargement is seen as a multiwave process in which the EU will absorb a handful of new members every few years until it has a maximum likely membership of around 30. The question of how to institutionalise stable relations between single currency 'ins' and 'outs' will therefore be a continuing one. To recapitulate from previous chapters, the following arrangements have thus far been put in place.

First, all countries will be members of the European System of Central Banks, and subject to certain common treaty obligations. Second, all member states will be members of Ecofin, and therefore all will participate in the mutual surveillance procedures. 'Outs' will not, however, be bound by the rules of the Stability Pact, though they will, curiously, have some role in determining its operation. Their exact rights of access to the Euro Council are unclear, and will probably only emerge through custom and practice.

Third, there will be an ERM2 in which 'out' currencies will be linked to the euro in fluctuation bands. Indeed one interpretation of the treaty is that this is a legal requirement if 'outs' are to be given the opportunity of qualifying for stage three. Given the enormous weight that the euro will have in the ERM2, it could be far more asymmetric than its predecessor. On the other hand it is likely to be based on the same wide and permissive bands which have characterised the ERM since 1993. The argument that has been made for an ERM2 is that it will help the EU to cope with the geographical mismatch between the single market and the euro zone by limiting currency volatility between the two. There is, however, an important counterargument, which has been summarised as follows. What is needed to prevent dislocation to the single market is real exchange rate stability (steady exchange rates after allowing for inflation). In targeting nominal exchange rates (those without any adjustment for inflation), the ERM can even produce divergence between the inflation performance of the member states. It would be better, therefore, for a European Union of many different currency regimes to concentrate on agreeing inflation targets in the Council of Ministers (evidence of the governor of the Bank of England to House of Lords Select Committee on the EU, June 1996).

So to conclude, monetary union is likely to be strikingly different from existing federal models for the management of a single currency. Unlike its main counterparts – those in Germany and the United States – it will be based in a supranational political system rather than a national one. It will also be introduced to a pattern of multilevel governance that is far less settled and more contested. This could well affect relationships between the ECB and the national central banks, as well as attempts to institutionalise macroeconomic coordination between the member states. A final complication that has been the subject of this present section is that other systems do not have to find institutional solutions to the problem of differential integration: the system may be federal, but the relationship between the whole and its parts is a fairly uniform one. Monetary union has probably confronted the EU with its greatest challenge of flexible integration to date. At the heart of this problem has always been the fundamental choice between institutionalising flexible integration as a temporary phenomenon in which there is an expectation that all members will eventually converge on full membership of the policy regime in question (the multispeed approach), and conceding that differences may become permanent (the two-tier approach). Countries without a derogation from stage three are clearly expected to fall into the former category, though we have seen that the process may be more voluntaristic in practice. The institutional mechanisms for managing 'insider–outsider' relations could pan out either way: it is unclear how far common membership of an ERM2, the ESCB and the mutual surveillance procedure will produce economic convergence and policy socialisation, or whether exclusion from the full ECB and Euro Council will produce tensions or incentives for the 'outs' to work for full membership of the monetary union.

Bibliography

Alesina, A. and Bayoumi, T. (1996) 'The Costs and Benefits of Fiscal Rules: Evidence from U.S. States', *NBER Working Paper*, no. 5614. Cambridge, Mass., NBER.

Alesina, A. and Grilli, V. (1992) 'The European Central Banks Reshaping Monetary Politics in Europe', in M. Canzoneri, V. Grilli, and P. Masson. (eds) *Establishing a Central Bank: Issues on European Monetary Union and Lessons from The US.* Cambridge, Cambridge University Press.

Allsopp, C. and Vines, D. (1996) 'Fiscal Policy and EMU', *National Institute Economic Review*, October.

Amato, G. (1988) 'Un Motore per lo SME', *Il Sole 24 Ore*, 25 February 1988.

Anderson, J. and Goodman, J. (1993) 'Mars or Minerva? A United Gemany in a Post-Cold War Europe', in R. Keohane, J. Nye and S. Hoffmann (eds), *After the Cold War: Politics and Institutions in Europe.* Cambridge, Mass., pp. 23–62.

Andrews, D. and Willett, T. (1997) 'Financial Interdependence and the State: International Monetary Relations at Century's End', *International Organisation*, vol. 51, no. 3, pp. 479—511.

Arrow, K. (1963) *Social Choice and Individual Values.* New York, Wiley.

Arrowsmith, J. and Taylor, T. (1996) 'Moving Towards EMU: The Challenges Ahead', *National Institute Economic Review*, October.

Artis, M. and Winkler, B. (1998) 'The Stability Pact: Safeguarding the Credibility of the European Central Bank', *National Institute Economic Review*, no. 163, pp. 87–98.

Association for the Monetary Union of Europe (1990) *A Strategy for the ECU.* London, Kogan Page.

Association for the Monetary Union of Europe (1994) *Preparing for the Transition to the Single Currency, a Report on the Practical Implications for Banks and Businesses.* Paris.

Attali, J. (1995) Verbatim III: *Chronique des années 1988–1991, Deuxième Partie.* Paris, Fayard.

Baldwin, R. (1991) 'On the Microeconomics of European Monetary Union', *European Economy*, Special Issue, vol. 19, p. 35.

Balladur, E. (1988) *La Construction Monétaire Européenne.* Paris, Ministère d'Économie et des Finances.

Bank of England (1990) 'The Hard ECU in Stage 2: Operational Requirements', mimeo. London, Bank of England.

Bark, D. and Gress, D. (1992) *Histoire De L'Allemagne 1945–91*, Paris, Laffont.

Barrell, R. (ed.) (1992) *Economic Convergence and Monetary Union in Europe*. London, Sage.

Barro, R. and Gordon, D. (1983) 'Rules, Discretion and Reputation in a Model of Monetary Policy', *Journal of Monetary Economics*, vol. 12, pp. 101–21.

Bayoumi, T. (1994) 'A Formal Model of Optimum Currency Areas', *IMF Staff Papers*, no. 41. Washington, DC, IMF.

Bayoumi, T. and Eichengreen, B. (1994) 'Shocking Aspects of European Monetary Integration', in F. Giavazzi and F. Tores (eds), *Adjustment and Growth in the European Monetary Union*. Cambridge, CEPR/Cambridge University Press.

Bayoumi, T. and Eichengreen, B. (1996) *Operationalising the Theory of Optimum Currency Areas*, CEPR paper no. 1480. London, Centre for Economic Policy Research.

Bayoumi, T. and Eichengreen, B. (1997) 'Ever Closer to Heaven, An Optimum Currency Area Index for European Countries', *European Economic Review*, vol. 41.

Bayoumi, T. and Masson, P. R. (1994) 'Fiscal Flows in the United States and Canada: Lessons for Monetary Union in Europe', *CEPR Discussion Paper* no. 1057. London, Centre for Economic Policy Research.

Beetham, D. and Lord, C. (1998) *Legitimacy and the European Union*. London, Addison, Wesley and Longman.

Begg, D., De Grauwe, P., Giavazzi, F., Uhlig, H. and Wyplosz, C. (1998) *The ECB: Safe At Any Speed?* London, Centre for Economy Policy Research.

Begg, D., Giavazzi, F., Von Hagen, J. and Wyplosz, C. (1997) *EMU Getting the End Game Right*. London, Centre for Economic Policy Research.

Begg, D. and Wyplosz, C. (1987) 'Why the EMS? Dynamic Games and the Equilibrium Policy Regime', in R. Bryant and R. Portes (eds), *Global Macroeconomics: Policy Conflict and Co-operation*. New York, St. Martin's Press.

Berger, H. and De Haan, J. (1997) *A State Within the State: An Event Study of the Bundesbank*. Munich, CES.

Bergsten C. (1998) *Weak Dollar, Strong Euro?* London, Centre for European Reform.

Bernhard, W. and Leblang, D. (1999) 'Domestic Institutions and Exchange Rate Commitments', *International Organisation*, vol. 53, no. 1, pp. 71–97.

Bini-Smaghi, L. and Vori, S. (1993) *Rating the EC as an Optimal Currency Area: is it worse than the US?*, Rome, Banca d'Italia Discussion Paper, no. 1987. Rome, Banca d'Italia.

Bofinger, P. (1992) 'Commentary on Alesina and Grilli', in M. Canzoneri. V. Grilli. and P. Masson (eds), *Establishing a Central Bank: Issues on European Monetary Union and Lessons from the US*. Cambridge, Cambridge University Press.

Boltho, A. (1994) 'A Comparison of Regional Differentials in the European Community and the United States', in J. Mortensen (ed.), *Improving Economic and Social Cohesion in the European Community*. New York, St Martin's Press.

Branson, W. (1994) 'German reunification, the breakdown of the EMS, and the path to Stage Three', in D. Cobham (ed.), *European Monetary Upheavals*. Manchester, Manchester University Press.

Briault, C., Haldane, A. and King, M. (1996) *Independence and Accountability*, Working Paper no. 49. London, Bank of England.

Britton, A. and Mayes, D. (1992) *Achieving Monetary Union in Europe*. London, Sage.

Buiter, W. (1999a) 'Alice in Euroland', *Journal of Common Market Studies*, vol. 37, no. 2, pp. 181–209.

Buiter, W. (1999b) 'Price of Independence', *Financial Times*, 17 June 1999.

Buiter, W., Corsetti, G. and Roubini, N. (1993) 'Excessive Deficits. Sense and Nonsense in the Treaty of Maastricht', *Economic Policy*, vol. 16, pp. 57–100.

Bundesverfassungsgericht (1993) 'Maastricht-Urteil', *Juristische Zeitschrift*, vol. 22, pp. 1100–12.

Buti, M. and Sapir, A. (1998) *Economic Policy in EMU*. Oxford, Clarendon Press.

Calleo, D. (1982) *The Imperious Economy*. Cambridge, Mass., Harvard University Press.

Canzoneri, M., Grilli, V. and Masson, P. (1992) (eds) *Establishing a Central Bank: Issues on European Monetary Union and Lessons from the US*. Cambridge, Cambridge University Press.

Ceccini, P. with Catinat, M. and Jacquemin, A. (1988) *The European Challenge 1992: The Benefits of a Single Market*. Aldershot, Gower.

Cerny, P. (1997) 'The dynamics of political globalisation', *Government and Opposition*, vol. 32, no. 2, pp. 251–74.

Chennells, L. and Griffiths, R. (1997) *Taxing Profits in a Changing World*. London, Institute for Fiscal Studies.

Cobham, D. (ed.) (1994) *European Monetary Upheavals*. Manchester, Manchester University Press.

Cole, A. (1997) *François Mitterrand: A Study in Political Leadership*. London, Routledge.

Connelly, B. (1995) *The Rotten Heart of Europe: The Dirty War for Europe's Money*. London, Faber and Faber.

Council of Ministers of the European Community (1978) 'Resolution of the European Council on the Establishment of the European Monetary System'. Brussels, Council of Ministers.

Council of Ministers of the European Union (1998) 'Joint Communiqué on the Determination of the Irreversible Conversion Rates for the Euro', 2 May. Brussels, Council of Ministers.

Cowles, M. (1995) 'The European Round Table of Industrialists: The Strategic Player in European Affairs', in J. Greenwood (ed.), *European Case Book on Business Alliances,* Hemel Hempstead, Prentice Hall, pp. 225–36.

Cukierman, A. (1992) *Central Bank Strategy, Credibility and Independence.* Cambridge, Mass., MIT Press.

Currie, D. (1997) *The Pros and Cons of EMU.* London, Economist Intelligence Unit.

Currie, D. and Whitley, J. (1994) 'What route to European Monetary Integration?', in D. Cobham (ed.), *European Monetary Upheavals.* Manchester, Manchester University Press.

De Grauwe, P. (1994a) *The Economics of Monetary Integration.* Oxford, Oxford University Press.

De Grauwe, P. (1994b) 'Towards Monetary Union without the EMS', *Economic Policy,* vol. 18, pp. 149–74.

De Grauwe, P. (1995) 'An easier road to monetary union', *Financial Times,* 17 October 1995.

De Grauwe, P. (1996) The Economics of Monetary Integration. Oxford, Oxford University Press.

De Grauwe, P. and Vanhaverbeke, W. (1993) 'Is Europe an Optimum Currency Area?', in P. Masson and M. Taylor (eds), *Policy Issues in the Operation of Currency Unions.* Cambridge, Cambridge University Press.

De la Dehesa, G. and Krugman, P. (1992) *EMU and the Regions,* Occasional Paper no. 39, Washington DC, Group of Thirty.

De Silguy, Y.-T. (1998), *L'Euro,* Paris, Livres de Poches.

Dehousse, R. (1995) *Institutional Reform in the European Community: are there Alternatives to the Majoritarian Avenue?,* EUI Working Paper, Florence, EUI.

Dehousse, R. (1997) 'European Integration and the Nation-State', in M. Rhodes, P. Heywood and V. Wright (eds), *Developments in West European Politics.* London, Macmillan, pp. 37–57.

Delors, J. (1994) *L'Unité d'un Homme.* Paris, Odile Jacob.

Deutsche Bundesbank (1998) *Opinion of the Central Bank Council Concerning Convergence in the European Union in view of Stage III of Economic and Monetary Union.* Frankfurt, Deutsche Bundesbank.

Dornbusch, R. (1988) 'The EMS, the dollar and the Yen' in F. Giavazzi., S. Nicossi and M. Miller (eds), *The European Monetary System.* Cambridge, Cambridge University Press, pp. 23–41.

Dornbusch, R. (1990) 'Problems of European Monetary Unification' in A. Giovanni. and C. Mayer (eds), *European Financial Integration.* Cambridge, Cambridge University Press.

Dornbusch, R., Favero, C. and Giavazzi, F. (1998) 'Immediate Challenges for the European Central Bank', *Economic Policy,* vol. 26.

Dowd, K. and Greenaway, K. (1993) 'Currency Competition, Network Externalities and Switching Costs: Towards an Alternative View of Optimum Currency Areas', *Economic Journal,* vol. 103.

Duff, A. (1997) *The Amsterdam Treaty. Text and Commentary.* London, Federal Trust.

Dyson, K. (1994) *Elusive Union: The Process of Economic and Monetary Union in Europe.* London, Longman.

Eichengreen, B. (1990) 'One Money for Europe? Lessons from U.S. Currency Union', *Economic Policy,* vol. 10.

Eichengreen, B. (1991) 'Is Europe an Optimum Currency Area', NBER Working Paper no. 3759. Cambridge, Mass., NBER.

Eichengreen, B. (1992) 'Designing a Central Bank for Europe: A Cautionary Tale from the Early Years of the Federal Reserve System', in M. Canzoneri, V. Grilli and P. Masson (eds), *Establishing a Central Bank: Issues on European Monetary Union and Lessons from the US.* Cambridge, Cambridge University Press.

Eichengreen, B. (1993) 'Labour Markets and European Monetary Unification', in P. Masson and M. Taylor (eds), *Policy Issues in the Operation of Currency Unions,* Cambridge, Cambridge University Press.

Eichengreen, B. and Frieden, J. (eds) (1994) *The Political Economy of European Monetary Integration.* Boulder, CO, Westview.

Eichengreen, B. and Von Hagen, J. (1995) *Fiscal Policy and Monetary Union: Federalism, Fiscal Restrictions and the No-Bail Out Rule,* CEPR Discussion Paper no. 1247. London, CEPR.

Eichengreen, B. and Wyplosz, C. (1998) 'The Stability Pact: more than a minor nuisance', *Economic Policy,* vol. 26.

Eiffinger, S. and de Haan, J. (1996) 'The Political Economy of Central Bank Independence', *Special Papers in International Economics 19.* Princeton, NJ, Princeton University Press.

Eizenga, W. (1987) 'The Independence of the Deutsche Bundesbank and the Netherlands Bank with Regard to Monetary Policy: Comparative Study' *SUERF Papers on Monetary Policy and Financial Systems 2.* Tilburg, SUERF.

Esping-Andersen, G. (1990) *The Three Worlds of Welfare Capitalism.* Princeton, NJ, Princeton University Press.

European Central Bank (1998a) *The Single Monetary Policy in Stage Three.* Frankfurt, ECB General Documentation.

European Central Bank (1998b) *The President's Statement, 13th October 1998.* Frankfurt, ECB.

European Commission (1957) *The Treaty of Rome.* Luxembourg, European Commission.

European Commission (1962) *Action Programme of the Community for the Second Stage,* Brussels, European Commission.

European Commission (1970) 'Report to the Council and Commission on the Realisation by Stages of Economic and Monetary Union in the Community', *OJ* C 136/1, 8 October 1970.

European Commission (1988) 'Presidency Conclusions from Hannover European Council', Bulletin 6.

European Commission (1989) *Committee for the study of Economic and Monetary Union* (the Delors Report). Luxembourg, Office for Official Publications.

European Commission (1990) 'One Market, One Money', *European Economy*, Luxembourg, no. 44.

European Commission (1992) Treaty of European Union.

European Commission (1995) *One Currency for Europe, Green Paper on the Practical Arrangements for the Introduction of the Single Currency.* Luxembourg, Office for Official Publications of the EC.

European Commission (1996), *European Economy*, vol. 62.

European Commission (1997a) *External Aspects of Economic and Monetary Union*, Euro Paper no. 1. Brussels, DG II.

European Commission (1997b) *Accounting for the Introduction of the Euro*, Euro Paper no. 2. Brussels, DG XV.

European Commission (1997c) *Legal Framework for the Use of the Euro – Questions and Answers on the Euro Regulations*, Euro Paper no. 2. Brussels, DG II.

European Commission (1997d) *The Impact of the Introduction of the Euro on Capital Markets*, Euro Paper no. 3. Brussels, DG II.

European Commission (1997e) *Legal Framework for the Use of the Euro*, Euro Paper no. 4. Brussels, DG II.

European Commission (1997f) *The Introduction of the Euro – Compilation of Community Legislation and Related Documents*, Euro Paper no. 7. Brussels, DG II.

European Commission (1997g) *Practical Aspects of the Introduction of the Euro*, Euro Paper no. 8. Brussels, DG II.

European Commission. (1997h) *Impact of the Changeover to the Euro on Community Policies, Institutions and Legislation*, Euro Paper no. 9. Brussels, DG II.

European Commission (1998a) *The Legal Implications of the European Monetary Union Under U.S. and New York Law*, by Niall Lenihan, Euro Paper no. 15. Brussels, European Commission.

European Commission (1998b) *Euro 1999, Report on Progress Towards Convergence and Recommendation with a View to the Transition to the Third Stage of Economic and Monetary Union, Part 1 Recommendation, Part 2 Report.* Luxembourg, Office for Official Publications of the EC.

European Monetary Institute (1997a) *The Single Monetary Policy in Stage III: the Operational Framework.* Frankfurt, EMI.

European Monetary Institute (1997b) *Elements of the Monetary Policy Strategy of the ESCB in Stage III of EMU.* Frankfurt, EMI.

European Monetary Institute (1998) *Convergence Report, Report Required by Article 109J of the Treaty Establishing the European Community.* Frankfurt, EMI.

European Parliament (1998a) *La Monnaie Unique et le Parlement Européen.* Luxembourg, Parlement Européen.

European Parliament (1998b) 'Resolution on democratic accountability in the third phase of EMU' (the Randzio-Plath report). Brussels, European Parliament.

European Parliament (1998c) 'Nominations to the Executive Board of the European Central Bank: European Parliament Confirmation Hearings', 7–8 May. Brussels, European Parliament.

European Parliament (1998d) *The Role of the Euro as an International Currency*, Working Paper Economics, no. 101. Luxembourg, European Parliament Directorate General for Research.

European Parliament (1999) *Rules of Procedure.* Brussels, European Parliament.

Fatas, A. (1998) 'Does EMU Need a Fiscal Federation?' in D. Begg, J. von Hagen, C. Wyplosz and K. Zimmermann (eds), *EMU: Prospects and Challenges for the Euro.* London, Blackwell, CEPR.

Fischer, S. (1996) 'Why Are Central Banks Pursuing Long Run Price Stability?', in Federal Reserve Bank of Kansas City, *Achieving Price Stability.* Kansas City, Federal Reserve Bank of Kansas.

Folkerts-Landau and Garber, P. (1992) 'The ECB: A Bank or a Monetary Policy Rule?' in M.Canzoneri, V. Grilli, and P. Masson (eds), *Establishing a Central Bank: Issues on European Monetary Union and Lessons from the US.* Cambridge, Cambridge University Press.

Forster, A. (1999) *Britain and the Maastricht Negotiations.* London, Macmillan.

Frattiani, M. and von Hagen, J. (1992) *The European Monetary System and European Monetary Union.* Boulder, CO, Westview Press.

Fritsch-Bournazel, R. (1991) *L'Allemagne Unie Dans La Nouvelle Europe*, Paris, Editions Complexe.

Gaddum, E. (1994) *Die Deutsche Europapolitik in den 80er Jahren: Interessen, Konflikte und Entscheidungen der Regierung Kohl.* Paderborn.

Garton-Ash, T. (1993) *In Europe's Name: Germany and the Divided Continent.* London, Jonathan Cape.

Gilpin, R. (1987) *The Political Economy of International Relations.* Princeton, NJ, Princeton University Press.

Goodhart, C. (1991) 'The Draft Statute of the European System of Central Banks', *Special Paper 37, Financial Markets Group.* London School of Economics, London.

Goodhart, C. (1995) *The Central Bank and the Financial System.* London, Macmillan.

Goodman, J. (1992) *Monetary Sovereignty: The Politics of Central Banking in Western Europe*. Ithaca, NY, Cornell University Press.

Grant, C. (1994) *Jacques Delors: Inside the House that Jacques Built*. London, Nicholas Brealey.

Greenwood, J. (1997) *Representing Interests in the European Union*. London, Macmillan.

Greenwood, M. (1975) 'Research on Internal Migration in the United States', *Journal of Economic Literature*, vol. 13.

Gros, D. (1990) 'Seigniorage and EMS Discipline' in P. De Grauwe and L. Papademos (eds), *The European Monetary System in the 1990s*. London, Longman.

Gros, D. (1995) 'Excessive Deficits and Debts', CEPS Paper 65. Brussels, Centre for European Policy Studies.

Gros, D. (1996a) 'A Reconsideration of the Optimum Currency Area Approach: The Role of External Shocks and Labour Mobility', *National Institute Economic Review*, vol. 4.

Gros, D. (1996b) 'Towards Economic and Monetary Union: Problems and Prospects', CEPS Paper no. 65. Brussels, Centre for European Policy Studies.

Gros, D. and Lannoo, K. (1996) 'A Passage to the Euro', CEPS Working Party Report 6 July, CEPS Paper no. 65. Brussels, Centre for European Policy Studies.

Gros, D. and Thygesen, N. (1992) *European Monetary Integration: From the European Monetary System to European Monetary Union*. London, Longman.

Gros. D. and Thygesen, N. (1998) *European Monetary Integration*, 2nd edn. London, Longman.

Haas, E. (1958) *The Uniting of Europe: Political, Social and Economic Forces*. London, Stevens and Sons.

Haas, E. (1964) *Beyond the Nation State*. Stanford, CA, Stanford University Press.

Haas, P. (1992) 'Epistemic Communities and International Policy Co-ordination', *International Organisation*, vol. 46, no. 1, pp. 1–35.

Harden, I. (1993) 'The European Central Bank and the Role of National Central Banks in Economic and Monetary Union', in K. Gretschmann (ed.), *Economic and Monetary Union: Implications for National Policy Makers*. Dordrecht, Martinus Nijhoff.

Hartmann, P. (1996) *The Role of the Euro as an International Currency*, CEPS Research Report, no. 20. Brussels, Centre for European Policy Studies.

Hayes-Renshaw, F. and Wallace, H. (1997) *The Council of Ministers*. London, Macmillan.

Helleiner, E. (1995) 'Explaining the Globalization of Financial Markets: Bringing States Back', *Review of International Political Economy*, vol. 2, pp. 315–41.

Helpman, E. and Krugman, P. (1985) *Market structure and foreign trade: increasing returns, imperfect competition and the international economy.* Cambridge, Mass., MIT Press.

Henning, C. (1994) *Currencies and Politics in the United States, Germany and Japan.* Washington, DC, Institute for International Economics.

Héritier, A. (1997) 'Policy-making by subterfuge: interest accommodation, innovation and substitute democratic legitimation in Europe – perspectives from distinct policy areas', *Journal of European Public Policy*, vol. 4, no. 2, pp. 171–89.

Hill, C. (1993) 'The capability-expectations gap, or conceptualising Europe's international role', *Journal of Common Market Studies*, vol. 31, no. 3, pp. 305–28.

Hix, S. (1998) 'The Study of the European Union II: the "new governance" agenda and its rival', *Journal of European Public Policy*, vol. 5, no. 1, pp. 38–65.

Hix, S. (1999) *The Political System of the European Union.* London, Macmillan.

Hix, S. and Lord, C. (1997) *Political Parties in the European Union.* London, Macmillan.

HM Treasury (1989) 'An Evolutionary Approach to Economic and Monetary Union'. London, HMSO.

Hoffmann, S. (1966) 'Obstinate or Obsolete? The Fate of the Nation State and the Case of Western Europe', *Daedalus*, vol. 95, no. 3, pp. 882–97.

Hogg, S. and Hill, J. (1995) *Too Close to Call.* London, Little, Brown.

Issing. O. (1998) 'Open for business', *Financial Times*, 22 September 1998.

Issing, O. (1999) 'The Eurosystem: Transparent and Accountable or "Willem in Euroland"', *Journal of Common Market Studies*, vol. 37, no. 3, pp. 503–19.

Jachtenfuchs, M. (1997) 'Democracy and Governance in the European Union', *European Integration Online Papers*, vol. 1, no. 2, http://eiop.or.at/eiop/texte/1997-002a.htm.

Jachtenfuchs, M. and Kohler-Koch, B. (eds) (1996) *Europäische Integration*, Opladen, Leske und Budrich.

Jacquet, P. (1998) 'EMU: a worthwhile gamble', *International Affairs*, vol. 74, no. 1.

Jacquémin, A. and Sapir, A. (1989) *The European Internal Market: Trade and Competition*, Oxford, Oxford University Press.

Jenkins, R. (1989) *European Diary 1977–81.* London, Collins.

Joerges, C. and Neyer, J.(1997) 'Transforming strategic interaction into deliberative problem-solving: European comitology in the foodstuffs sector', *Journal of European Public Policy*, vol. 4, no. 4, pp. 609–25.

Kenen, P. (1995) *Economic and Monetary Union in Europe, Moving Beyond Maastricht.* Cambridge, Cambridge University Press.

Kenen, P. (ed.) (1996) *Making EMU Happen, Problems and Proposals: Symposium Essays in International Finance 199*, August. Princeton, NJ, Princeton University Press.

Keohane, R. (1984) *After Hegemony: Cooperation and Discord in the World Political Economy*. Princeton, NJ, Princeton University Press.

Kielmansegg, P. (1996) 'Integration und Demokratie', in M. Jachtenfuchs, and B. Kohler-Koch (eds) *Europäische Integration*, Opladen: Leske und Budrich.

Kingdon, J. (1995) *Agendas, Alternatives and Public Policies*. New York, HarperCollins.

Kohl, H. (1991) *Bilanzen und Perspektiven: Regierungspolitik 1989–91*. Bonn, Presse und Informationsamt der Bundesregierung.

Kohler-Koch, B. (1996) 'Catching up with Change: the Transformation of Governance in the European Union', *Journal of European Public Policy*, vol. 3, no. 3, pp. 359–80.

Krugman, P. (1991) *Geography and Trade*. Cambridge, Mass., MIT Press.

Kydland, F. and Prescott, E. (1977) 'Rules rather than Discretion: The Inconsistency of Optimal Plans', *Journal of Political Economy*, vol. 85.

Lannoo, K. (1998) *From 1992 to EMU, The Implications for Prudential Supervision*. Brussels, Centre for European Policy Studies.

Lawson, N. (1992) *The View From No 11: Memoirs of a Tory Radical*. London, Bantam.

Levitt, M. (1994) 'Introducing a Single Currency', in *The Single Currency, An Immense Challenge for Banks, Conference Proceedings, European Financial Management Association*. Paris, EFMA.

Levitt, M. (1995) *Economic and Monetary Union, Stage III: The Issues for Banks*. London, Centre for the Study for Financial Innovation.

Levitt M. (1997) *Fixing Conversion Rates at the Start of EMU*. London, Centre for the Study for Financial Innovation.

Lindberg, L. (1963) *The Political Dynamics of European Integration*. Oxford, Oxford University Press.

Lohmann, S. (1997) 'Political Accountability in an Economic and Monetary Union', *Aussenwirtschaft*, vol. 52, pp. 159–77.

Ludlow, P. (1982) *The Making of the European Monetary System*. London, Butterworth.

MacDougall, D. (1997) 'Report of the Study Group on the Role of Public Finance in European Integration'. Brussels, Commission of the European Communities.

McKay, D. (1999) 'The Political Sustainability of Monetary Union', *British Journal of Political Science*, vol. 29, pp. 463–85.

Majone, G. (1996a) 'Regulatory legitimacy', in G. Majone (ed.), *Regulating Europe*. London, Routledge, pp. 284–301.

Majone, G. (1996b) in J. Richardson (ed.), *European Union: Power and Policy-Making*. London, Routledge.

March, J. and Olsen, J. (1984) 'The New Institutionalism: Organisational Factors in Political Life', *American Political Science Review*, vol. 78, pp. 734–49.

Marks, G., Hooghe, L. and Blank, K. (1996) 'European Integration from the 1980s: State-Centric vs Multi-Level Governance', *Journal of Common Market Studies*, vol. 34, no. 3, pp. 341–78.

Marsh, D. (1992) *The Bundesbank: The Bank that Rules Europe*. London, Heinemann.

Masson, P., Krueger, T. and Turtleboom, B. (1998) *EMU and the International Monetary System*. Washington, DC, International Monetary Fund.

McNamara, K. (1998) *The Currency of Ideas: Monetary Politics in the European Union*. Ithaca, NY, Cornell University Press.

Meade, J. and Weale, M. (1995) 'Monetary Union and the Assignment Problem', *Scandinavian Journal of Economics*, vol. 97.

Melitz, J. (1997) *Some Cross-Country Evidence About Debt, Deficits and the Behaviour of Monetary and Fiscal Authorities*, CEPR Discussion Paper, no. 1653. London, Centre for Economic Policy Research.

Milesi, G. (1998) *Le Roman de l'Euro*. Paris, Hachette.

Milward, A. (1992) *The European Rescue of the State*. London, Routledge.

Minford, P. (1994) in D. Cobham (ed.) *European Monetary Upheavals*. Manchester, Manchester University Press.

Monticelli, C. and Papi, U. (1996) *European Integration, Monetary Co-ordination and the Demand for Money*. Oxford, Oxford University Press.

Moravcsik, A. (1993a) 'Preferences and power in the European Community: a liberal intergovernmentalist approach', *Journal of Common Market Studies*, vol. 31, no. 4, pp. 473–524.

Moravcsik, A. (1993b) 'Idealism and Interest in the European Community: The Case of the French Referendum', *French Politics and Society*, vol. 11, no. 1, pp. 57–69.

Moravcsik, A. (1999) *The Choice for Europe: Social Purpose and State Power from Messina to Maastricht*. London, UCL Press.

Mortensen, J. (1990) *Federalism vs Co-ordination: Macroeconomic Policy in the European Community*, CEPS Paper, no. 47, London, Centre for European Policy Studies.

Mundell, R. (1961) 'A Theory of Optimum Currency Areas', *American Economic Review*, vol. 51, pp. 657–65.

Neumann, M. (1991) 'Central Bank Independence as a Pre-Requisite of Price Stability', *European Economy Special Issue*. Brussels, pp. 77–88.

Nolan, C. and Schaling, E. (1996) *Monetary Policy Uncertainty and Central Bank Accountability*, Working Paper no. 54. London, Bank of England.

Nordhaus, W. (1975) 'The Political Business Cycle', *Review of Economic Studies*, vol. 42, pp. 169–90.

Obstfeld, M. and Peri, G. (1998) 'Regional Non-Adjustment and Fiscal Policy', *Economic Policy*, no. 26. Oxford, Blackwell.

Odell, J. (1982) *US International Monetary Policy: Markets, Power and Ideas as Sources of Change*. Princeton, NJ, Princeton University Press.

Olsen, J. (1995) 'The Changing Political Organisation of Europe: An Institutional Perspective on the Role of Comprehensive Reform Efforts', in J.-J. Hesse, and A. Toonen (eds), *The European Yearbook of Comparative Government and Public Administration*. Baden-Baden, Nomos.

Olsen, J. (1997) 'European Challenges to the Nation State', in B. Steunenberg, and F. Van Vught (eds), *Political Institutions and Public Policy*. Amsterdam, Kluwer, pp. 157–88.

Padoa-Schioppa, T. (1987) *Efficiency, Stability and Equity: A Strategy for the Evolution of the Economic System of the European Community*. Oxford, Oxford University Press.

Padoa-Schioppa, T. (1994) *The Road to Monetary Union in Europe*. Oxford, Clarendon Press.

Page, E. and Wouters, L. (1994) 'Bureaucratic Politics and Political Leadership in Brussels', *Public Administration*, vol. 72, no. 3, pp. 445–59.

Pelkmans, J. and Winters, L. (1988) *Europe's Domestic Market*. London, RIIA.

Peters, G. B. (1996) 'Agenda-setting in the European Union', in J. Richardson (ed.), *European Union: Power and Policy-Making*. London, Routledge, pp. 61–76.

Peters, G. B. (1997) 'Escaping the Joint-Decision Trap: Repetition and Sectoral Politics in the European Union', *West European Politics*, vol. 20, no. 2, pp. 22–36.

Peterson, J. (1995) 'Decision-Making in the European Union: towards a framework for analysis', *Journal of European Public Policy*, vol. 2, no. 1, pp. 69–93.

Pierson, P. (1996) 'The Path to European Integration: A Historical Institutionalist Analysis', *Comparative Political Studies*, vol. 29, no. 2, pp. 123–63.

Pollack, M. (1997) Delegation, agency and agenda setting in the European Community, *International Organisation*, vol. 51, no. 1, pp. 99–134.

Portes, R. and Rey, H. (1998) 'The Emergence of the Euro as an International Currency in EMU; Prospects and Challenges for the Euro', in D. Begg , J. Von Hagen, G. Wyplosz, and K. Zimmermann (eds), *EMU: Prospects and Challenges for the Euro*. Oxford, Blackwell.

Posen, A. (1992) 'Why Central Bank Independence Does Not Cause Low Inflation', in R. O'Brien (ed.), *Finance and the International Economy*. Oxford, Oxford University Press.

Rhodes, M. (1997) 'The Welfare State: Internal challenges, external constraints', in M. Rhodes, P. Heywood and V. Wright (eds), *Developments in West European Politics*. Basingstoke, Macmillan.

Richardson, J. (1996) 'Policy-making in the EU: interests, ideas and garbage cans of primeval soup', in J. Richardson (ed.), *European Union: Power and Policy-Making*. London, Routledge.

Riker, W. (1982) *Liberalism against Populism: A Confrontation between the Theory of Democracy and the Theory of Social Choice*. San Francisco, W. H. Freeman.

Ritter, G. (1962) *Das Deutsche Problem. Grundfragen deutschen Staatslebens Gestern und Heute*. München, Oldenberg.

Rogoff, K. (1985) 'The Optimal Degree of Commitment to an Intermediate Monetary Target', *Quarterly Journal of Economics*, vol. 100, pp. 169–90.

Ross, G. (1995) *Jacques Delors and European Integration*. Cambridge, Polity Press.

Rovelli, R. (1994) 'Reserve Requirements, Seigniorage and the Financing of the Government in an Economic and Monetary Union', *European Economy*, vol. 1.

Sandholtz, W. (1993) 'Choosing Union: Monetary Politics and Maastricht', *International Organisation*, vol. 47, no. 1, pp. 1–39.

Sandholtz, W. (1996) 'Membership Matters: Limits of the Functional Approach to European Institutions', *Journal of Common Market Studies*, vol. 34, no. 3, pp. 403–29.

Scharpf, F. (1988) 'The Joint Decision Trap: Lessons from German Federalism and European Integration', *Public Administration*, vol. 66, no. 3.

Schönfelder, W. and Thiel, E. (1994) *Ein Markt – Eine Währung: Die Verhandlung zur Europäischen Wirtschafts und Währungsunion*. Baden-Baden.

Sebenius, J. (1992) 'Challenging Conventional Explanations of International Co-operation: Negotiation Analysis and the Case of Epistemic Communities', *International Organisation*, vol. 46, no. 1, pp. 323–65.

Selsdon, A. (1997) *John Major: A Political Life*. London, Phoenix.

Shepsle, K. (1989) 'Studying Institutions: Some Lessons from the Rational Choice Approach', *Journal of Theoretical Politics*, vol. 1, no. 2, pp. 131–47.

Smyrl, M. (1998) 'When and How Do the Commission's Preferences Matter', *Journal of Common Market Studies*, vol. 36, no. 1, pp. 79–99.

SPD/Grüne (1998), *Koalitionsvertrag*. Bonn, SPD.

Strange, S. (1988) *States and Markets*. London, Pinter.

Stubb, A. (1996) 'A Categorisation of Differentiated Integration', *Journal of Common Market Studies*, vol. 34, no. 2.

Szukala, A. and Wessels, W. (1997) 'The Franco-German Tandem', in G. Edwards and A. Pijpers (eds), *The Politics of European Treaty Reform: The 1996 Intergovernmental Conference and Beyond*. London, Pinter.

Taylor, C. (1997) 'A Common Currency Route to EMU: the Hard ECU revisited', National Institute of Economic and Social Science Research, Discussion Paper no. 119. London, NIESR.

Teltschik, H. (1991) *Innenansichten der Einigung*, Berlin.

Thatcher, M. (1993) *The Downing Street Years*. New York, HarperCollins.

Thygesen, N. (1996) 'Interpreting the Exchange Rate Criterion', in P. Kenen (ed.), *Making EMU Happen, Essays in International Finance*. Princeton, NJ, Princeton University Press.

Tietmeyer, H. (1994) 'The Relationship Between Economic, Monetary and Political Integration', in A. Bakker, H. Boot, O. Sleijpen and W. Vanthoor (eds), *Monetary Stability Through International Co-operation – Essays in Honour of Andre Szasz*. Dordrecht, Kluwer.

Tinbergen, J. (1965) *International Economic Integration*. Amsterdam, Elsevier.

Tranholm-Mikkelsen. J. (1991) 'Neofunctionalism: obstinate or obsolete? A reappraisal in the light of the new dynamism of the EC', *Millennium*, vol. 20, no. 1, pp. 1–22.

Tsebelis, G. (1990) *Nested Games: Rational Choice in Comparative Politics*. Berkeley, University of California Press.

Tsebelis, G. (1995) 'Conditional Agenda-Setting and Decision-Making Inside the European Parliament', *Journal of Legislative Studies*, vol. 1, no. 1, pp. 65–93.

Tsoukalis, L.(1977) *The Politics and Economics of European Monetary Integration*. London, George Allen and Unwin.

Tsoukalis, L. (1993) *The New European Economy: The Politics and Economics of Integration*. Oxford, Oxford University Press.

Vaubel, R. (1994) 'The Political Economy of Centralisation and the European Community', *Public Choice*, vol. 59, no. 1, pp. 151–85.

Vinals J. and Jimeno, J. (1996) *Monetary Union and European Unemployment*, CEPR Discussion Paper no. 1485. London, Centre for European Policy Studies.

Von Hagen, J. and Suppel, R. (1994) *Central Bank Constitutions for Monetary Unions*, CEPR Discussion Paper, no. 919. London, Centre for European Policy Studies.

Wallace, H. and Young, A. (1996) 'The Single Market: A New Approach to Policy' in H. Wallace and W. Wallace (eds) *Policy-Making in the European Union*. Oxford, Oxford University Press.

Wessels, W. (1991)'Staat und (westeuropaische) Integration: die Fusionsthese', *Politische Vierteljahresschift*, Sonderheft, no. 23, pp. 36–61.

Wessels, W. (1997) 'A Dynamic Macropolitical View on Integration Processes', *Journal of Common Market Studies*, vol. 35, no. 2, pp. 267–99.

Winkler, B. (1999) 'Is Maastricht a Good Contract', *Journal of Common Market Studies*, vol. 37, no. 1, pp. 39–59.

Wolf, M., Scharrer, H.-E. and Johnson, C. (1997) *The Politics and Economics of a Single Currency, Three Views*. London, Royal Institute of International Affairs.

Index